The LNICST series publishes ICST's conferences, symposia and workshops.
LNICST reports state-of-the-art results in areas related to the scope of the Institute.
The type of material published includes

- Proceedings (published in time for the respective event)
- Other edited monographs (such as project reports or invited volumes)

LNICST topics span the following areas:

- General Computer Science
- E-Economy
- E-Medicine
- Knowledge Management
- Multimedia
- Operations, Management and Policy
- Social Informatics
- Systems

Sanjay Goel · Shuchi Sinha · Agam Gupta
Editors

Artificial Intelligence for Communications and Networks

5th EAI International Conference, AICON 2025
New Delhi, India, April 25–27, 2025
Proceedings

 Springer

Editors
Sanjay Goel
State University of New York
Albany, NY, USA

Shuchi Sinha
Indian Institute of Technology Delhi
Hauz Khas, Delhi, India

Agam Gupta
Indian Institute of Technology Delhi
Hauz Khas, Delhi, India

ISSN 1867-8211 ISSN 1867-822X (electronic)
Lecture Notes of the Institute for Computer Sciences, Social Informatics
and Telecommunications Engineering
ISBN 978-3-032-14804-9 ISBN 978-3-032-14805-6 (eBook)
https://doi.org/10.1007/978-3-032-14805-6

Preface

We are delighted to introduce the proceedings of the Fifth edition of the European Alliance for Innovation (EAI) International Conference on Artificial Intelligence for Communications and Networks (AICON 2025). The conference was organized by the Indian Institute of Technology, Delhi and held online from April 25–27, 2025. The conference brought together researchers and practitioners from around the world who are leveraging machine learning, deep learning, and artificial intelligence for a smarter and more efficient world.

The technical program of EAI AICON 2025 consisted of 13 papers across the following tracks: Track 1 - Deep Learning Applications; Track 2 - AI Impact; and Track 3 - AI Behavior and Society. These papers were selected from 56 submissions. Each submission received one review in a double-blind process. Aside from the technical paper presentations, the technical program also featured two keynote speeches. The two keynote speeches were by Yuksel Celik, Massry School of Business, University at Albany, State University of New York, and Pradeep Atrey, State University of New York. In addition, three workshops were conducted – 1) AI for Business by Sanjay Goel, 2) The Behavioral Implications of Generative AI by Shuchi Sinha and Smridhi Saluja, 3) Using Generative AI for Research by Agam Gupta and Zaid-Bin Ahsan. The workshops together aimed to address how generative AI could be leveraged in Business and Research (focusing on management and social sciences).

We sincerely appreciate the support lent by the Technical Program Committee. It was also a great pleasure to work with an excellent organizing committee team which worked hard toward organizing and supporting the conference. We are also grateful to the reviewers and all the authors who submitted their papers to the EAI AICON 2025 conference.

We believe that EAI AICON provides a good forum for all researchers, developers, and practitioners to discuss all science and technology aspects. We also look forward to future AICON conferences, which will bring together researchers and practitioners from around the world and strengthen the discussions in the field.

Sanjay Goel
Shuchi Sinha
Agam Gupta

Organization

Organizing Committee

General Chairs

Sanjay Goel   University at Albany – SUNY, USA
Shuchi Sinha   Indian Institute of Technology Delhi, India
Agam Gupta   Indian Institute of Technology Delhi, India

Workshops Chairs

Shuchi Sinha   Indian Institute of Technology Delhi, India
Agam Gupta   Indian Institute of Technology Delhi, India
Sanjay Goel   University at Albany – SUNY, USA

Publicity and Social Media Chair

Akanksha Malik   London Metropolitan University, UK

Publications Chairs

Sanjay Goel   University at Albany – SUNY, USA
Shuchi Sinha   Indian Institute of Technology Delhi, India
Agam Gupta   Indian Institute of Technology Delhi, India

Technical Program Committee

Zaid Bin Ahsan   Indian Institute of Technology Delhi, India
Smridhi Saluja   Indian Institute of Technology Delhi, India
Sakshi Sharma   Indian Institute of Technology Delhi, India
Pragati Singh   Indian Institute of Technology Delhi, India
Yuksel Celik   University at Albany – SUNY, USA
Lakshika Vaishnav   University at Albany – SUNY, USA
Sakshi Singh   University at Albany – SUNY, USA
Akanksha Malik   London Metropolitan University, UK
Swati Garg   Keele University, UK
Srishti Gupta   University at Albany – SUNY, USA

Contents

Deep Learning Applications

Deep Learning Based Automatic Classification of Cloud Images Using
Segmentation Network Model 3
    S. Sudharson, R. Annamalai, Bachu Ganesh,
    and Tekumudi Vivek Sai Surya Chaitanya

Internet of Things-Enabled System to Monitor Leaf Structure and Increase
Crop Yield 22
    Ankit Khare, Bramah Hazela, Awanish Mishra,
    and Brijesh Kumar Chaurasia

A Machine Learning Based Drone Surveillance for Safer Railways 40
    K. R. Swetha, M. P. Hemadarshini, C. R. Nagarathna, G. Nandini,
    Karthik Dinesh Vernekar, B. K. Chiran, and Aman Kumar Verma

A Comprehensive Approach to Adaptive Multi-model Architecture
for Heterogeneous Data Sources 51
    E. Anbazhagan, S. Sudharson, R. Annamalai, and V. Vamsi Krishna

Beyond Classification: Understanding Why URLs Are Malicious
with Transparent Convex Optimization and Interpretable XAI 70
    Yi Anson Lam, Kam-Pui Chow, and Siu-Ming Yiu

Forecasting Cyber Vulnerabilities: A Critical Analysis of ARIMA Models'
Efficacy and Efficiency 85
    N. H. M. Arafat and Weiqing Sun

Watchguard: Real Time Women Safety Detection System 108
    Seema Srinivas, B. C. Divakara, C. R. Nagarathna, G. Nandini,
    M. Ramya, R. B. Suchithra, and T. Suchithra

AI Impact

A Survey of AI-Enhanced Augmented Reality in Phobia Treatment:
Innovations, Challenges, and Societal Impacts 119
    M. Abinaya and G. Vadivu

Exploring Sustainability in Artificial Intelligence: Balancing Innovation
and Environmental Impact? 138
    Maria Bartekova, Helena Majduchova, and Anita Romanova

The Productivity Paradox: Job Crafting in the Context of Generative
Artificial Intelligence 150
    Akanksha Malik Jamwal and Swati Garg

The Role of Generative AI in Supporting Neurodiverse Individuals:
Literature Insights and Future Directions 159
    Srishti Gupta and Sanjay Goel

AI Behavior and Society

Exploring the Potential of Voice Interaction for Gamified Education
in Children with ADHD 173
    Rithvik Hariprasad, Aryamann Anand, and T. M. Navamani

Virtual Character-Based Study of the Combined Effect of Turn-Taking
Behavior and Speech Speed on Conversational Atmosphere 182
    Masahide Yuasa

Author Index 193

Deep Learning Applications

Deep Learning Based Automatic Classification of Cloud Images Using Segmentation Network Model

S. Sudharson[1]([⊠]), R. Annamalai[2], Bachu Ganesh[2],
and Tekumudi Vivek Sai Surya Chaitanya[2]

[1] School of Computer Science and Engineering, Vellore Institute of Technology,
Chennai 600127, India
`sudharson.s@vit.ac.in`
[2] Department of Computer Science and Engineering, Amrita School of Computing,
Amrita Vishwa Vidyapeetham, Chennai 601103, India

Abstract. Global warming intensifies daily, prompting individuals, NGOs, environmental groups, and governments to combat it through various strategies, such as building va. However, the impact of these efforts on climate change remains understudied. One critical approach involves examining shallow clouds—key to Earth's radiation balance yet poorly represented in climate models. Changes in low-level cloud frequency and radiative effects suggest global warming may reshape shallow cloud structures. This study analyzes four mesoscale cloud types— Sugar, Flower, Fish, and Gravel—using a method combining SENet feature extraction and U-Net segmentation architecture. State-of-the-art deep learning models, trained on a NASA-curated standard dataset, are fine-tuned for image segmentation, with U-Net serving as the encoder-decoder backbone. The models undergo diverse pre-processing techniques and are assessed via multiple metrics. The top-performing model achieves an F1-Score of 0.663 and a mean IoU score of 0.411.

Keywords: Segmentation · Mesoscale · Pre-trained models · Fine-tuning · Satellite images

1 Introduction

New research identifies four shallow convection patterns—Flowers, Fish, Gravel, and Sugar—in the tropical western Atlantic, using satellite infrared data. Analyzing 19 years, it ties these cloud patterns to regional factors, low-level cloud cover, and radiative effects. Global warming may alter shallow cloud structures, emphasizing their role in low-cloud feedback [1].

Shallow clouds critically influence climate change by affecting Earth's energy balance. Their impact on temperature and humidity profiles can either amplify or reduce the greenhouse effect, with water vapor feedback serving as a key measure. Sensitive to environmental shifts, these clouds significantly alter Earth's

© ICST Institute for Computer Sciences, Social Informatics and Telecommunications Engineering 2026
Published by Springer Nature Switzerland AG 2026. All Rights Reserved
S. Goel et al. (Eds.): AICON 2025, LNICST 672, pp. 3–21, 2026.
https://doi.org/10.1007/978-3-032-14805-6_1

radiation imbalance and climate sensitivity. Discrepancies in cloud feedback estimates from climate models largely stem from the response of trade-wind clouds to warming [2].

Clouds regulate solar energy and atmospheric radiation. As the atmosphere absorbs more energy, polar ice melts, raising sea levels and warming the globe. Less trapped energy cools temperatures. Studying cloud structure helps climatologists better understand Earth's weather [3]. Satellite cloud photos offer a detailed view of the atmosphere, revealing planetary conditions. Unlike ground-based shots, they track cloud changes, climatic zone shifts, and cover vast areas in one image. Rising Earth temperatures likely increase ocean evaporation, forming more varied clouds [4].

Clouds appear uneven and amorphous from below. Monitoring climate change requires assessing their shape, volume, density, and altitude. Cirrus clouds, resembling curls of hair, dominate high altitudes. Though shallow clouds show varied mesoscale structures, their role in cloud feedback remains unclear. Debate persists on whether their mesoscale structure affects responses to warming, often overlooked in models and small-domain simulations [5].

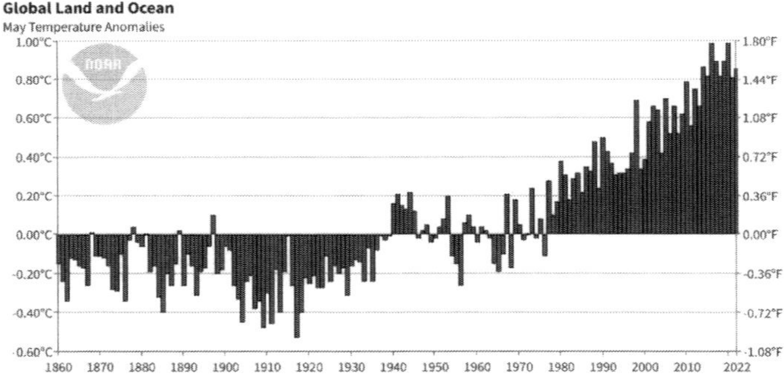

Fig. 1. Average rise in Global temperatures [7].

Figure 1 shows the average global temperature rise over years, highlighting the need to predict climate change to curb global warming. Studies suggest shallow clouds significantly influence climate shifts, linking global warming and climate change. Pattern recognition persists despite challenges in defining traits, as many patterns complicate clear, objective methods. Machine learning, especially deep learning, mimics human pattern recognition in satellite cloud imagery, but complex data collection limits its use and evaluation in cloud research [8].

Pre-trained models have revolutionized image segmentation, enabling researchers to adapt them to diverse datasets and challenges. Previously, effective segmentation required large annotated datasets and significant computing power. Now, models pre-trained on vast datasets like ImageNet reduce the need for labeled data, allowing fine-tuning and parameter transfer to new problems with fewer resources.

A 2020 study provides a detailed analysis of deep learning for image segmentation [9], covering designs and applications in fields like remote sensing, intrusion detection [10], autonomous driving, and medical imaging [11]. It explores challenges and opportunities. Deep learning excels in biomedical segmentation, aiding early disease detection like cancer, using models like SegAN, SegNet, and U-Net. SegAN, a GAN variant, segments brain tumors and skin lesions, tested on BraTs 2017 and ISIC 2018 datasets, with strong Jaccard and Dice scores [?], [12].

2 Dataset Description

The dataset is made up of satellite photos obtained from the Kaggle competition-understanding clouds from satellite images with the help of NASA Worldview and the Max Planck Institute for Meteorology. The dataset includes photographs of clouds which consists of four classes, namely Fish, Flowers, Sugar, and Gravel [13].

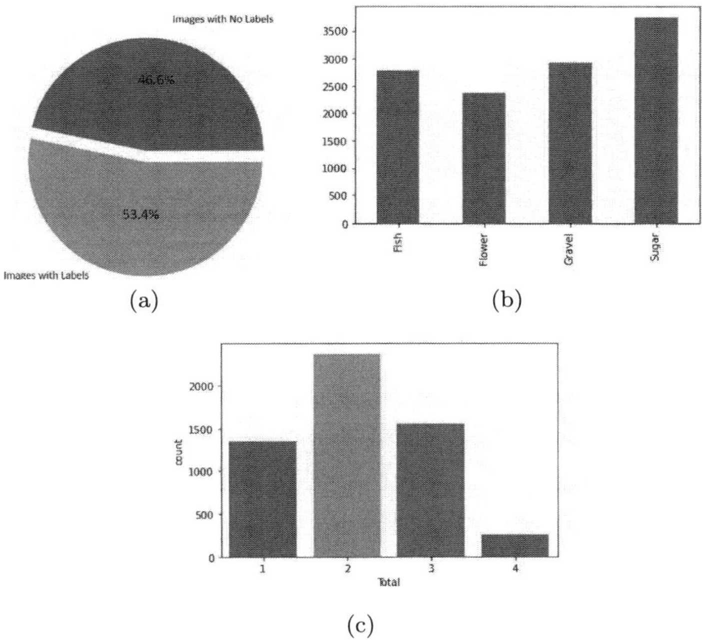

Fig. 2. (a) Null Value percentage (b) Distribution of class counts in the dataset (c) Number of labels per image.

Figure 2 shows class counts and label distribution in images from three trade wind region sites east of Barbados, spanning 21^0 longitude and 14^0 latitude. Full-color photos were taken by Terra and Aqua satellites using MODIS, which has a small footprint, allowing dual-orbit image stitching. The dataset, split 80:20 for training and testing, includes 22,184 training images (5,546 per class), with 53.4% having mask encoding. The 11,836 training images are balanced. Each image, uniquely named, comes with an Excel sheet detailing cloud class masks, shown in Fig. 3. Images contain 1 to 4 shape encodings, sized 1400 × 2100 pixels. Three scientists labeled 68 training images. Augmentation, using Scikit-Learn for noise and OpenCV2 for denoising, artificially expands the dataset, boosting model generalization.

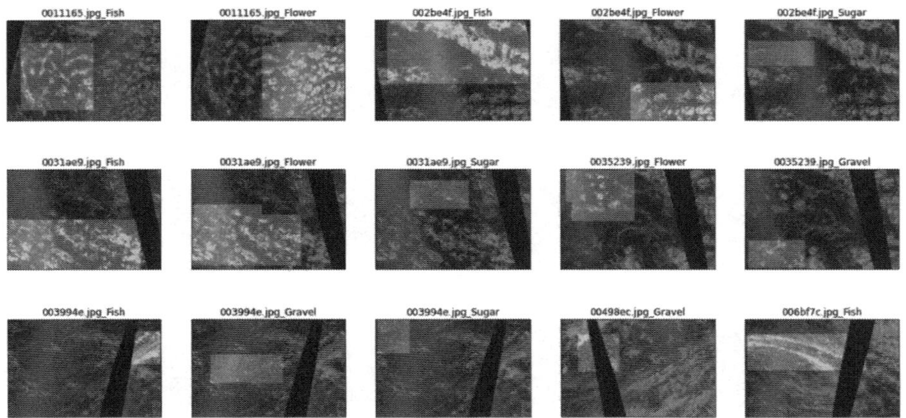

Fig. 3. Masked images of different samples.

2.1   Shapes

Fish. Fish shapes are elongated skeletal cloud formations, stretching up to 1,000 km lengthwise. Per [14], they resemble aciniform clouds [15]. These structured clouds appear across ocean basins, often downwind of stratocumulus-rich areas. Fish may be more common than thought if they're variants of actinoform clouds identified in 2004.

Flowers. Flowers shapes are isotropic cloud patterns, 50âŞ200 km in diameter, with large cloud-free gaps between. They overlap with closed-cell Mesoscale Cellular Convection (MCC) but are less dense, featuring small cloud-free edges, and occur beyond stratocumulus zones [16]. They may evolve from denser closed-cell MCC breaking apart.

Sugar. Sugar refers to large, fine cumulus cloud regions that are less reflective, lack significant cloud-free pockets, and show minimal mesoscale structure. Integrated into larger-scale flow, they gain some form. Strong flow can shape sugar into fine veins or feathers, once called dendritic clouds [17].

Gravel. Gravel denotes granular fields with arcs or rings, typically 20 km wide, likely formed by cold pools from raining cumulus clouds [18]. Unlike open-cell MCC, which has larger cells driven by shear-layer circulations, gravel differs, though the line between them can blur.

3 State-of-the-Art Pre-trained Models for Image Segmentation

Pre-trained models have excelled in image segmentation recently, with some out-performing in medical image classification [19, 20]. Image segmentation divides images into parts representing distinct objects or backgrounds. Trained on vast datasets like ImageNet, these models learn complex features, enabled by powerful GPUs and TPUs. While beneficial, choosing the optimal model is tricky. This study evaluated public pre-trained models, selecting the best based on assessment metrics from extensive segmentation research.

3.1 MobileNetV2

MobileNetV2, a popular deep-learning model, is known for its lightweight design and precise segmentation. Ideal for real-time use, it achieved 62.9% accuracy on the Cityscapes dataset for semantic segmentation in 2019 [21]. It also scored a 69.1% IoU on street scene segmentation, matching more complex models [22].

3.2 ResNet101

ResNet101, with its skip connections, is widely used for image segmentation. Its residual connections prevent degradation, enabling deep network training [23]. It excels in medical imaging, achieving over 99% accuracy in liver segmentation from CT scans in the LiTS Challenge [24]. In 2021, it outperformed others in lung nodule segmentation from liver CTs, hitting 90% accuracy, 3% higher than prior models [25].

3.3 VGG19

VGG19, a deep CNN, is widely used for image segmentation with high accuracy. In a 2021 study [26], it segmented lung nodules in CT images, achieving 97.83% accuracy and 98.2% sensitivity. In 2022, another study [27] used VGG19 to identify plant diseases via tomato leaf images, reaching 99.72% accuracy with a 0.00001 learning rate.

3.4 Inception-Resnetv2

Inception-ResNet-v2, a deep CNN, merges Inception and ResNet strengths, excelling in image classification and segmentation. A study used it for brain tumor classification via an Adaptive Eroded Deep CNN, achieving a 0.79 Dice score and 0.99 Jaccard score [28]. Another study on chest X-ray classification found Inception-ResNet-v2 with average pooling outperformed others, with 0.9402 sensitivity and 0.9263 accuracy [29].

3.5   SENet154

In a study comparing nine pre-trained models for pneumonia detection from chest X-rays, SENet154 achieved 97.5% accuracy, 98.5% sensitivity, 97.1% specificity, and 0.989 AUC-ROC, proving highly effective [30]. In 2019, SENet154, paired with feature pyramid networks, semantically segmented sub-surface salt targets for oil drilling, recording a top mean IoU of 86.6% [31].

3.6   DenseNet201

In a 2021 study, researchers applied DenseNet201 to segment skin lesions in the ISIC 2018 dataset, a collection featuring skin lesion photos with pixel-level annotations. They surpassed established models like U-Net and DeepLabv3+, securing a dice coefficient of 0.865 on test data [32].

4   Methodology

Satellite data collection is expensive, time-consuming, and often restricted due to national security concerns. This study serves as an initial exploration using publicly available data, providing insights into mesoscale cloud patterns. While validation with real-time meteorological datasets would improve reliability, these findings lay the groundwork for future research.

The dataset comprises high-resolution images, though acquiring such quality demands significant computational power and storage, and these are often hard to obtain. This study aims to train pre-existing models to detect data features amidst noise. By introducing and then filtering out noise, we add variance and subtle distortions to the data. For this, speckle noise is applied across all images at three levels—low, medium, and high—with variances of 0.02, 0.06, and 0.1, respectively, and a consistent mean of 0. Denoising employs a bilateral filter across all levels, using a uniform 50×50 neighborhood area. Post-processing, the images exhibit minor deviations from their originals—slight shifts due to noise addition and removal. These minimal changes preserve core image features while introducing subtle variations. Such alterations are pivotal for model training, forcing focus on dominant features within these micro-cloud patterns, rather than minor details muted by the noise process. The noise-added and denoised images, across all levels, then undergo contrast enhancement to amplify color brightness.

The proposed architecture model's framework is outlined in Fig. 4. High-quality data isn't needed, as it's tough to acquire, demands heavy computational resources, and requires substantial storage—complicating real-world application integration. Instead, the approach leverages U-Net as both encoder and decoder to cut down on computation time and resource use. In U-Net, data is initially down-sampled (encoding), yielding key feature maps. These maps feed into a neural network using pre-trained models. The output is then up-sampled and decoded within the proposed model.

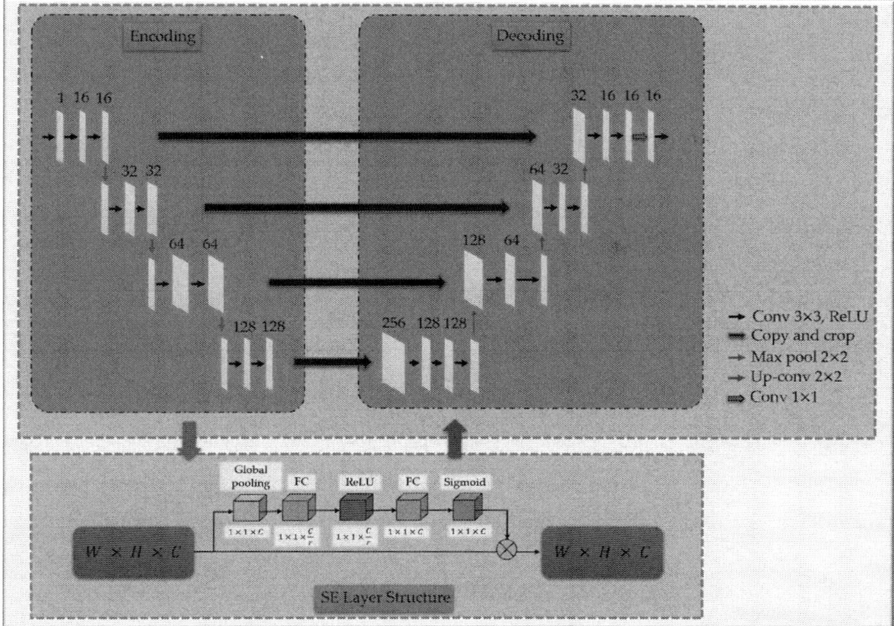

Fig. 4. Framework of the proposed architecture model.

4.1 Speckle Noise

Speckle noise prevails in satellite images, rendering them grainy or speckled due to coherent wave interference, which creates constructive and destructive patterns. This noise degrades the quality of satellite image viewing and analysis, hindering the detection and extraction of critical details.The noise model is multiplicative in nature and noise is multiplied by the input image. The noisy image is created by adding the speckle noise to the original image. The speckle noise model equation is presented as follows,

$$I\left(x,y\right) = R\left(x,y\right) * N(x,y) \tag{1}$$

Several filtering methods—like the Lee filter, Frost filter, and Gamma MAP filter—have been devised to tackle speckle noise in satellite images. These filters employ diverse strategies to suppress speckle noise while preserving the images' spatial details. Figure 5a presents the original image, a high-quality, noise-free visual benchmark. Figure 5b depicts the same image post-speckle noise addition, serving as a key baseline for assessing our proposed denoising method's efficacy. Machine learning approaches, such as convolutional neural networks and deep belief networks, have also been applied to denoise satellite images, yielding promising results in speckle noise reduction while retaining image integrity [33].

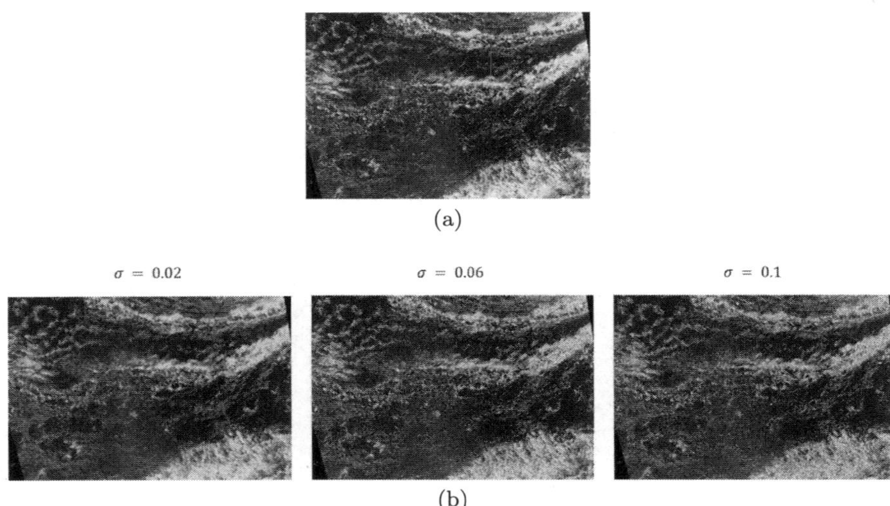

Fig. 5. (a) Original Image (b) After adding Speckle noise to the original image.

4.2   Bilateral Filter

A popular despeckling technique for satellite photos is the bilateral filter, which tries to eliminate noise while retaining the image edges and features. By applying a weighted average of the nearby pixels—whose weights depend on both the spatial separation and the intensity difference between the pixels—the bilateral filter operates [34].

The following is the bilateral filter formula:

$$I\_filtered(x,y) = \frac{1}{W} * \sum_{(x',y')\in\Omega} exp^{-\sqrt{\frac{(x'-x)^2+(y'-y)^2}{2*\sigma_s{}^2}} - \sqrt{\frac{I(x',y')^2 - I(x,y)^2}{2*2*\sigma_r{}^2}}} * I(x',y') \quad (2)$$

In satellite imaging, it curbs speckle noise—multiplicative noise from ultrasound-tissue interaction—maintaining structural details. Figure 6a shows noisy images with added noise levels; Fig. 6b displays denoised results from our bilateral filter, proving its efficacy in noise reduction and detail restoration across contamination levels.

4.3   Dice Co-efficient

The Dice coefficient is the assessment measure utilized in this study. The following equation was used to assess the pixel-wise agreement between a projected segmentation and related ground truth (Eq. 3):

$$\frac{2 * |X \cap Y|}{|X| + |Y|} \quad (3)$$

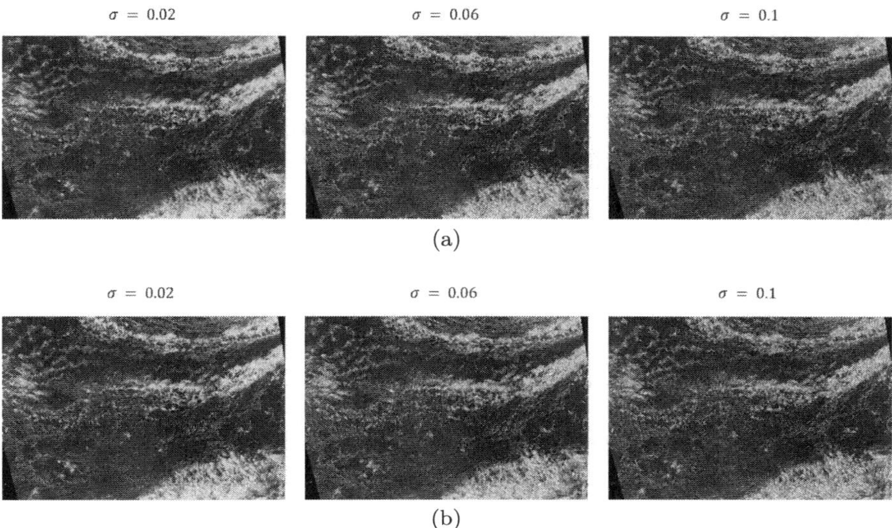

Fig. 6. (a) Noisy Images at different levels (b) Denoised images at different levels.

Here, X represents the predicted pixel set, and Y the actual training data set. The Dice coefficient equals 1 when both X and Y are empty. Unlike the typical accuracy metric, Dice coefficients assess image segmentation performance uniquely. Images are pre-labeled with ground truth regions before an automated system segments them. The Dice score, calculated as the overlap of two segmentations divided by their combined size, validates the approach [35]. Its ease of differentiation makes it superior for segmentation, outperforming Jaccard's index, a similar metric [36].

4.4 ADAM

The Adam optimizer, prized for its high classification accuracy, is employed here [37]. Widely adopted in semantic segmentation within neural networks, it excels in applications like hyperspectral image analysis [38]. Adam's superior performance stems from two key features:

4.5 Categorical Cross-Entropy

Categorical Cross-entropy (CCE) is used as a loss function in multi-class classification problems. Categorical Cross-entropy, commonly referred to as SoftMax Loss, is used to compare two probability distributions [39].

The formula for CCE is written as (Eq. 4):

$$Loss = -\sum_{i=1}^{N} y_i \times \log(\widehat{y_i}) \tag{4}$$

4.6 SoftMax

SoftMax is recommended as an activation function with CCE as it adjusts the model's output to ensure desired properties, favoring positive values so each output y_i is valid. This loss function aims to compare two probability distributions. The loss score combines CCE for classification and $CCE0.6 + DICE0.4$ for segmentation. The Dice coefficient measures overlap between predicted and ground truth pixel values, ranging from 0 to 1—higher values indicating better alignment. Thus, Dice Loss (DICE) seeks to maximize this overlap between predicted and ground truth sets [40].

4.7 F1-Score

The F1 score is a widely used metric in segmentation models to evaluate classification performance, particularly valuable when datasets are imbalanced, with one class far outnumbering the other. It merges precision and recall—key classification measures. Precision gauges the ratio of true positives among all predicted positives, while recall measures the ratio of true positives among all actual positives. The F1 score formula is given in (Eq. 5):

$$F1 - Score = \frac{2 * (precision * recall)}{(precision + recall)} \tag{5}$$

Ranging from 0 to 1, a higher F1 score signals better performance: 1 indicates perfect precision and recall, while 0 suggests random-guess-level accuracy.

4.8 IoU

The IOU (Intersection over Union) score is a standard metric for evaluating image segmentation models. It's calculated as the ratio of the intersection area to the union area between the predicted and ground truth masks, reflecting their overlap. An IOU score of 1 requires perfect alignment of the predicted and ground truth masks, while 0 indicates no overlap. The IOU score for an image is expressed as (Eq. 6):

$$IOU = \frac{intersection\ area}{union\ area} \tag{6}$$

Here, the intersection area counts pixels correctly identified as positive by both masks, and the union area includes all pixels marked positive by either. Widely used in image segmentation, the IOU score provides a simple, effective way to gauge prediction accuracy. It's often paired with metrics like accuracy, recall, and F1 score for a comprehensive performance assessment.

4.9   Proposed Architecture

The proposed architecture is built by integrating SENet-154 and U-Net. Here The U-Net is used to reduce the image size without suppressing the features present in the image and with the help of the U-Net, the image segmentation process is accelerated with better results. SENet-154 is used for extracting the hidden features present in the output of the U-Net encoder.

SENet-154. SENet-154 is an enhanced architecture combining Squeeze-and-Excitation (SE) blocks with the ResNeXt framework [41]. ResNeXt, a ResNet variant, uses grouped convolutions to enrich the network's representational power. SE blocks recalibrate channel importance by adaptively weighting each feature map based on its task relevance. The SENet-154 architecture is depicted in Fig. 7.

A deep neural network leveraging SENet-154 was developed for image classification and segmentation. Building on the original SENet's SE block, it adaptively tunes feature responses by significance. In this design, the SE block integrates into a deep, layered network, structured around four key modules: stem, stage, transition, and classifier.

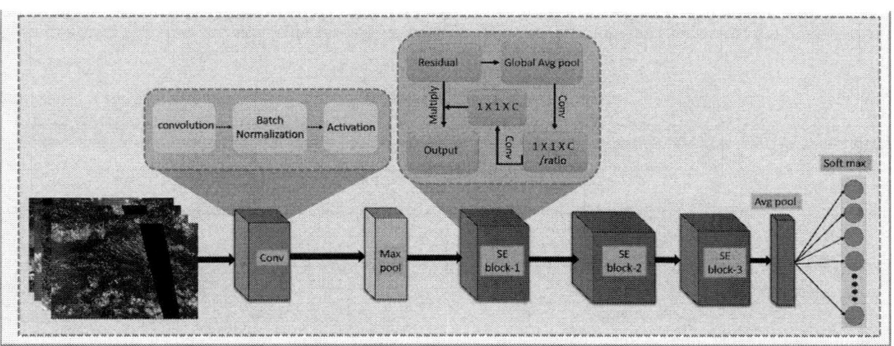

Fig. 7. SENet Architecture.

Stem module: The stem module processes the input image with a convolutional layer, batch normalization, and ReLU activation, feeding its output to the first stage module.

Stage module: SENet-154 has four stage modules, each with convolutional layers and SE blocks. SE blocks perform squeeze (global average pooling to form a channel descriptor vector) and excitation (scaling factors applied to feature maps), enhancing discrimination by amplifying key features and suppressing irrelevant ones.

Transitions module: Three transition modules reduce spatial size and increase channel count using convolutional layers, batch normalization, and ReLU, placed after each stage module for efficiency.

Classifier module: The final classifier module predicts via a global average pooling layer, fully connected layer, and softmax, outputting a probability distribution over classes.

SENet-154, a deep hierarchical network, excels at complex pattern recognition, with channel counts rising from 64 to 1024 across stages and spatial size shrinking to cut computational cost. SE blocks in stage modules boost performance by focusing on vital data [41]. Evaluated on ImageNet, SENet-154 achieves top accuracy, with ablation studies confirming SE blocks' critical role. Variants like SENet-50, SENet-101, and SENet-Inception follow the same principles, differing in depth and SE block use. Overall, SENet-154 is a powerful tool for image classification and segmentation, inspiring further SE block research in neural networks.

4.10   U-Net

In computer vision, U-Net is a favored architecture for image segmentation tasks [42]. It features a contracting path and an expanding path, as shown in Fig. 8. The contracting path, akin to a standard convolutional neural network, downsizes the image via convolutional and pooling layers. The expanding path restores the image to its original size using deconvolutional layers.

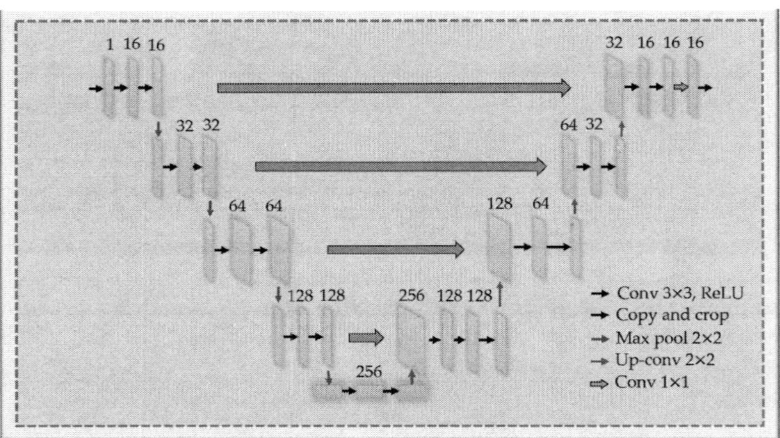

Fig. 8. U-Net Architecture.

Skip connections link feature maps from the contracting path to their counterparts in the expanding path, preserving high-resolution details during up-sampling and boosting segmentation quality. Widely applied in fields like medical image analysis, remote sensing, and object detection, U-Net has seen numerous enhancements, including added layers, attention mechanisms, and spatial context integration into the segmentation process.

4.11   Contrast Enhancement

Contrast enhancement sharpens an image by amplifying color and light differences across its regions, highlighting task-relevant details for easier interpretation. Techniques like histogram equalization and contrast stretching are commonly used. Figure 9a displays denoised images at varying noise levels, while Fig. 9b shows their contrast-enhanced counterparts.

In medical imaging, contrast enhancement boosts visibility of structures or conditions, such as blood vessels, tumors, or abnormalities, often unseen without it, as in contrast-enhanced CT or MRI scans [43,44]. It also differentiates tissue types based on contrast properties, like gadolinium-enhanced MRI scans for brain tumor detection.

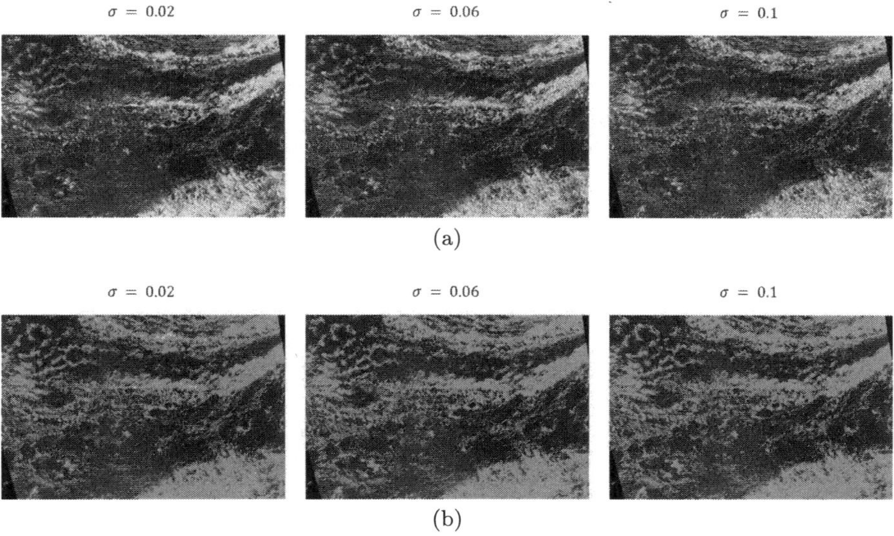

Fig. 9. (a) Denoised Images at different noise levels (b) Contrast enhancement to the denoised images.

5   Results

This research is done by using 6 different architectures. All the architectures are built by integrating them with U-Net, which are MobileNetV2, ResNet101,

VGG19, Inception-Resnetv2, SENet154, and DenseNet201. Each architecture has been fine-tuned at 3 different noise levels. Each model has been evaluated on its F1-score (Sect. 4.7), IoU-score (Sect. 4.8) and Loss. Each model is trained for 25 epochs with a learning rate of 0.02.

The F1 score, as a harmonic mean of Precision and Recall, makes reporting them separately unnecessary. Accuracy, Recall, and Precision are classification-centric and less relevant to this segmentation-based study. IoU and Dice Coefficient are closely related, with the Dice Coefficient being approximately $2 \times$ IoU, making both metrics interchangeable for assessing segmentation performance.

Table 1. Performance comparison of proposed model with the existing state-of-the-art models at different speckle noise levels

	No Noise($\sigma = 0$)			$\sigma = 0.02$			$\sigma = 0.06$			$\sigma = 0.1$		
Models	F1-Score	IoU-Score	Loss	F1-Score	IoU-Score	Loss	F1-Score	IoU-Score	Loss	F1-Score	IoU-Score	Loss
MobileNetV2 + U-Net	0.541	0.384	0.824	0.592	0.391	0.812	0.623	0.387	0.801	0.604	0.375	0.811
ResNet101 + U-Net	0.531	0.378	0.841	0.560	0.377	0.845	0.598	0.371	0.832	0.588	0.362	0.843
VGG19 + U-Net	0.522	0.373	0.859	0.578	0.379	0.855	0.585	0.374	0.846	0.581	0.368	0.852
Inception-ResNetV2 + U-Net	0.466	0.322	0.893	0.487	0.341	0.889	0.512	0.345	0.874	0.504	0.339	0.886
DenseNet201 + U-Net	0.540	0.392	0.841	0.569	0.410	0.848	0.577	0.404	0.837	0.559	0.391	0.844
SENet+U-Net(Proposed Model)	**0.612**	**0.398**	**0.814**	**0.628**	**0.401**	**0.815**	**0.663**	**0.411**	**0.798**	**0.635**	**0.408**	**0.801**

From the analysis in Table 1, the proposed model surpasses other network architectures in F1-score and IoU-score. This research reveals that the training F1-score peaks at 0.85 when images undergo the proposed method—adding speckle noise, denoising, and applying contrast enhancement—compared to a mere 0.65 when feeding images directly to the model. This elevated F1-score indicates the model better captures image features with preprocessing. Further scrutiny of the low IoU-score reveals that cloud masks, shaped as geometric rectangles, include both clouds and background (water in this dataset) in training images. With most images featuring black spaces, this likely contributes to the low IoU-score and high loss. The primary aim of this experiment was to concretely show that the proposed model alone yields unsatisfactory results on such a dataset. This study proves that adding and removing noise, paired with contrast enhancement, delivers superior outcomes compared to solely fine-tuning models. Observing plots Fig. 10a and Fig. 10b, the F1-score dips slightly to minimize architecture loss. Closer analysis shows optimal results at $\sigma = 0.06$, indicating this noise level extracts more features than the original image.

Figure 11 illustrates the average time taken for each model. We demonstrated that using the architectures in this way allows for faster performance for memory-intensive datasets and can be applied to a variety of fields, including medical image analysis and cellular image classification for cancer detection, where the data are typically segmented. Figure 12(b) shows the segmentation of meso cloud structure of a sample image presented in Fig. 12(a). The proposed approach has demonstrated better performance in terms of F1-Score and IoU scores. This process also has one more advantage when the models are trained in the presence of a small amount of noise.

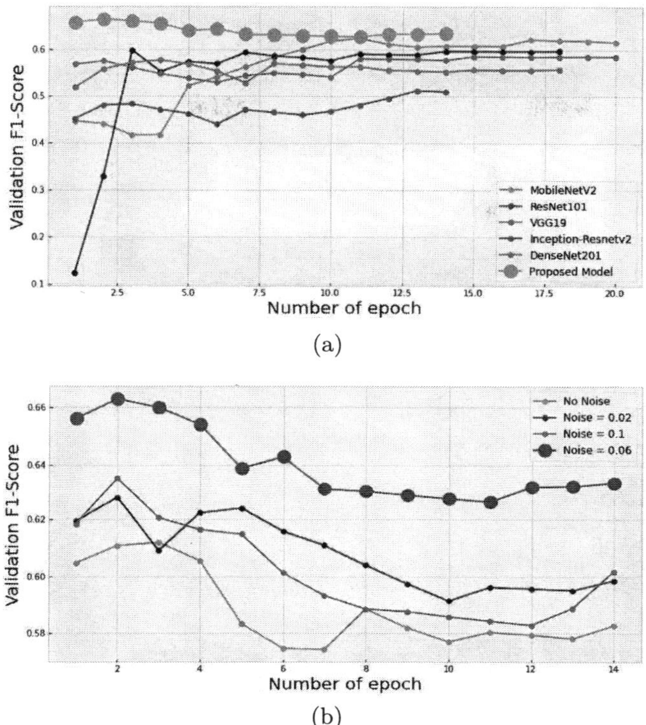

(a)

(b)

Fig. 10. (a) Different models with $\sigma = 0.06$ (b) Performance of proposed model with different noise levels.

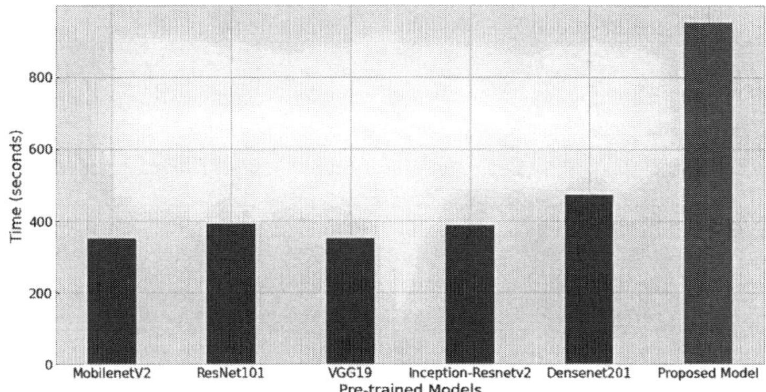

Fig. 11. Average Time taken for Pre-trained Models.

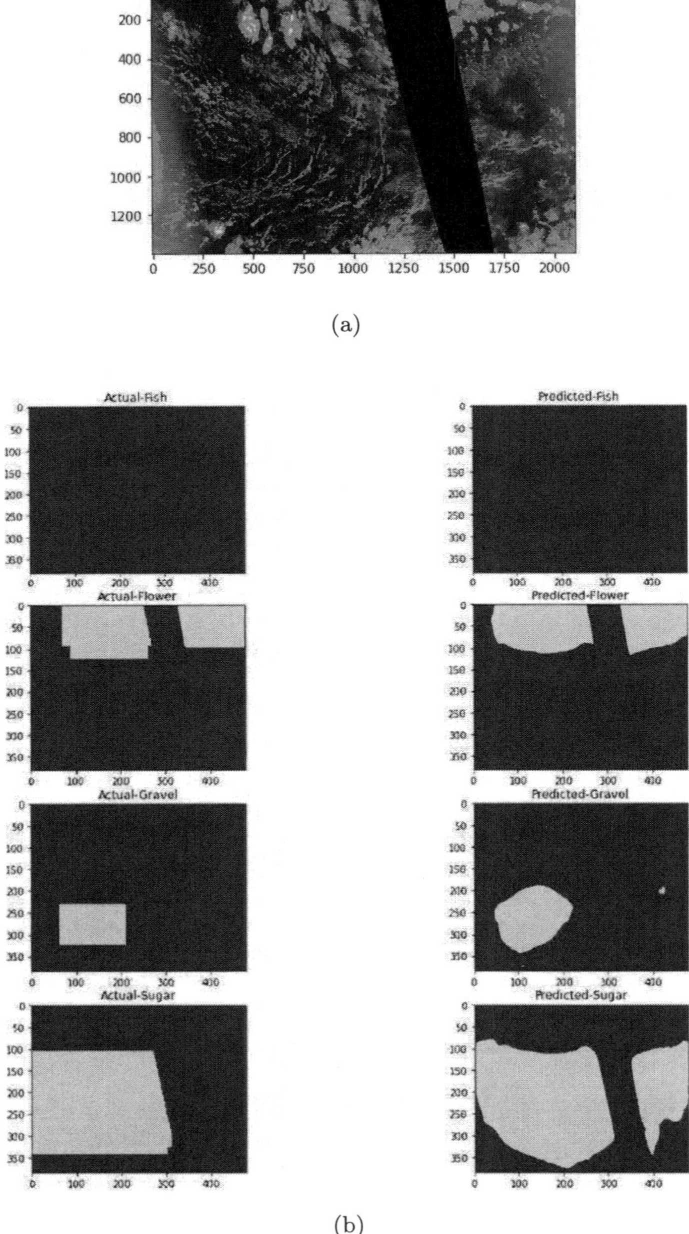

(a)

(b)

Fig. 12. (a) Sample Input Image to the Best performing model (b) Output of the model.

6 Conclusions

This study has illustrated that deep neural networks make miniature cloud segmentation possible. This proposed approach considers four different classes of cloud structures: Sugar, Flower, Fish, and Gravel. The proposed method is based on SENet feature extraction followed by U-Net segmentation architecture. The proposed method outperforms the existing approaches in terms of F1 and IoU scores. It is illustrated that good performance can be achieved by the hybrid combination of pre-trained and segmentation architecture. In the future, the work may be extended by modifying the network architecture to enhance performance. Exploring the pre-processing step with neural network-based despeckling filters may improve the performance. Fine-tuning the parameters of the network model will improve the classification performance of the system. AI-driven climate predictions must be reliable for policy decisions. Addressing biases in dataset labeling and model generalization is crucial for trustworthiness. Incorporating ethical AI principles and model interpretability enhances transparency in climate analytics.

References

1. Bony, S., et al.: Sugar, gravel, fish, and flowers: Dependence of mesoscale patterns of trade-wind clouds on environmental conditions. Geophy. Res. Letters **47**(7), e2019GL085988 (2020)
2. Bony, S., Jean-Louis, D.: Marine boundary layer clouds at the heart of tropical cloud feedback uncertainties in climate models. Geophy. Res. Letters **32**(20) (2005)
3. Turner, D., et al.: Thin liquid water clouds: Their importance and our challenge. Bulletin Am. Meteorol. Soc. **88**(2), 177–190 (2007)
4. Leconte, J., et al.: Increased insolation threshold for runaway greenhouse processes on Earth-like planets. Nat. **504**(7479), 268–271 (2013)
5. Dowling, D.R., Radke, L.F.: A summary of the physical properties of cirrus clouds. J. Appl. Meteorol. Climatol. **29**(9), 970–978 (1990)
6. Malkus, J.S., Riehl, H.: Cloud structure and distributions over the tropical Pacific Ocean 1. Tellus **16**(3), 275–287 (1964)
7. Global Time Series. https://www.ncei.noaa.gov/access/monitoring/climate-at-a-glance/global/time-series/globe/land_ocean/1/5/1860-2022
8. Rasp, S., et al.: Combining crowdsourcing and deep learning to explore the mesoscale organization of shallow convection. Bulletin Am. Meteorol. Soc. **101**(11), E1980–E1995 (2020)
9. Minaee, S., et al.: Image segmentation using deep learning: A survey. IEEE Trans. Pattern Anal. Mach. Intell. **44**(7) 3523–3542 (2021)
10. Ganesh, B., Sridevi, S.: Analysis of hybrid deep learning models for efficient intrusion detection. In: 2023 International Conference on Networking and Communications (ICNWC). IEEE, (2023)
11. Sachin, T.K., Saj, V.S., Soman, K.P.: Performance analysis of deep learning models for biomedical image segmentation. Deep Learning for Biomedical Applications. CRC Press, 83–100 (2021)

12. eshu Babu, G., Sachin Saj, T.K., Sowmya, V., Soman, K.P. (2021). Tuberculosis Classification Using Pre-trained Deep Learning Models. In: Komanapalli, V.L.N., Sivakumaran, N., Hampannavar, S. (eds) Advances in Automation, Signal Processing, Instrumentation, and Control. Select Proceedings of i-CASIC 2020. Vol. 700, Springer Singapore (2021). https://doi.org/10.1007/978-981-15-8221-9_71
13. Stephan, R., Hauke, S., Walter, R., Maggie, D.: Understanding Clouds from Satellite Images. Kaggle. (2019). https://kaggle.com/competitions/understanding_cloud_organization
14. Stevens, B., et al.: Sugar, gravel, fish and flowers: Mesoscale cloud patterns in the trade winds. Quart. J. Royal Meteorol. Soc. **146**(726), 141–152 (2020)
15. Garay, M.J., et al.: Actinoform clouds: Overlooked examples of cloud self-organization at the mesoscale. Bulletin Am. Meteorol. Soc. **85**(10), 1585–1594 (2004)
16. Norris, J.R.: Low cloud type over the ocean from surface observations. Part II: Geographical and seasonal variations. J. Clim. **11**(3), 383–403 (1998)
17. Nicholls, S.D., Young, G.S.: Dendritic patterns in tropical cumulus: An observational analysis. Mon. Weather Rev. **135**(5), 1994–2005 (2007)
18. Rauber, R.M., et al.: Rain in shallow cumulus over the ocean: The RICO campaign. Bulletin Am. Meteorol. Soc. **88**(12) 1912–1928 (2007)
19. Sudharson, S., Priyanka, K.: An ensemble of deep neural networks for kidney ultrasound image classification. Comput. Method. Prog. Biomed. **197**, 105709 (2020)
20. Dwarakanath, B., et al.: A novel feature selection with hybrid deep learning based heart disease detection and classification in the e-healthcare environment. Comput. Intelli. Neurosci. **2022** (2022)
21. Sandler, M., et al.: Mobilenetv2: Inverted residuals and linear bottlenecks. In: Proceedings of the IEEE Conference on Computer Vision and Pattern Recognition (2018)
22. Hu, P., et al.: Real-time semantic segmentation with fast attention. IEEE Robot. Autom. Letters **6**(1) 263–270 (2020)
23. He, K., et al.: Deep residual learning for image recognition. In: Proceedings of the IEEE Conference on Computer Vision and Pattern Recognition (2016)
24. Sirco, A., et al.: Liver tumour segmentation based on ResNet technique. In: 2022 IEEE 12th International Conference on Control System, Computing and Engineering (ICCSCE). IEEE (2022)
25. Zhang, Q.: A novel ResNet101 model based on dense dilated convolution for image classification. SN Appl. Sci. **4**, 1–13 (2022)
26. Khan, M.A., et al.: VGG19 network assisted joint segmentation and classification of lung nodules in CT images. Diagnostics **11**(12), 2208 (2021)
27. Nguyen, T.-H., Nguyen, T.-N., Ngo, B.-V.: A VGG-19 model with transfer learning and image segmentation for classification of tomato leaf disease. AgriEng. **4**(4), 871–887 (2022)
28. Sunsuhi, G.S., Albin Jose, S.: An Adaptive Eroded Deep Convolutional neural network for brain image segmentation and classification using Inception ResnetV2. Biomed. Sign. Process Cont. **78**, 103863 (2022)
29. Ahmet, D., Feyza, Y.: Inception-ResNet-v2 with LeakyReLU and averagepooling for more reliable and accurate classification of chest X-ray images. In: 2020 Medical Technologies Congress (TIPTEKNO). IEEE (2020)
30. Hashem, M., et al.: Detection of pneumonia by using nine pre-trained transfer learning models based on deep learning techniques. Iraqi J. Comput. Inf. **47**(1), 18–26 (2021)

31. Liu, B., et al.: Image segmentation of salt deposits using deep convolutional neural network. In: 2019 IEEE International Conference on Systems, Man and Cybernetics (SMC). IEEE (2019)
32. Khan, M.A., et al.: Skin lesion segmentation and multiclass classification using deep learning features and improved moth flame optimization. Diagnostics **11**(5), 811 (2021)
33. Singh, P., Shree, R.: Speckle noise: modelling and implementation. Int. J. Cont. Theo. Appl. **9**(17), 8717–8727 (2016)
34. Choi, H., Jeong, J.: Despeckling algorithm for removing speckle noise from ultrasound images. Symmetry **12**(6), 938 (2020)
35. Dice, L.R.: Measures of the amount of ecologic association between species. Ecol. **26**(3), 297–302 (1945)
36. Niwattanakul, S., et al.: Using of Jaccard coefficient for keywords similarity. In: Proceedings of the International Multiconference of Engineers and Computer Scientists. Vol. 1. No. 6. (2013)
37. Diederik, P.K.: Adam: A Method for Stochastic Optimization. (2014)
38. Paoletti, M.E., et al.: Deep learning classifiers for hyperspectral imaging: A review. ISPRS J. Photogr. Rem. Sens. **158**, 279–317 (2019)
39. Gordon-Rodriguez, E., et al.: Uses and Abuses of the Cross-Entropy Loss: Case Studies in Modern Deep Learning. 1–10 (2020)
40. Sudre, C.H., et al.: Generalised dice overlap as a deep learning loss function for highly unbalanced segmentations. In: Cardoso, M., et al.(eds) Deep Learning in Medical Image Analysis and Multimodal Learning for Clinical Decision Support: Third International Workshop, DLMIA 2017, and 7th International Workshop, ML-CDS 2017, Held in Conjunction with MICCAI 2017, Québec City, QC, Canada, September 14, Proceedings 3. Springer International Publishing, (2017). https://doi.org/10.1007/978-3-319-67558-9_28
41. Hu, J., Li, S., Gang, S.: Squeeze-and-excitation networks. In: Proceedings of the IEEE Conference on Computer Vision and Pattern Recognition. (2018)
42. Ronneberger, O., Fischer, P., Brox, T.: U-Net: Convolutional Networks for Biomedical Image Segmentation. In: Navab, N., Hornegger, J., Wells, W.M., Frangi, A.F. (eds.) MICCAI 2015. LNCS, vol. 9351, pp. 234–241. Springer, Cham (2015). https://doi.org/10.1007/978-3-319-24574-4_28
43. O'connor, J.P.B., et al.: Dynamic contrast-enhanced imaging techniques: CT and MRI. Br. J. Radiol. **84**(2), S112–S120 (2011)
44. Eisele, P., et al.: Characterization of contrast-enhancing and non-contrast-enhancing multiple sclerosis lesions using susceptibility-weighted imaging. Front. Neurol. **10**, 1082 (2019)
45. Simonyan, K.: Very Deep Convolutional Networks for Large-Scale Image Recognition. arXiv preprint arXiv:1409.1556 (2014)
46. Szegedy, C., et al.: Inception-v4, inception-resnet and the impact of residual connections on learning. In: Proceedings of the AAAI conference on artificial intelligence. Vol. 31. No. 1. (2017)
47. Huang, G., et al.: Densely connected convolutional networks. In: Proceedings of the IEEE Conference on Computer Vision and Pattern Recognition (2017)

Internet of Things-Enabled System to Monitor Leaf Structure and Increase Crop Yield

Ankit Khare[1]([⊠]), Bramah Hazela[2] [iD], Awanish Mishra[2],
and Brijesh Kumar Chaurasia[2] [iD]

[1] Department of Computer Science and Engineering, Amity School of Engineering and Technology, Amity University, Lucknow, Uttar Pradesh, India
`ankit.khare@s.amity.edu`
[2] Department of Computer Science and Engineering, Pranveer Singh Institute of Technology, Kanpur, U.P, India
`bhazela@lko.amity.edu, brijeshchaurasia@ieee.org`

Abstract. Sustainable farming and higher agricultural yields may arise from IoT adoption in agriculture. This research creates an IoT-based system to track leaf structures, a key indicator of plant health and growth. The system uses sensors to measure environmental conditions, leaf temperature, moisture, and chlorophyll content. Due to advanced data analytics and machine learning algorithms, the system provides accurate and useful crop health insights. By making smart irrigation, fertilization, and pest management decisions with real-time data, farmers can maximize resource utilization and productivity. This strategy boosts agricultural yield, lowers input costs, and promotes sustainable farming. Empirical results show that accuracy is achieved by up to 98.50%. This article also covers IoT monitoring system design, deployment, and performance evaluation. Technology-driven precision farming could alter modern agriculture with this technique.

Keywords: Internet of Things (IoT) · Agriculture · Leaf Structure Monitoring · Crop Yield · Precision Farming · Real-time Data · Sensors · Data Analytics

1 Introduction

Growing population, changing weather, and natural resource scarcity are causing agricultural difficulties that require more efficient and environmentally friendly production methods [1]. Internet of Things (IoT), which uses cutting-edge technology to monitor and manage agricultural operations, could solve these issues. Traditional approaches to measuring plant health, especially leaf structure [2], can take time and effort to obtain continuous and complete insights. Using a network of sensors to measure leaf temperature, moisture [3], and chlorophyll content [4], this study provides an IoT-enabled system that analyzes leaf structures in real-time, addressing these limitations [5]. This data is processed using modern analytics and machine learning (ML) algorithms to help farmers make irrigation and pest management decisions [6, 28]. IoT technology

S. Goel et al. (Eds.): AICON 2025, LNICST 672, pp. 22–39, 2026.
https://doi.org/10.1007/978-3-032-14805-6_2

enhances agricultural output, resource use, and precision farming, enabling more sustainable agriculture. The system's design, deployment, and evaluation highlight its potential to enhance modern agriculture with technology-driven solutions.[7].

IoT connects devices to the internet, enabling data collection, sharing, and response. This network drives data-driven decision-making and automation across various applications, from home appliances to industrial systems. IoT sensors and communication technology enhance efficiency and connectivity [8], and computational capabilities enable real-time monitoring, analysis, and control of many applications. IoT might transform farming by providing real-time soil, crops, and environmental data [9]. Minimizing waste and optimizing resources enhances production, efficiency, and sustainability. Emerging IoT technology can transform industries by addressing challenges and creating new opportunities. Environmental factors like soil nutrients and humidity influence production [10], and temperature. Sensor devices are designed for open environments to gather data from soil, water, and air. To endure weather, humidity, and temperature fluctuations, smart agricultural devices require specific durability features.[11]. Figure 1 shows IoT devices are ideal for smart agriculture solutions.

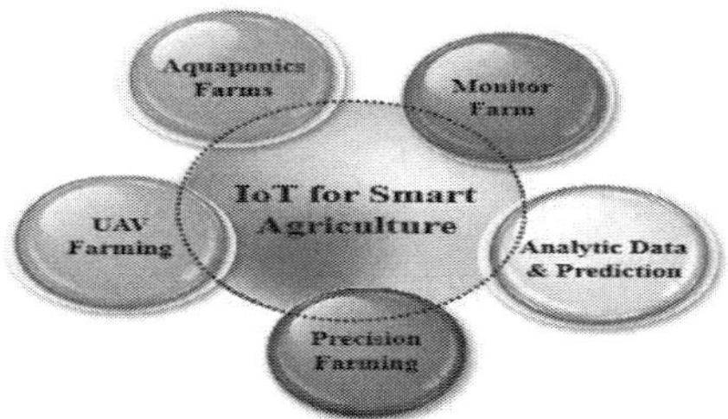

Fig. 1. IoT for Smart Agriculture

Precision agriculture uses cutting-edge technology to fine-tune crop and soil management [12]. Precision agriculture treats each field area differently, unlike conventional farming, which uses standard methods throughout fields [13]. Figure 2 illustrates IoT-enabled smart precision farming. This GPS-based remote sensing and data analytics system monitors soil moisture, nutrients, and crop health in real time. By integrating data and insights, precision agriculture enhances irrigation, fertilization, and pest management, boosting efficiency, sustainability, and yields [14]. This method reduces waste and maximizes inputs, improving efficiency and the environment [15]. Figure 3 highlights the key components of a leaf's structure. The midrib runs through the center, providing support, while the tip marks the topmost point. Vein extends from the midrib to transport water and nutrients. The lamina is a broad, flat surface, and the margin forms the outer edge. The petiole connects the leaf to the stem, aiding nutrient flow.

Modern farming relies on leaf structure to assess plant health [16]. This involves studying leaf anatomy and physiology. The plant's productivity and crop yield depend on the leaves' photosynthesis [17], transpiration, and respiration. Leaf health monitoring used to involve laborious hand examinations and sampling [18, 19].

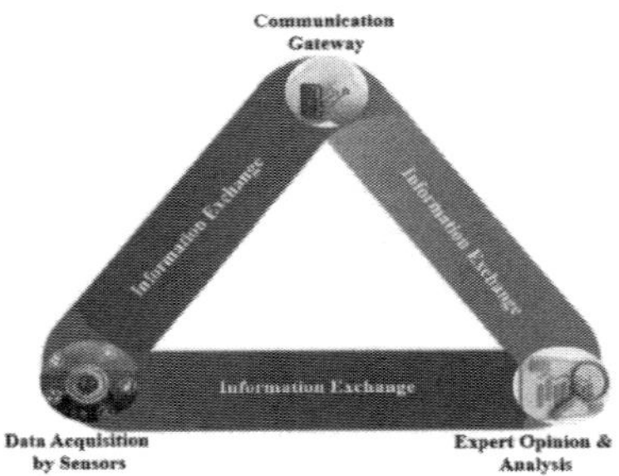

Fig. 2. Smart precision farming

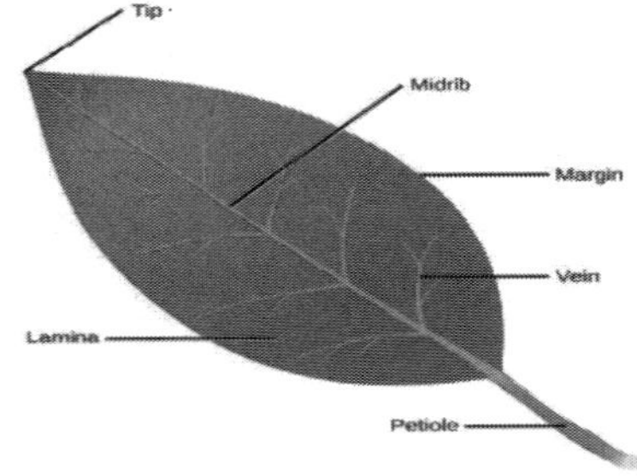

Fig. 3. Leaf Structure Monitor

IoT makes leaf structure monitoring automatic, precise, and real-time, making plant health evaluation easier than ever [20]. A network of IoT sensors and devices can continuously measure plant properties [21] including chlorophyll, leaf temperature, and moisture content. This system seamlessly transmits [22] and analyzes data [23] from high-tech sensors connected to wireless communication networks to eliminate human inspections. Farmers utilize IoT to monitor crops in real time, enabling more precise treatments and better resource use [24]. This boosts agricultural output, quality, and monitoring efficiency. Intelligent farming technology enabled by IoT can improve sustainable agriculture by improving decision-making and reducing waste [25–27].

Random Forest (RF) is an ensemble classifier designed to enhance IDS accuracy and performance. It consists of multiple decision trees and classifies intrusions more accurately than other classifiers. RF split nodes based on trees, features, and minimum node size, offering benefits like saving forests for future use and resolving fitting issues. It is a robust ML algorithm that prevents overfitting, handles high-dimensional data, and supports both classification and regression tasks with minimal preprocessing. RF reduces variance by averaging multiple trees, manages missing data effectively, and identifies key predictive features, making it superior in handling class imbalance.

An IoT-enabled system for monitoring leaf structure enhances agricultural productivity by addressing key farming challenges. It provides real-time data on leaf temperature, moisture, and chlorophyll levels to optimize fertilization and pest management. This innovation promotes sustainable agriculture by improving crop yields, reducing input costs, and minimizing waste. By demonstrating IoT's role in precision leaf monitoring, this study advances precision agriculture and sets the stage for future smart farming technologies.

Why has RF been chosen?

Random Forest (RF) was selected for its high accuracy, low computational cost, and robustness to noisy data, making it ideal for IoT-enabled precision agriculture. While CNNs excel in image analysis, RF is better suited for processing structured sensor data, ensuring efficient real-time monitoring and decision-making. The distinctions between the various machine learning approaches for IoT-enabled precision agriculture are summarized in Table 1.

By integrating blockchain-based security mechanisms, encryption, and robust access control, IoT-enabled precision agriculture can significantly enhance data privacy,

Table 1. Comparison of ML Algorithms for IoT-Enabled Precision Agriculture

Criteria	CNN (Deep Learning)	SVM (Traditional ML)	RF (Ensemble Learning - Proposed)
Accuracy	High (especially for image-based data)	Moderate to High (depends on kernel choice)	High (suitable for structured tabular data)
Computational Complexity	Very High (requires GPUs/TPUs)	Moderate (depends on dataset size)	Low (efficient on CPU, suitable for IoT)
Training Time	Long (requires extensive training)	Moderate	Short (faster training with ensemble learning)
Inference Speed	Slow (high latency in real-time applications)	Moderate	Fast (suitable for real-time IoT applications)
Suitability for IoT	Not ideal (resource-intensive)	Moderate (may struggle with large datasets)	Highly suitable (low resource consumption)
Robustness to Noisy Data	Low (sensitive to overfitting, requires large labeled datasets)	Moderate (performance depends on kernel selection)	High (handles missing/noisy data effectively)
Interpretability	Low (black-box model)	Moderate (depends on kernel function)	High (feature importance ranking available)
Scalability	Limited (requires large labeled datasets)	Moderate	High (efficient with large feature sets)
Cost & Deployment	High (expensive GPUs/TPUs needed)	Moderate	Low (runs efficiently on edge IoT devices)

integrity, and protection against cyber threats, ensuring reliable and secure data-driven decision-making. To identify privacy and data security vulnerabilities with IoT-enabled precision agriculture are outlined in Table 2.

The rest of the proposed paper is structured as follows: Sect. 2 includes literature survey. Problem formulation is discussed in Sect. 3.In Sect. 4, proposed methodology is discussed. And lastly in Sect. 5, result evaluation also discussed followed by a conclusion in Sect. 6.

Table 2. Data Security and Privacy Challenges in IoT-Enabled Precision Agriculture

Security Challenge	Potential Vulnerabilities	Proposed Solution
Cyberattacks	DDoS attacks, malware injections, botnet attacks	Implement **intrusion detection systems (IDS)** and **firewalls** to detect and prevent malicious traffic
Unauthorized Data Access	Data breaches, hacking attempts, lack of authentication	Use **blockchain-based access control**, multi-factor authentication (MFA), and **role-based access control (RBAC)**
Sensor Manipulation	Tampering with IoT devices, falsification of agricultural data	Implement **digital signatures** and **tamper-proof sensor hardware** to verify data authenticity
Data Integrity Issues	Corruption or alteration of sensor data during transmission	Utilize **blockchain ledger** for immutable data storage and **hashing techniques** for integrity verification
Privacy Concerns	Leakage of sensitive farm data (e.g., soil conditions, yields)	Employ **end-to-end encryption (AES-256, RSA)** and **zero-trust architecture**
Edge Device Vulnerabilities	Insecure firmware, unpatched software, remote exploits	Regular **firmware updates**, **secure boot mechanisms**, and **sandboxing** to isolate threats
Scalability of Security Measures	High computational overhead security in large IoT networks	Use **lightweight cryptographic algorithms** like ECC (Elliptic Curve Cryptography) for efficiency
Compliance and Regulations	Lack of adherence to GDPR, HIPAA, or agricultural data policies	Ensure **compliance with regulatory standards** and **periodic security audits**

2 Literature Survey

New developments in IoT have significantly influenced farming methods, aiming to make them more efficient and environmentally friendly. Research by Fan et *al.* (2021) on IoT in agricultural high-throughput phenotypic platforms showed significant advancements in crop management and plant phenotyping [1]. The advantages of these technologies for improving the efficiency and sustainability of farming operations were emphasized in a recent study of IoT advancements in agriculture by Kour et *al.* (2020) [2]. In their investigation of IoT solutions for sustainable agriculture, Dhanaraju et *al.* (2022) demonstrated how these technologies improve crop monitoring and optimize resource management, hence bolstering sustainable agricultural methods [3]. The efficacy of IoT systems in managing growth conditions and enhancing crop quality was highlighted in Devare and Hajare's (2019) analysis of numerous IoT applications for crop growth monitoring along with quality control [4]. An IoT-based SAM system was created by Sekaran et *al.* (2020). This system improves agricultural management by collecting and analyzing real-time data [5]. In their review of smart agriculture's background and potential future developments, Jararweh et *al.* (2023) found that cutting-edge IoT breakthroughs and technologies are essential to enhancing smart agricultural practices [6, 28]. While IoT has many potential advantages, it also has some drawbacks that can reduce its usefulness in smart agriculture, as Thilakarathne et *al.* (2021) pointed out [7]. To demonstrate how IoT can optimize water use and enhance crop management in dry places, Mohamed Firdaus et *al.* (2018) used it for sustainable dry zone agriculture [8]. IoT and sensor technologies improve agricultural sustainability and food security, according to Morchid et *al.* (2024), who also examined the pros and cons of these technologies [9]. To improve soil diagnostics and management and increase crop output, Wu et *al.* (2023) created a multi-sensor MS for soil information [10]. An IoT system for verifying urban agricultural parameters was developed by Podder et *al.* (2021),enabling efficient urban agriculture through precise parameter verification [11]. To improve soil health management, Kalantzopoulos et *al.* (2024) used AI and IoT to create a soil information system for Western Greece [12]. To improve land usage and agricultural planning, Mohammad El-Basioni et *al.* (2024) developed an IoT-based system for assessing site suitability [13]. Through in-depth data analysis showed how AI significantly improves crop management and production prediction in precision agriculture [14]. AI and ML in precision agriculture, Shaikh et *al.* (2022) proved that these technologies improve agricultural methods and boost output per acre [15].To identify the research gap, we have summarized the analysis of existing techniques in Table 3. The gap problem formulation is discussed in the next section on behalf of the existing approach.

Table 3. Summary of Existing Techniques.

Ref	Authors	Year	Objective(s)	Technique(s)	Summary / Outcome
[1]	Fan et *al*	2021	Discover IoT applications in agricultural high-throughput phenotypic systems	IoT-based phenotypic analysis	IoT improves plant phenotyping, improving crop management and production estimates
[2]	Kour et *al*	2020	Review recent agricultural IoT advances	Survey of IoT applications	IoT technologies can boost agriculture's efficiency and sustainability

(continued)

Table 3. (*continued*)

Ref	Authors	Year	Objective(s)	Technique(s)	Summary / Outcome
[3]	Dhanaraju et *al*	2022	Explore IoT-based sustainable agriculture solutions	IoT-based smart farming	IoT improves agriculture monitoring and resource management, promoting sustainability
[4]	Devare and Hajare	2019	Survey Monitoring agricultural growth and quality using IoT	Literature review	IoT technologies improve crop quality and grow environment control
[5]	Sekaran et *al*	2020	Create smart agriculture management	IoT-based smart management system	Technology aids agricultural management through data analysis and real-time monitoring
[28]	Jararweh et *al*	2023	Examine smart agricultural basics and future directions	Overview of enabling technologies	Smart agriculture's future is bright thanks to IoT and other cutting-edge technology
[7]	Thilakarathne et *al*	2021	Discuss smart agricultural IoT difficulties and prospects	Conference presentation	The IoT opportunities along with challenges impact smart agriculture
[8]	Mohamed Firdhous et *al*	2018	Use IoT for dry-zone agriculture sustainability	Experimental implementation	IoT enhances agricultural management and water optimization
[9]	Morchid et *al*	2024	Explore IoT and sensor food security and sustainability innovations	Analysis of benefits and challenges	IoT along with sensors increase food sustainability along with security

(continued)

Table 3. (*continued*)

Ref	Authors	Year	Objective(s)	Technique(s)	Summary / Outcome
[10]	Wu et *al*	2023	Create a soil monitoring system with many sensors and an IoT-based system for urban farming parameter verification	IoT-based multiple-sensor system	Technology improves soil diagnosis and management, increasing crop yield
[11]	Podder et *al*	2021	Create an IoT and AI soil information system for Western Greece	IoT-based smart agrotech system	Technology verifies farming factors, making urban agriculture more efficient
[12]	Kalantzopoulos et *al*	2024	Create an IoT land suitability system	IoT and AI integration	Superior data collection and processing make the system useful for soil health management
[13]	Mohammad El-Basioni and Abd El-Kader	2024	Explore AI-driven precision agriculture	IoT-based assessment system	Land appropriateness can be assessed using the technique, improving land use and planning
[15]	Ghosh et *al*	2024	AI and machine learning for precision and smart farming	AI-based precision agriculture	AI's data processing makes crop management and yield prediction easier
[16]	Shaikh et *al*	2022	Discover IoT applications in agricultural high-throughput phenotypic systems	Machine learning and AI techniques	AI and ML have made farming more productive and efficient

3 Problem Formulation

System design, along with the implementation of IoT leaf structure monitoring systems, provides significant obstacles. The lack of precision in existing technology makes integrating high-tech sensors with IoT systems for leaf analysis difficult. The fact that diverse plant species and climates may affect sensor accuracy and data reliability worsens the issue. Scalability is another challenge. IoT technologies are interesting but must be more expensive, sophisticated, and hard to integrate for broad use, especially in agriculture. The fact that these cutting-edge technologies may be too pricey for small and medium-sized farms makes matters worse. There has also been no long-term study on IoT devices' operational and maintenance costs. As this interdisciplinary integration is still developing, further research is needed to fully employ IoT, AI, and ML to improve crop management and leaf structure monitoring. There is a need to consider the shape, edge structure, vein structure, color, texture, structure traits, curvature, and growth pattern features of a leaf during crop monitoring. Identification of all these features is another issue while monitoring leaf structure. The proposed system ensures scalability, efficiency, and security for real-world IoT agriculture deployment. Strategies for overcoming obstacles in the large-scale deployment of real-world systems are shown in Table 4.

Table 4. Addressing Challenges in Large-Scale Real-World Deployment

Challenges	Conventional Issues	Proposed Solutions
Scalability	Struggles with large sensor data processing	Uses cloud & edge computing for efficiency
Latency	Delays in decision-making	Fog computing & optimized ML models for real-time processing
Sensor Integration	Difficulty in handling multiple sensors	Standardized protocols (MQTT, LoRaWAN) ensure interoperability
Real-Time Decisions	Lacks predictive capabilities	AI-driven analytics enable adaptive responses
Energy Efficiency	High power consumption	Energy-efficient routing & duty-cycling optimize usage
Network Reliability	Weak connectivity in remote areas	5G, LPWAN, satellite communication ensure stability
Security & Privacy	High risk of cyberattacks	Blockchain & encryption enhance security
Cost Efficiency	High infrastructure costs	Hybrid cloud-edge model lowers expenses
Environmental Adaptability	Accuracy affected by weather changes	Adaptive ML models adjust dynamically
User Adoption	Complex systems limit use by farmers	Mobile dashboards & AI assistants enhance usability

4 Methodology

This section explores a multi-stage research procedure to develop an IoT-enabled leaf structure analysis system to boost agricultural output. The design phase includes: designing software. Combining sensors with an IoT platform to acquire and process data. Selecting the correct sensors to study leaf structure. A model is built and tested in greenhouses or experimental plots to study leaf structure, environmental conditions, and harvest success.

Figure 4 presents an IoT-enabled system where the leaf monitoring node considers temperature, humidity, light, and images captured by sensors and cameras. Then, this data is preprocessed to filter and normalize. Then, feature extraction takes place for leaf structure analysis. Different features considered during training are shape, edge structure, vein structure, color, texture, structure traits, curvature, and growth pattern. Shape features include leaf length, width, aspect ratio, leaf area, and perimeter. Edge structure considers leaf margin type and number of lobes. The ML model supports classification using RF. Random Forest algorithms are parallelized, allowing them to take advantage of multiple cores in modern processors and providing quicker training times than other algorithms that require more complex computations. It is less sensitive to noise in the data than algorithms like k-Nearest Neighbors (kNN) or single decision trees. RF also has flexibility with hyperparameter tuning, making it easier to use and tune than more complex algorithms.

A cloud-based database stores results, and the decision support system performs prediction and shows disease alerts. Finally, the user interface is accessed *via* a mobile app. A cost-benefit analysis follows this data evaluation of the system's accuracy, dependability, and crop output impact. We thoroughly publish our study and ask end-user feedback to develop the system. New ways to study advanced technologies and their prospective applications have been found. The proposed IoT-enabled system improves agricultural yield through leaf structure monitoring using leaf monitoring nodes equipped with sensors and image capture devices to collect environmental data and plant leaf images. The data is preprocessed for accuracy and consistency, and feature extraction techniques are applied to identify relevant attributes. This data is fed into ML algorithms to classify plant health, detect diseases, and predict potential yield. The information is stored in a cloud-based or local data storage system for easy access and analysis. A decision support component generates recommendations, such as yield predictions and alerts for disease outbreaks. A user-friendly interface, including dashboards or mobile applications, allows farmers and managers to monitor real-time data, visualize trends, and make well-versed decisions to optimize crop management along with enhance yield outcomes.

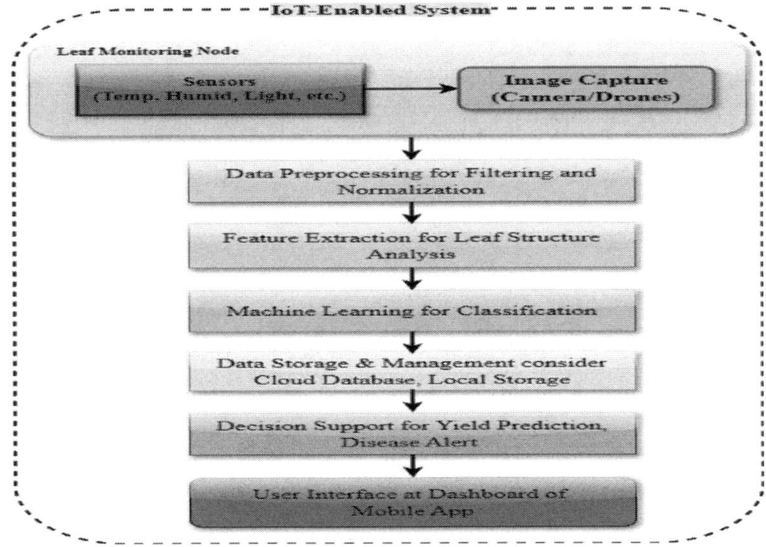

Fig. 4. The Proposed Model

5 Results and Analysis

In this section, the efficacy of the proposed model is evaluated. We have used four leaf datasets: the Fossil Leaf Dataset, Leaf Snap Dataset, Plant CLEF Dataset, and Oxford Flowers 102. The Fossil Leaf Dataset contains 800 images of fossilized leaves, ideal for paleobotany and fossil analysis. The Leaf Snaps Dataset provides 30,000 high-resolution images from 180 plant species, aiding in plant species classification. The Plant CLEF Dataset contains 500,000 images supporting plant identification and classification research (Table 5).

Table 5. Four leaf datasets and its descriptions.

Dataset	URL	Description	Details	Data size
Fossil Leaf Dataset	http://www.laght.com/fossil-leaf-dataset/	Contains images of fossilized leaves, used for leaf classification and fossil identification studies	Includes various fossil leaf types with images and metadata	Approximately 800 images
Leafsnap Dataset	https://github.com/Leafsnap/leafsnap	A dataset of high-resolution leaf images from different plant species, used for plant species classification	Contains images from over 180 plant species with species annotations	About 30,000 images

(continued)

Table 5. (*continued*)

Dataset	URL	Description	Details	Data size
The Plant CLEF Dataset	https://www.ima geclef.org/lifeclef/ 2021 /plant	Part of the Plant CLEF competition, featuring a large collection of plant images including leaves	Includes images of plant leaves, flowers, and other parts for diverse plant species	Around 500,000 images
Oxford Flowers 102	https://www.robots. ox.ac.uk/~vgg/data /flowers/102/	Primarily a flower dataset but includes leaf images of some flower species, used for plant recognition	Contains images of 102 flower categories, with some including leaves	Approximately 8,189 images

Python has been used over Collaborator to program a ML model for an IoT-enabled system that monitors leaf structure to improve agricultural yield and makes predictions accordingly. The process starts with data generation, which includes synthetic data representing environmental factors and leaf attributes, along with a binary label indicating plant health. The data is formatted into a Pandas Data Frame for easy processing. The preprocessing step involves scaling features to standardize their ranges, improving ML algorithms' performance. Metrics attributed to a numerical value that is used for training and testing the dataset are shown below in Table 6.

Table 6. Metrics Used for Training and Testing.

Feature Category	Feature Name	Metric
Shape	Leaf Length	Length in millimeters (mm)
	Leaf Width	Width in millimeters (mm)
	Aspect Ratio	Dimensionless (Leaf Length / Leaf Width)
Edge Structure	Leaf Margin Type	Categorical values encoded numerically
Vein Structure	Vein Density	Veins per square millimeter (veins/mm^2)
	Primary Vein Angle	Angle in degrees
	Vein Length	Length in millimeters (mm)
	Vein Thickness	Thickness in millimeters (mm)
Color	Leaf Color (RGB/HSV)	Numerical values for RGB or HSV components
	Chlorophyll Content	Measured in mg/cm^2 or by a relative index
Texture	Surface Texture	Categorical values encoded numerically
Structural Traits	Leaf Thickness	Thickness in millimeters (mm)
	Leaf Mass per Area (LMA)	Mass per area in g/cm^2

(continued)

Table 6. (continued)

Feature Category	Feature Name	Metric
Curvature	Leaf Curvature	Curvature index (e.g., ratio of curved length to straight length)
	Leaf Flexibility	Measured by force applied for deformation (Newtons)
Growth Patterns	Leaf Orientation	Angle in degrees
	Leaf Phyllotaxy	Categorical values encoded numerically

Dataset is divided into training along with testing subsets, and a RF classifier is used for feature extraction and classification. Figure 5 illustrates a confusion matrix frequently employed to estimate a model's performance in classification issues. The forecasted labels are laid out across the columns, and the matrix includes two labels—Leaf and Non-Leaf—representing the actual class. The model accurately categorized 2,600 non-leaf occurrences and 17,100 Leaf cases. However, although no leaf occurrences were misclassified, they were designated as non-leaf. In addition, the results also show that 300 non-leaf cases are misclassified as leaf class.

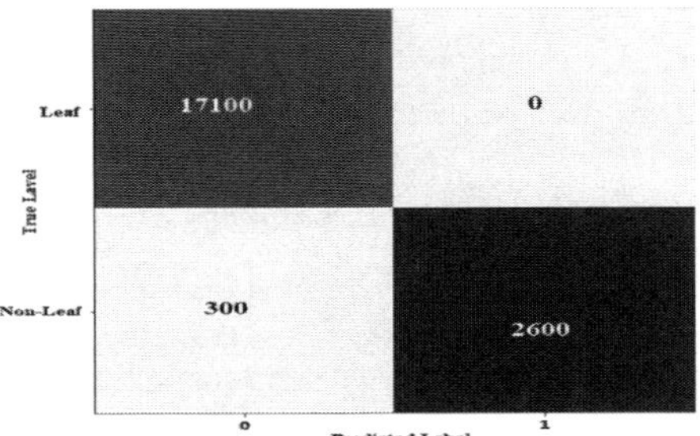

Fig. 5. Confusion Matrix

Model's performance is assessed through an organization report along with confusion matrix, providing metrics like precision, recall, along with F1-score. The results are visualized to offer insight into model's effectiveness, showing feature importance and predictions versus actual labels. In a real-world application, actual data from IoT sensors and image analysis would provide precise insights for improving agricultural practices.

The impact of several characteristics for recognizing leaf diseases is illustrated in Fig. 6. Temperature, humidity, light intensity, leaf size, and leaf color are among the characteristics that are examined. The graph reveals that temperature and humidity are the most significant factors in disease detection after leaf size. Leaf color also makes a major contribution, with light intensity having the least. These insights can help prioritize features in models or systems intended to identify leaf diseases.

The outcome of a suggested model appears in Fig. 7 over four distinct datasets: Oxford Flower 102, Plant CLEF, Leaf snap, and Fossil Leaf. The y-axis represents the predictability percentage, and all datasets exhibit model performance in the 80–90% range. The most accurate is Fossil Leaf; the other three do almost as well. The graph highlights the model's dependability in discriminating against leaves and other plant-related information by showcasing its consistency over various datasets.

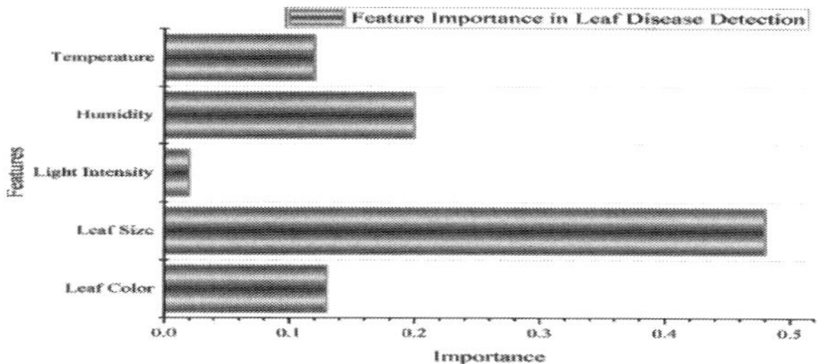

Fig. 6. Feature Importance in Leaf Disease Prediction

The accuracy of a suggested model is shown in Fig. 8, evaluated over four distinct datasets: Oxford Flower 102, Plant CLEF, Fossil Leaf, and Leaf snap. With an interval of about 85–95%, every dataset reveals excellent accuracy. The result shows 95% height accuracy on the Oxford Flower 102 dataset. However, 85% accuracy is achieved on the Leaf snap dataset.

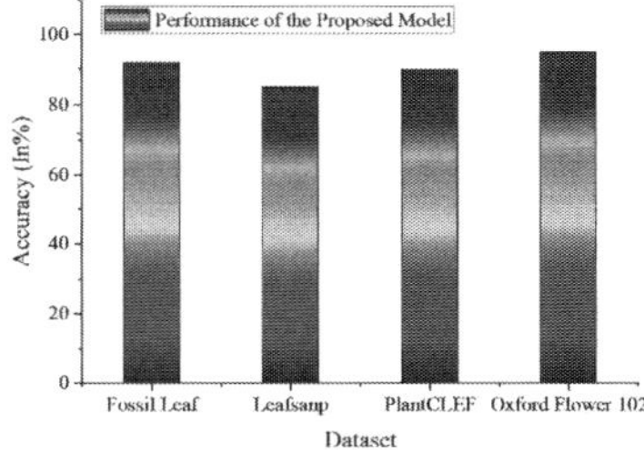

Fig. 7. Accuracy of the Proposed Model

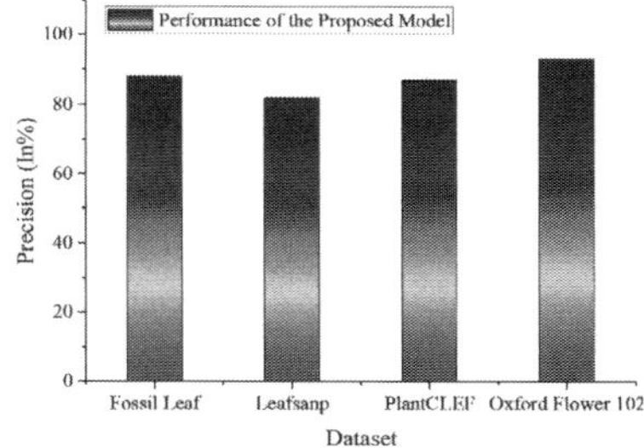

Fig. 8. Precision of the Proposed Model

The precision,F1-Score, and recall are depicted in Figs. 8, 9, and 10, respectively. These parameters are also evaluated on four datasets, as shown in the figure: Oxford Flower 102, Fossil Leaf, Leaf snap, and Plant CLEF. The Precision, F1-Score, and Recall values are 93%, 94%, and the same 94% on the Oxford Flower 102 dataset, respectively. Moreover, all three parameters have 82 to 84% performance on the Leaf snap dataset. Out of three parameters, the Precision value is the lowest at 82% on the Leaf snap dataset and 93% on the same dataset. The accuracy, effectiveness, affordability, and scalability of many machine learning models (CNN, SVM, and RF) in IoT-enabled precision agriculture are contrasted in Table 7.

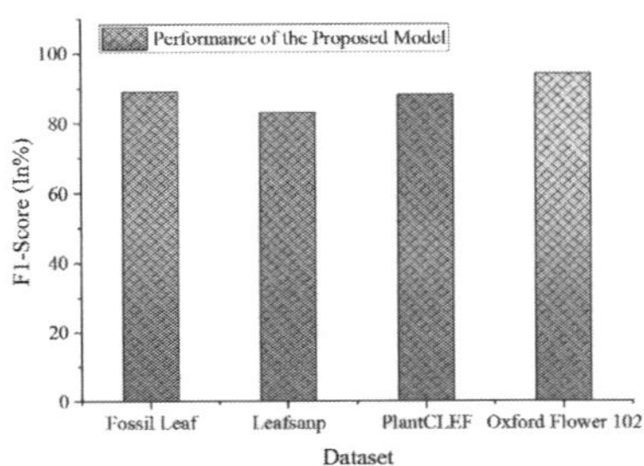
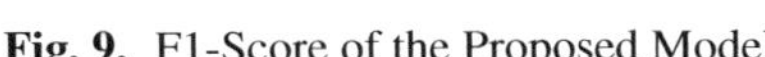

Fig. 9. F1-Score of the Proposed Model

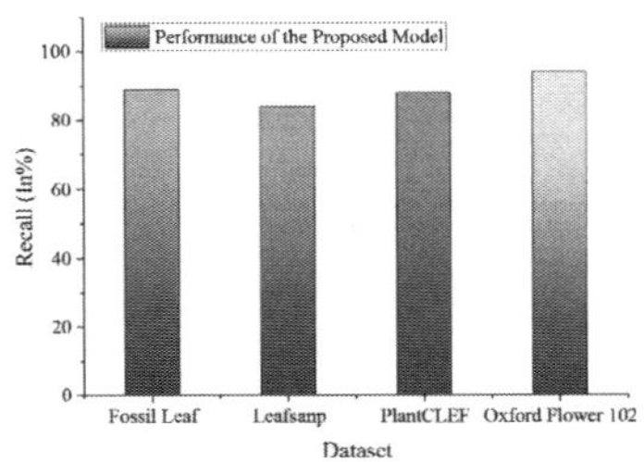

Fig. 10. Recall of the Proposed Model

Table 7. Four leaf datasets and their descriptions.

Model	Accuracy (%)	Efficiency (Processing Speed & Resource Usage)	Cost (Computational & Implementation Cost)	Scalability (Adaptability to Large Datasets & IoT Applications)
Convolutional Neural Network (CNN)	94.5	Moderate (High computational power required)	High (Expensive due to GPU/TPU needs)	Moderate (Scales well but requires high-end infrastructure)
Support Vector Machine (SVM)	89.2	Low (Slowfor large datasets)	Moderate (Less costly than deep learning but expensive for high-dimensional data)	Low (Struggles with large-scale IoT data due to computational complexity)
Random Forest (RF)	92.7	High (Fast training and inference with low resource usage)	Low (Cost-effective as it runs efficiently on standard hardware)	High (Easily scales to large IoT datasets and heterogeneous agricultural environments)
Proposed Hybrid Model (RF + Optimization Techniques)	96.8	Very High (Optimized feature selection and parallel processing reduce complexity)	Moderate (Optimized for cost-effectiveness while maintaining performance)	Very High (Adaptable to real-time IoT applications and large-scale data integration)

6 Conclusion and Future Scope

An IoT-enabled leaf structure tracking gadget with the potential to revolutionize precision agriculture by enhancing harvest productivity and lowering environmental effects is studied in this paper. The system integrated real-time data collection and analysis with modern sensor technology to give farmers deep plant health information. The work also allows precise and timely interventions. This strategy increased agricultural yields and reduced overhead costs by optimizing irrigation and fertilizer systems. The approach helped farmers practice sustainability by reducing waste and improving environmental care. Advanced agricultural leaf structure monitoring technology using IoT offered significant potential. Research demonstrated that Random Forest outperformed other models in terms of accuracy when dealing with big datasets, resistance to overfitting, and handling missing data. The feature significance rankings also provided insightful data. Random Forest was the best model for complicated and noisy datasets because it aggregated various trees to increase resilience and predictive performance, unlike single decision trees or simpler models. Additional environmental and plant health parameters from soil sensors, weather stations, and crop growth models could have improved the system. ML and AI algorithms could have enhanced data processing, enabling more accurate predictive analytics and targeted agricultural recommendations. The system could have interfaced with drones and autonomous vehicles and been modified to handle different crop varieties and agricultural settings, from small farms to substantial commercial enterprises. As IoT expanded, its infrastructure needed to be upgraded to protect consumers' data.

Future studies may use blockchain technology to verify data quality and traceability. Advanced IoT technology and ML should stimulate more farming inventions, improving efficiency, longevity, and resistance to changing environmental and climatic circumstances.

References

1. Fan, J., Zhang, Y., Wen, W., Gu, S., Lu, X., Guo, X.: The future of Internet of Things in agriculture: plant high-throughput phenotypic platform. J. Clean. Prod. **280**, 123651 (2021). https://doi.org/10.1016/j.jclepro.2020.123651
2. Kour, V.P., Arora, S.: Recent developments of the internet of things in agriculture: a survey. IEEE Access **8**, 129924–129957 (2020). https://doi.org/10.1109/ACCESS.2020.3009298
3. Dhanaraju, M., Chenniappan, P., Ramalingam, K., Pazhanivelan, S., Kaliaperumal, R.: Smart farming: internet of things (IoT)-based sustainable agriculture. Agriculture **12**(10), 1745 (2022). https://doi.org/10.3390/agriculture12101745
4. Devare, J., Hajare, N.: A survey on IoT based agricultural crop growth monitoring and quality control. In: International Conference on Communication and Electronics Systems (ICCES), pp. 1624–1630 (2019).https://doi.org/10.1109/ICCES45898.2019.9002533
5. Sekaran, K., Meqdad, M.N., Kumar, P., Rajan, S., Kadry, S.: Smart agriculture management system using internet of things. TELKOMNIKA (Telecommun. Comput. Electron. Control) **18**(3), 1275 (2020). https://doi.org/10.12928/telkomnika.v18i3.14029
6. Singh, Y.P., Chaurasia, B.K., Shukla, M.M.: Deep transfer learning driven model for mango leaf disease detection. Int. J. Syst. Assur. Eng. Manag. **15**(10), 4779–4805 (2024). https://doi.org/10.1007/s13198-024-02480-y
7. Thilakarathne, N.N., Yassin, H., Bakar, M.S.A., Abas, P.E.: Internet of Things in smart agriculture. challenges, opportunities and future directions. In: IEEE Asia-Pacific Conference on Computer Science and Data Engineering (CSDE), pp. 1–9 (2021). https://doi.org/10.1109/CSDE53843.2021.9718402

8. Mohamed Firdhous, M.F., Sudantha, B.H., Karunaratne, P.M.: IoT-powered sustainable dry zone agriculture: an experimental implementation. In: 3rd International Conference on Information Technology Research (ICITR), pp. 1–6 (2018). https://doi.org/10.1109/ICITR.2018.8736148

9. Morchid, A., El Alami, R., Raezah, A.A., Sabbar, Y.: Applications of internet of things (IoT) and sensors technology to increase food security and agricultural sustainability: benefits and challenges. Ain Shams Eng. J. **15**(3), 102509 (2024). https://doi.org/10.1016/j.asej.2023.102509

10. Wu, Y., Yang, Z., Liu, Y.: Internet-of-things-based multiple-sensor monitoring system for soil information diagnosis using a smartphone. Micromachines **14**(7), 1395 (2023). https://doi.org/10.3390/mi14071395

11. Podder, A.K., et al.: IoT based smart agrotech system for verification of Urban farming parameters. Microprocess. Microsyst. **82**, 104025 (2021). https://doi.org/10.1016/j.micpro.2021.104025

12. Kalantzopoulos, G., Paraskevopoulos, P., Domalis, G., Liopa-Tsakalidi, A., Tsesmelis, D.E., Barouchas, P.E.: The Western Greece soil information system (WESIS)—a soil health design supported by the internet of things, soil databases, and artificial intelligence technologies in Western Greece. Sustainability **16**(8), 3478 (2024). https://doi.org/10.3390/su16083478

13. Mohammad El-Basioni, B.M., Abd El-Kader, S.M.: Designing and modeling an IoT-based software system for land suitability assessment use case. Environ. Monit. Assess. **196**(4), 380 (2024). https://doi.org/10.1007/s10661-024-12483-8

14. Pandey, J.K. et al.: Investigating role of IoT in the Development of smart application for security enhancement. In: IoT Based Smart Applications, pp. 219–243. Springer, Heidelberg (2022). https://doi.org/10.1007/978-3-031-04524-0_13

15. Ghosh, D., Siddique, M.A., Pal, D.: AI-driven precision agriculture approach. AI Agric. Sustain. Econ. Manag. **67** (2024)

16. Shaikh, T.A., Rasool, T., Lone, F.R.: Towards leveraging the role of machine learning and artificial intelligence in precision agriculture and smart farming. Comput. Electron. Agric. **198**, 107119 (2022)

17. Muthugurunathan, G., Padmapriya, S., Leelavathy, L., Talukdar, V., Gupta, A., Mittal, M.: Smart conversations: enhancing user engagement through NLP in IoT environments. In: 11th International Conference on Reliability, Infocom Technologies and Optimization (Trends and Future Directions) (ICRITO), pp. 1–6 (2024). https://doi.org/10.1109/ICRITO61523.2024.10522332

18. Naresh, R.K., et al.: The prospect of artificial intelligence (AI) in precision agriculture for farming systems productivity in sub-tropical India: a review. Curr. J. Appl. Sci. Technol. **39**(48), 96–110 (2020)

19. Talaviya, T., Shah, D., Patel, N., Yagnik, H., Shah, M.: Implementation of artificialintelligence in agriculture for optimization of irrigation and application of pesticides and herbicides. Artif. Intell. Agric. **4**, 58–73 (2020)

20. Malo, M.: Artificial intelligence in agriculture: strengthening the future of farming. Agric. Food e-Newslett. **71** (2020)

21. Comegna, A., Hassan, S.B.M., Coppola, A.: Development and application of an IoT-based system for soil water status monitoring in a soil profile. Sensors **24**(9), 2725 (2024). https://doi.org/10.3390/s24092725

22. Prasad, R., Tiwari, R., Srivastava, A.K.: Internet of Things-based fuzzy logic controller for smart soil health monitoring: a case study of semi-arid regions of India. ECSA **58**, 85 (2023). https://doi.org/10.3390/ecsa-10-16208

23. Venkateshwari, P., Veeraiah, V., Talukdar, V., Gupta, D.N., Anand, R., Gupta, A.: Smart city technical planning based on time series forecasting of IOT data. In: 2023 International

Conference on Sustainable Emerging Innovations in Engineering and Technology (ICSEIET), pp. 646–651 (2023). https://doi.org/10.1109/ICSEIET58677.2023.10303480
24. Senapaty, M.K., Ray, A., Padhy, N.: IoT-enabled soil nutrient analysis and croprecommendation model for precision agriculture. Computers **12**(3), 61 (2023)
25. Maity, T., Roy, A., Das, O., Kashyap, R., Mishra, A., Samanta, J.: Design and development of IoT-based smart health monitoring system for greenhouse cultivation. In: Studies in Autonomic, Data-driven and Industrial Computing, pp. 173–185. Springer, Singapore (2024). https://doi.org/10.1007/978-981-99-5435-3_12
26. Raza, A., et al.: Artificial intelligence-enabled precision agriculture: a review of applications and challenges. In: Presented at the 2nd International Electronic Conference on Agriculture, vol. 1, p. 15 (2023)
27. Adewusi, O., Asuzu, O.F., Olorunsogo, T., Iwuanyanwu, C., Adaga, E., Daraojimba, D.O.: AI in precision agriculture: a review of technologies for sustainable farming practices. World J. Adv. Res. Rev. **21**(1), 2276–2285 (2024)
28. Jararweh, Y., Fatima, S., Jarrah, M., AlZu'bi, S.: Smart and sustainable agriculture: fundamentals, enabling technologies, and future directions. Comput. Electr. Eng. **110**, 108799 (2023). https://doi.org/10.1016/j.compeleceng.2023.108799

A Machine Learning Based Drone Surveillance for Safer Railways

K. R. Swetha[1], M. P. Hemadarshini[1], C. R. Nagarathna[2(✉)], G. Nandini[3],
Karthik Dinesh Vernekar[3], B. K. Chiran[3], and Aman Kumar Verma[3]

[1] Computer Science and Engineering, BGS Institute of Technology, Adhichunchanagiri
University, Mandya, Karnataka, India
[2] Department of Artificial Intelligence and Machine Learning, BNM Institute of Technology,
Bengaluru, India
Nagarathna.binu@gmail.com
[3] Department of Information Science and Engineering, BNM Institute of Technology,
Bengaluru, India

Abstract. Severe compromise is brought to integrity and functionality of the rail systems problems like, inoperable tracks, poor welds and unseen blocking. The inspection methods used presently are extremely time-consuming as they are primarily manual and yield no real-time data about what is happening, particularly towards directions that are way gone and out of reach. The system to be proposed is an drone-based solution for railway track monitoring to detect anomalies like cracks, welding flaws, and blockages in real-time. AI models such as YOLO and high-resolution camera-enabled drones capture data across different environments, and detected problems are geotagged. Hybrid 4G/5G and LoRa network ensures fault-tolerant data transmission. A Real-time dashboard displays and indicates anomalies and actionable insights. The system is better in terms of maintenance efficiency by monitoring the railway precisely, scalable, and reliably.

Keywords: Drone equipped with AI · Computer Vision · Real-time defect detection · Train safety.

1 Introduction

1.1 A Subsection Sample

Indian Railway networks are important for making the transportation of passengers and freight smooth and efficient. They are in fact the backbones of most global transportation systems. Their safety and reliability, however, depend largely on railway track structure. Cracks, welding problems, or unexpected obstacles on the tracks put serious risks of derailment, delay in operations, or even loss of life in some cases.

Traditionally, Indian railway inspections are always a largely manual operation: track-walking personnel observe the tracks and infrastructures with naked eyes to identify defects and obstructions. Maintenance personnel would observe cracks, loose fittings,

S. Goel et al. (Eds.): AICON 2025, LNICST 672, pp. 40–50, 2026.
https://doi.org/10.1007/978-3-032-14805-6_3

and worn-out conditions using mainly minimal instruments and limited instrumentation. It was very clumsy and took quite a lot of time. Not to mention, it had room for much human error along that expanse of area in India. However, problems remained concerning limited coverage, slow inspection speeds, and Indian Railways majorly uses the present system of track mounted cars provided with ultrasonic UV sensors to inspect the track conditions. The systems identify inner rail defects such as crack initiation, weld failures, and other structural damage that takes place by sending back waves through the internal sound reflection inside the rail. In manual mode, they are semi-automatics; thus, their usability delivers very good knowledge on track integrity. However, these systems have weaknesses such as slower inspection speed, reliance on human intervention, and inability to cover such a vast railway network properly. Moreover, unfavorable climatic conditions and inability to continuously monitor the tracks degrade their efficiency, making a need for advanced automated technologies.

Fig. 1. Oscillation carts for railway inspection

An oscillation car used by Indian Railways for railway track inspection is seen in Fig. 1. This is a track-running vehicle that may be driven by hand or by a motor. It includes simple seating and all the equipment needed to physically check the track's geometry, alignment, and other features. It facilitates maintenance personnel's site-level inspection, which helps them find obvious flaws like cracks or uneven surfaces. Its drawbacks, however, include the possibility of errors in manual observation, the incapacity to detect internal or microscopic flaws, and inefficiency when used across long distances or in extremely difficult environmental circumstances.

By processing recorded data to produce highly accurate anomaly identification and classification using sophisticated object detection models, this suggested solution combines the agility and adaptability of drones with the analytical power of artificial intelligence. Regardless of network coverage zones, the system's strong integration with dependable communication technologies guarantees real-time transmission. A safer and more dependable railway network will result from this as it has also optimised the field of maintenance activities and lowered operational costs with less delay.

2 Literature Review

In order to improve safety and operational efficiency, a great deal of research has been done on using drones and artificial intelligence for railway track surveillance. With an emphasis on real-time data processing, anomaly categorization, and defect identification, a wide range of approaches, methods, and systems have been put forth. The purpose of this review is to evaluate various methods, compile important findings, and pinpoint important gaps in order to guide the creation of a reliable and effective drone-based railway surveillance system.

P. Aela et al. (2022) [1] examined the use of UAVs in railway infrastructure monitoring by employing drones equipped with cameras and sensors to detect anomalies in real time. Although the technique was effective at analyzing images, long-term monitoring was impacted by the drones' limited range and battery life. In a similar vein, G. Gugan and A. Haque (2023) [2] investigated autonomous drone path planning, focusing on algorithms for navigating dynamic settings. However, the prototypes were not tested in real complicated contexts as part of the study.

A drone-based railway inspection system that used machine learning to diagnose problems with high accuracy was described by El-Sayed et al. (2023) [3]. However, its range and workflow integration were restricted. In order to track invasions, Guan et al. (2020) [4] used a saliency detection method using UAV footage. This provided new detection techniques, but it was not applicable in real-time and could not handle unfavorable weather conditions. This suggests that UAVs may be used to monitor railroads, but it also brings up concerns about scalability, operational limitations, and integration difficulties.

The use of UAVs in railway track inspection was demonstrated by Equinox's Drones (2021) [5], which demonstrated how their ability to capture incredibly detailed images may aid in defect detection and maintenance scheduling. Although operational efficiency was observed by the study, regulatory issues and the integration of drone-collected data into existing maintenance workflows were not thoroughly covered. Using drones, Banić et al. (2019) [6] developed an intelligent machine vision-based inspection system and made notable progress in image processing. It still had scaling problems for huge railway networks, though, because there were no reliable fleet management strategies in place.

The viability of employing drone technology to inspect distant BART rail systems was shown by Banh Lau et al. (2018) [7], but they also highlighted the challenge of contrasting the operational effectiveness and safety of drone-based inspection with traditional techniques. It doesn't address scalability or if long-term adoption would be expensive.Useful for big networks. With an emphasis on the regulatory environment and adoption patterns in India, Dubey (2020) [8] carried out a qualitative study of drone applications in sectors including infrastructure monitoring. However, the study lacked economic impact analyses and technical details, which limited its applicability to railway applications.Falamarzi et al. (2019) [9] review sensors applied devices in railway infrastructure inspection and evaluate available technologies like ultrasonic and infrared sensors.

Although the research didn't go into great detail concerning economic viability or real-world applications, it did offer some insight into sensor performance. For efficiency, Flammini et al. (2016) [10] talked of using drones to automatically monitor trains by adding a sensor like LiDAR. The automation opportunity was emphasized more than the implementation's practical difficulties, such as data integration and legal restrictions.

A UAV-photogrammetry-based system for rail track inspection was shown by Ghassoun et al. 2021 [11], and it produced incredibly precise 3D models for problem diagnosis. However, the system was not scalable because to environmental constraints including weather and costly expenses. An overview of track geometry degradation models was provided by Higgins in 2017 [12]. These models were based on statistics and mechanics, but they lacked the integration of UAV data and thorough testing conditions under various operational settings.

The ROI of drone technology for airport surveillance, transportation, and infrastructure assessment was investigated by Karpowicz (2022) [13]. Although operational efficiency and cost reductions were discovered, no quantitative support was offered, and regulatory concerns were not taken into consideration. In order to inspect railway infrastructure, Lesiak (2020) [14] employed UAVs, concentrating on flaw detection through the use of high-resolution images. Its cost-effectiveness was impacted by limitations including its reliance on favorable weather and experienced operators.

CNNs were utilized with promising accuracy by Mittal and Rao (2017) [15] to analyze visual data from drones used for railway track surveillance. However, because to the variety of environmental circumstances the system encountered, the approach required a significant amount of labeled data for training, which was challenging to do. A technique for mapping land usage and railroad lines using UAVs that emphasizes aerial view photos was reported by Manatunga et al. (2017) [16]. The project faced issues with GPS errors and processing big data volumes, which made it unscalable.UAV-based visual inspection for bridges and railroad tracks was evaluated by Morgenthal and Hallermann (2014) [17], who found that high-resolution imagery showed promise. Nevertheless, the study emphasized the difficulties of flying endurance and susceptibility to external elements like wind. In order to identify plant species on railway embankments, Nyberg and Gupta (2013) [18] employed image processing, which provided some information about vegetation management. However, the inability to differentiate between similar plant species was a limitation of the study.

Using advanced machine learning techniques for vegetation detection in UAV data, Rahman and Mammeri (2021) [19] frequently achieved reliable classification. Congested environments and similarities between items and vegetation caused accuracy problems. The authors [20, 21], who concentrated on use cases including safety evaluations and track problem identification, detailed the benefits of UAVs for railway operations. The study had logistical and regulatory obstacles that prevented its broad application, in addition to the absence of quantitative data (Table 1).

Table 1. Literature Review Summary Table

Paper Name	*Summary*	*Limitations*	*Methods Used*
UAV-Based Studies in Railway Infrastructure Monitoring P. Aela, H-L. Chi, A. Fares, T. Zayed & M. Kim (2022) [1]	Makes use of real-time track inspection based on the image processing and anomaly detection using UAVs equipped with cameras and sensors	Drones have poor range and short battery life, a factor affecting the feasibility of long-term monitoring	UAVs, real-time image processing, anomaly detection
Path Planning for Autonomous Drones: Challenges and Future Directions G. Gugan & A. Haque (2023) [2]	Researches into Algorithms and Applications in Track Monitoring in Dynamic Environments	Poor testing and validation involving realistic scenarios of real-world railway	Path planning algorithms, simulation frameworks
Railway Track Monitoring Using Drones M. F. El-Sayed, H. Riad, H. Zohny & M. Zahran (2023) [3]	Utilize UAVs incorporating high-resolution camera and sensor technologies for detecting and classifying track defects utilizing machine learning for real- time inspection	Problems include battery life of drones, impact of weather, and the system integration into the workflows of railway maintenance	High-resolution cameras, sensors, machine learning algorithms
A Visual Saliency-Based Railway Intrusion Detection Method by UAV Remote Sensing Image L. Guan, X. Li, H. Yang & L. Jia (2020) [4]	Capture resolution remote sensing imagery using UAVs and apply saliency detection to identify obstructions or intrusion on railway tracks	It fails to discuss the applicability of real-time monitoring and is limited in addressing adverse environmental conditions, for instance low visibility	UAVs, saliency detection algorithm, anomaly detection
Railway Inspection & Monitoring Using UAV/Drone Technology Equinox's Drones (2021) [5]	It illustrates real-time defect detection and maintenance planning for the railway infrastructure with a camera- and sensor-equipped UAV	Lacks discussion on integrating drone data with existing systems and does not address regulatory challenges or large-scale deployment hurdles	High-resolution cameras, UAV-based data analysis

(continued)

Table 1. (*continued*)

Paper Name	Summary	Limitations	Methods Used
Intelligent Machine Vision- Based Railway Infrastructure Inspection Using UAV M. Banić et al. (2019) [6]	Explores image processing algorithms for inspecting railway infrastructure, focusing on drones capturing images of tracks and components	System does not scale well for large networks. There is no good fleet management strategy in place	UAVs, image processing algorithms
Evaluation of Feasibility of UAV Technologies for Remote Surveying BART Rail Systems Banh Lau et al. (2018) [7]	Compares drone-based data collection with traditional methods of surveying rail systems in terms of feasibility, efficiency, and safety	Limited focus on long-term scalability and integration challenges such as operational costs and regulatory compliance	Feasibility analysis, UAV-based data collection
Usage of Drone Technology in India: Changing Phases N. Dubey (2020) [8]	Provides qualitative analysis of the application of drones in industries with possibilities in infrastructure and surveillance	Very insufficient discussion on technical matters, plus insufficient consideration of specific railway applications	Case study analysis, qualitative review
A Review on Existing Sensors and Devices for Inspecting Railway Infrastructure A. Falamarzi et al. (2019) [9]	Very insufficient discussion on technical matters, plus insufficient consideration of specific railway applications	Has fewer real-world case studies, especially not considering economic or integration challenges for large-scale application	Sensor technology review (ultrasonic, laser, infrared)
Towards Automated Drone Surveillance in Railways: State-of-the-Art and Future Directions F. Flammini et al. (2016) [10]	Highlights that cameras and LiDAR are used by UAVs to automate the process of data collection and analysis for railway monitoring	Lacks discussion on the regulatory constraint, integration challenge, and the high launch cost of automated UAV	UAVs, LiDAR, sensor integration

(continued)

Table 1. (*continued*)

Paper Name	Summary	Limitations	Methods Used
Implementation and Validation of a High-Accuracy UAV-Photogrammetry-Based Rail Track Inspection System Y. Ghassoun et al. (2021) [11]	UAVs and photogrammetry software were used to process the rail track images into 3D models for the detection of defects against traditional measurement methods	Limited by environmental factors, high costs, and complexity, hindering large- scale adoption	UAVs, high-resolution cameras, photogrammetry software
Modeling of Track Geometry Degradation and Decisions on Safety and Maintenance C. L. Higgins (2017) [12]	Analyzes statistical, mechanistic, and hybrid models for predicting track geometry degradation to improve safety and maintenance planning	Does not integrate actual real-time data from modern technologies and limits model accuracy in dynamic operation conditions	Statistical and mechanistic models, track geometry analysis
The ROI of Drone Technology in Infrastructure, Transportation, and at Airports J. Karpowicz (2022) [13]	Explores how drones can reduce the operational costs, enhance the safety, and increase efficiency of infrastructure inspection and transportation management	Lacks quantitative data to validate its ROI claims and does not address regulatory or logistical challenges.	Business analysis, drone case studies
Inspection and Maintenance of Railway Infrastructure with the Use of Unmanned Aerial Vehicles P. Lesiak (2020) [14]	Highlights UAV applications in railway inspections, using high-resolution cameras to detect and document infrastructure defects	Battery limitations, dependency on weather, and high costs for UAV operation and skilled workforce are significant barriers	UAVs, high-resolution cameras, aerial inspection
Development of a Methodology to Map Railway Lines and Surrounding Land Use Using UAVs U. Manatunga et al. (2017) [15]	This presents a method of collecting and analyzing UAV-based aerial imagery of railway lines and their environment with better planning for the infrastructure	GPS errors, big data handling difficulties, and the reliance of good weather	UAVs, GIS-based analysis, aerial imagery processing

(*continued*)

Table 1. (*continued*)

Paper Name	*Summary*	*Limitations*	*Methods Used*
Vision-Based Railway Track Monitoring Using Deep Learning S. Mittal & D. Rao (2017) [16]	Employs convolutional neural networks (CNNs) to analyze visual data from UAVs or train-mounted cameras for the detection of railway defects	Requires extensive labeled data and struggles with environmental diversity affecting model accuracy	CNNs, deep learning, visual data analysis
Quality Assessment of UAV-Based Visual Inspection of Structures G. Morgenthal & N. Hallermann (2014) [17]	Explores UAV-based visual inspection methods for structural elements like bridges and towers, focusing on efficiency and accuracy	Limited flight endurance, susceptibility to environmental conditions like wind, and the need for specialized expertise	UAVs, visual inspection, structural monitoring

3 Proposed Methodology

The railway track monitoring system is modeled as an autonomous anomaly detection framework, with the drone as the primary agent. The goal of the system is to identify and report defects like cracks, welding problems, slag inclusions, undercuts, and obstructions on railway tracks. Main assumptions: Drones have high-resolution cameras and sensors that capture actual data in real time. Tracks and their surroundings have different environmental conditions, such as lighting and weather. It depends on the hybrid model of 4G/5G and LoRa when cellular networks are unstable. The operational environment is designed to simulate real-world railway conditions, and it includes:

- Track geometry data (e.g., alignments, joints).
- Dynamic environmental changes (e.g., low-light intensities, covered by vegetation).
- Network Conditions for Testing Communication Resiliency.

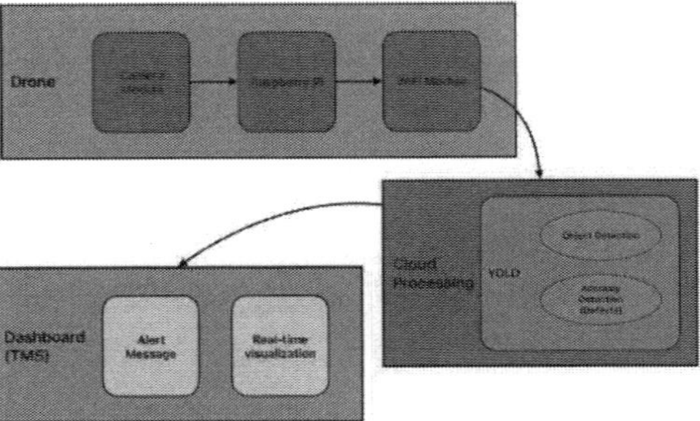

Fig. 2. Data Flow Diagram (Level 1)

Figure 2 depicts the system architecture diagram, which shows end-to-end communication flow for an autonomous drone-based railway track monitoring system. The Drone Module is designed to capture real-time video feeds with a high-resolution camera, transfer data to the Raspberry Pi, and then process raw input and prepare it for transmission. It utilizes a Wi-Fi module that transfers the processed data to the Cloud Processing Unit, in which YOLO algorithms identify crack defects or obstructions as well as anomalies. In real-time, the images or video frames are processed using the cloud server that contains a GPU-enabled setup; then it generates actionable insights. A system of alerts has also been provided to notify the operators through the Dashboard Module, abbreviated as TMS. This dashboard provides real-time visualization of detected defects and alert messages for prompt interventions. The architecture ensures a seamless flow of data from the drone to the cloud and ultimately to the station master, optimizing railway safety and maintenance.

4   Conclusion

The proposed drone-based railway track monitoring system offers a transformative approach to addressing the challenges of track inspection and maintenance. By leveraging the speed and flexibility of drones, the system can survey extensive railway tracks in a fraction of the time required by traditional methods. Integrating cutting-edge AI algorithms, ensures accurate and real-time detection of defects like cracks, welding issues, and obstructions, enabling timely interventions. The incorporation of hybrid communication technologies ensures seamless data transmission even in areas with poor network connectivity.

This framework not only enhances railway safety and operational efficiency but also optimizes resource utilization, reducing manual inspection efforts and associated costs. By processing data on the cloud and providing actionable insights via a real-time dashboard, the system empowers railway operators to make informed decisions, minimizing delays and preventing accidents. These contributions are particularly impactful in regions with vast railway networks, where timely maintenance is critical for uninterrupted service.

Future directions for this work include incorporating predictive analytics to foresee potential track failures, integrating blockchain for secure data management, and scaling the system for nationwide deployment. This solution represents a significant step toward modernizing railway infrastructure, aligning with broader goals of safety, efficiency, and sustainability, and setting a foundation for smarter transportation systems.

References

1. Aela, P., Chi, H.L., Fares, A., Zayed, T., Kim, M.: UAV-based studies in railway infrastructure monitoring. Autom. Constr. **167**, 105714 (2024)
2. Gugan, G., Haque, A.: Path planning for autonomous drones: challenges and future directions. Drones **7**(3), 169 (2023)
3. El-Sayed, M.F., Riad, H.S., Zohny, H.N., Zahran, M.S.: Railway track monitoring using drones. J. Phys. Conf. Ser. **2616**, 012056 (2023). https://doi.org/10.1088/1742-6596/2616/1/012056
4. Guan, L., Li, X., Yang, H., Jia, L.: A Visual saliency based railway intrusion detection method by uav remote sensing image, pp. 291–295. Institute of Electrical and Electronics Engineers Inc., Beijing (2020). https://doi.org/10.1109/SDPC49476.2020.9353141
5. Equinox's Drones. Railway Inspection & Monitoring Using UAV/Drone Technology (2021). Accessed 15 July 2022. https://www.equinoxsdrones.com/blog/railway-inspectionmonitoring-using-uav-drone-technology
6. Banić, M., Miltenović, A., Pavlović, M., Ćirić, I.: Intelligent machine vision based railway infrastructure inspection and monitoring using UAV. Facta Universitatis, Ser. Mech. Eng. **17**(3), 357–364 (2019). https://doi.org/10.22190/FUME190507041B
7. Banh Lau, M., et al.: Evaluation of Feasibility of UAV Technologies for Remote Surveying BART Rail Systems. UC Berkeley: Bay Area Rapid Transit (BART) (2018). Accessed 15 July 2022. https://escholarship.org/uc/item/3qr9v29d
8. Nagarathna, C.R., Kusuma, M.M.: Early detection of Alzheimer's Disease using MRI images and deep learning techniques. Alzheimers Dement. **19**, e062076 (2023)
9. Falamarzi, A., Moridpour, S., Nazem, M.: A Review on existing sensors and devices for inspecting railway infrastructure. Jurnal Kejuruteraan **31**(1), 1–10 (2019). https://doi.org/10.17576/jkukm-2019-31
10. Debnath, S., Preetham, A., Vuppu, S., Kumar, S.N.P.: Optimal weighted GAN and U-Net based segmentation for phenotypic trait estimation of crops using Taylor Coot algorithm. Appl. Soft Comput. **144**, 110396 (2023)
11. Flammini, F., Naddei, R., Pragliola, C., Smarra, G.: Towards automated drone surveillance in railways: state-of-the-art and future directions. Lect. Notes Comput. Sci. **10016**, 336–348 (2016). https://doi.org/10.1007/978-3-319-48680-2_30
12. Nagarathna, C.R., Chinnaswamy, C.N.: The technique to detect and avoid the denial of service attacks in wireless sensor networks. Int. J. Res. Eng. Technol. (IJRET) **3**(05), 1–4 (2014)
13. Bhavyashree, H.L., Nagarathna, C.R., Preetham, A., Priyanka, R.: Modified cluster based certificate blocking of misbehaving node in MANETS. In: 2019 1st International Conference on Advanced Technologies in Intelligent Control, Environment, Computing & Communication Engineering (ICATIECE), pp. 155–161. IEEE (2019)
14. Karpowicz, J.: The ROI of Drone Technology in Infrastructure, Transportation and at Airports (2022). Accessed 03 July 2022. https://www.commercialuavnews.com/infrastructure/the-roi-of-drone-technology-in infrastructure-transportation-and-at-airports
15. Chandana, S., Nagarathna, C.R., Amrutha, A., Jayasri, A.: Detection of image forgery using error level analysis. In: 2024 International Conference on Intelligent and Innovative Technologies in Computing, Electrical and Electronics (IITCEE), pp. 1–5. IEEE (2024)

16. Manatunga, U., Munasinghe, N., Premasiri, H.:. Development of a methodology to map railway lines and surrounding land use using UAVs. In: Proceedings of ISERME 2017, Sri Lanka, pp. 195–202 (2017). http://dl.lib.mrt.ac.lk/handle/123/12825
17. Mittal, S., Rao, D.: Vision Based Railway Track Monitoring using Deep Learning. arXiv preprint arXiv:1711.06423. https://doi.org/10.48550/arXiv:1711.06423 (2017)
18. Morgenthal, G., Hallermann, N.: Quality assessment of unmanned aerial vehicle (UAV) based visual inspection of structures. Adv. Struct. Eng. **17**(3), 289 (2014). https://doi.org/10.1260/1369-4332.17.3.289
19. Nagarathna, C.R., Kusuma, M.: Comparative study of detection and classification of Alzheimer's disease using Hybrid model and CNN. In: 2021 International Conference on Disruptive Technologies for Multi-Disciplinary Research and Applications (CENTCON), vol. 1, pp. 43–46. IEEE (2021)
20. Preetham, A., et al.: Instinctive recognition of pathogens in rice using reformed fractional differential segmentation and innovative fuzzy logic-based probabilistic neural network. J. Food Qual. **2022**(1), 8662254 (2022)
21. Rao, A., Kulkarni, S.B.: An improved technique of plant leaf classificaion using hybrid feature modeling. In: 2017 International Conference on Innovative Mechanisms for Industry Applications (ICIMIA), pp. 5–9. IEEE (2017)

A Comprehensive Approach to Adaptive Multi-model Architecture for Heterogeneous Data Sources

E. Anbazhagan[1], S. Sudharson[2(✉)], R. Annamalai[1], and V. Vamsi Krishna[1]

[1] Department of Computer Science and Engineering, Amrita School of Computing,
Amrita Vishwa Vidyapeetham, Chennai 601103, India
[2] School of Computer Science and Engineering, Vellore Institute of Technology,
Chennai 600127, India
sudharsonsriram@gmail.com

Abstract. Deep learning has revolutionized many domains, such as natural language processing, image recognition, and healthcare analysis, by providing accurate predictions and improved decision-making. However, choosing the best model architecture for a problem and selecting the problem domains is still a challenge. Convolutional neural networks (CNNs), long-short term memory networks (LSTMs), and dense neural networks are the models that have been used to build a conventional multi-model architecture for several problems. This study proposes a multimodel technique to determine the optimal model architecture based on the problem statement and input data type. The model selection process determines which model among the available models in the architecture is suitable for usage or in a combination of models. To assess the effectiveness of different models, we employ a diverse dataset comprising image data, text data, and numerical data. The proposed approach outperformed the existing state-of-the-art methods and obtained a maximum accuracy of 89% in image classification, which improved to 92% after our proposed ensemble technique, 90% in text sentiment analysis, and 88% in diabetes prediction with the standard datasets. The performance of the model was evaluated based on accuracy, sensitivity, selectivity, and training time. The proposed system helps in selecting the best for any type of input data samples.

Keywords: Multi-Model · Ensembling · Convolution Neural Network · Long Short-Term Memory

1 Introduction

The multi-model approach of deep learning architectures grows rigorously to be a broad spectrum that tries to cover all human aspects, unlike unimodal applications [1]. Extensive unimodal development is insufficient to fulfill human aspects. Modality associates objects, feelings, smells, and sounds with how they are experienced [2]. Generally, the environment around us is a multi-model where objects around us are captured through information in media formats of image, text, video, sound, and so on [3]. As the development of various deep learning models and approaches has become ample in order

© ICST Institute for Computer Sciences, Social Informatics and Telecommunications Engineering 2026
Published by Springer Nature Switzerland AG 2026. All Rights Reserved
S. Goel et al. (Eds.): AICON 2025, LNICST 672, pp. 51–69, 2026.
https://doi.org/10.1007/978-3-032-14805-6_4

to solve cross-domain problems, a better way of classifying and categorizing data has been limited.

Convolutional Neural Networks (CNNs), Recurrent Neural Networks (RNNs), and Fully-Connected Neural Networks (FCNs) are the keystones to building a multi-model, as most of the problems are being addressed around them. Building a model that selects the best parameters [4] for the specific type of data and using them in an optimized way is robust and efficient [5]. Several applications with heterogeneous data, such as emotion recognition and medical applications using visual, audio, and temporal data, are multiple sources semantically correlated. When constructing a naive multi-model by just stacking uni-models trained over type-specific input such as images, audio seems to fail as the corresponding models tend to highlight the patterns from the data they trained on, which shows they do not correlate [6].

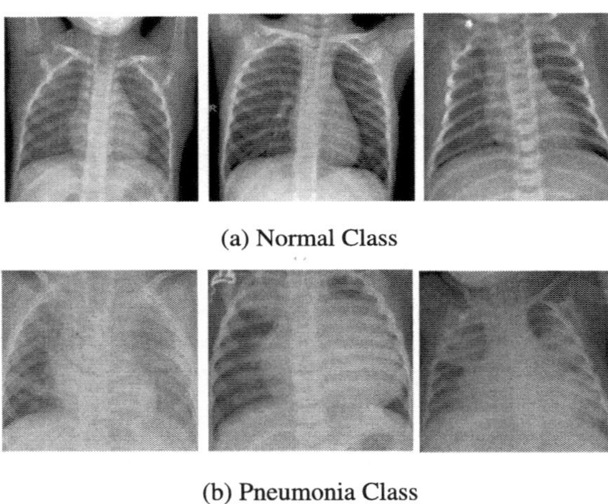

(a) Normal Class

(b) Pneumonia Class

Fig. 1. Chest X-ray images of normal pneumonia patients

Generating computer-aided radiology reports from a multi-model method, which involves CNN-RNN as an encoder-decoder architecture, and the data are collected from Indiana University. Plenteous approaches during the pandemic and in the arena of pneumonia infectious patients [7] from normal ones follow the trend of utilizing ImageNet models. Image segmentation, classification, object detection, and similar other patterns of problems in the medical and healthcare domain have a great deal of utilization of pre-trained ImageNet models such as AlexNet, ResNet, and VGG [8,9]. Ensembling these models along with other recursive and dense neural layers for the early stage of diagnosis using Chest Computed Tomography Images [10,11]. The crucial part of ensemble models is the voting strategy which has to be adaptive to complex instead of simple majority and average voting, like adaptive to the cost function [12]. Conventional classification problems have been improved by applications of Generative Adversarial Networks (GANs) [13].

Chest X-rays are non-invasive and painless, and they assist in modality development with fewer complications and efficiency. Pneumonia accounted for lots of lives, including children. It has a lot of factors playing along involved in its cause, like malnutrition, air pollution, and lack of immunity. Nothing more than a multi-model can be perfect to design and consider all factors in account [14]. In order to exhibit the proposed model with the spatial data pneumonia classification problem, it is taken into account as these have better performance with conventional ImageNet models. Sentiment analysis, object detection, named entity recognition, and many such similar problems are also dealt with cross-modal capabilities irrespective of supervised or unsupervised data [15]. They follow a peculiar trend down the path that illuminates them to perform versatile tasks and outperform uni-modals. Sentiment analysis and emotion detection diverge around various domains like natural language processing and speech processing, which help to understand the human mentality and emotions and build systems like recommendations and advertisements.

Sentiment is the opinion, views, and conduct of people and how they express themselves. This domain-specific research deals with temporal and sequential data that needs memory efficiency and high accuracy by using recursive layers like Long Short-Term Memory (LSTM) and Gated Recurrent Unit (GRU) [16]. The cross-modality of these recursive models with convolution and dense layers enhances the unimodal techniques with sequential data. This hybrid architecture [17] exclusively analyzes image cum textual information for sentimental analysis. As IMDB movie review text classification is another well-defined problem that has abundant research. In order to understand the functionality of the proposed architecture, we will experiment with IMDB data on LSTM layers. Apart from text as sequential data, audio-visual data also falls under this category. Audio-visual cross-modality feature extraction methods have been an initial thrust for multi-model architectures where they were well correlated for speech recognition techniques [18]. Complex and dynamic requirements of biomedical data outperform conventional unimodal methods by multimodal architecture [19]. Even an integrated multi-model with unimodal prediction to convey the multimodal nature of healthcare and clinical decision-making in the biomedical field [20]. In the field of healthcare, multimodal has proven to be a backbone of solving initial key research like diabetes prediction and diagnosis and retinopathy, which was a part of conventional machine learning models. Here, well-annotated data from diabetic patients are trained with FCNs for experimental purposes.

In this study, the focus is to determine the multimodality technique based on the problem statement and input data type. Selecting the model specific to data input may be an aspect to be addressed, unlike training a cross-modal with multi-type data (audio-visual, Image-Text). Model selection for multi-model architecture is based on stacking different models of unspecific types, like spatial, temporal, and sequential numerical data. The effectiveness of the model is tested on pneumonia classification (spatial data), IMDB sentiment analysis-text classification (temporal-sequential data), and diabetes prediction (numerical data) in this presented work. The remainder of the paper is structured as follows. Section 2 briefs the research related to the chosen experimental problems using transfer learning and multi-model approaches. The proposed methodology for the problem statement is discussed in Sect. 3, which comprises model selection, structural division of the model, and the ensemble technique. Section 4 deals with experimental result analysis and justifying them through discussion. Finally, conclusions and future work firections are derived in Sect. 5.

2 Related Works

This section deals with research related to the various multi-model, pneumonia classifications using chest X-rays, sentiment analysis, and diabetes prediction tasks. Deep Learning (DL) has been a dynamic and powerful way of implementing Machine Learning (ML) concepts [3]. Artificial Intelligence has been revolutionized by DL [21]. Multi-model advises that humans must understand and analyze better when it is required to engage a variety of senses. In any domain that implements a challenging task, it requires a great deal of assistance from deep learning. For instance, UAV object detection, Search And Rescue (SAR), and object detection of any kind might be an arduous job [22]. Cross-model architecture assists a lot in minute focuses on object detection and bounding.

A Deep Auto-Encoder (DAE) [23] is a model proposed to enhance the performance of unimodal, which reduces the computational cost. On the other hand, Bimodal Deep Auto-Encoder (BDAE) [23] is a multi-model facilitation construct that is superior to state-of-the-art methods in emotion recognition tasks. Stacking deep learning constructs would help create a multimodal, and if they are involved in feature extraction and reconstruction, it builds up an encoder. Therefore, multi-model constructs are versatile builds that engage in understanding human-like senses. Multi-Modality Learning (MML), Cross-Modality Learning (CML), and Multi-model Deep Learning (MDL) are three terms that correlate with one another. The development of multi-Model constructs from MML and CML. This kind of model shows better performance in remote sensing and geoscience, where the model intends to extract pixel and spectral features and learn them [24].

A Multi-model Extraction Network (Ex-Net) and Fusion Network (Fu-Net) is an end-to-end model approach of MDL. From geoscience to medical science, deep learning gives lots of holistic studies. However, a more cognitive construct provides a fusion of multiple data models in the healthcare sector. Clinical symptoms and disease diagnosis for various kinds of diseases, including Alzheimer's [25] and diabetic retinopathy, are assisted through multi-model analysis. Convo-LSTM is a cross-modal construct that works to diagnose diabetes [26,27]. This hyperglycemia diagnosis has been a conventional model that is trained with FCNs and validated over n-folds of cross-validation [28]. A feed-forward architecture [29] that extracts image features using ImageNet models and a dimensionality reduction using autoencoders using radiographic images includes chest x-rays, ultrasound, and CT scans. Ultrasound techniques are presumed to be less harmful than other techniques [30].

ImageNet models [31,32] are likely to perform well with the pneumonia classification task by freezing hidden layers along with concatenating the Global Average Pooling (GAP) layer and the other conventional addition of layers for multi-class classification problems. ConcatCNN [33] is a generic convolution layer with combinations of pooling layers, batch normalization, and regularization using dropout layers with a focus on extracting features with an optimal number of kernels. The optimization technique is applied to improvise the performance of adjusted layers to be used in ImageNet models and different optimizers like Stochastic Gradient Descent (SGD) [34]. The computer-aided diagnosis (CAD) systems revolve around the optimization of pre-trained 1000-class ImageNet model weights and achieved an average of 96% accuracy among all researchers. There are a few gaps that have to be addressed. The stepwise multimodal diagnostic system [35] is an efficient technique that tackles noisy and corrupted images. The feature maps are aggregated over successive steps adopting certain noise removal procedures like wavelet denoising and regularization-cum feature extraction. Faster Region-Based Convolutional Neural Network (Faster RCNN) [36], which is an advancement of the region proposal network (RPN) that does the feature map extraction from each proposal that has been extracted using selective search (segmentation + exhaustive search), finally, a support vector machine classifier would classify each proposal that makes the detection process faster.

Sentiment analysis through multimodal is also a possible outcome that yields high efficiency, unlike unimodal constructs. R-CNN also can perform sentiment analysis tasks. As a cross-modality technique, it can be applied to a variety of data types, including images, text, and audio. A tweet analysis [37] from Twitter has been proposed by this model that deals with image text segregation and aggregation features once they have been processed. This work exhibits exactly how the same modal can be a cross-modality component that helps us understand the deep learning [38] technique to modal human sense. Reviewing all these types of social media posts has built the ideology of analyzing them through various possible techniques, including machine learning approaches [39]. Even ensemble proposals recursive networks like LSTM, BiLSTM, and GRU that focus on textual data and sentimental analysis of them [40,41]. In our research, from knowledge acquired from the literature survey, we will experiment with our proposed model on the specific example described earlier in Sect. 1.

3 Material and Methodology

The motivation for proposing a multi-model is to automatically select a model for an appropriate task. Here we are implementing this multi-model for pneumonia classification, text classification for movie review, and diabetes prediction with the dense neural network. In this following section, we include Data collection, preprocessing, and transfer learning models for image classification such as ResNet50, VGG16, InceptionV3, and a pre-trained deep convolutional network. The details are explained in the subsections following.

3.1 Data Collection and Pre-Processing

In the proposed model, the CNN Architecture was trained and tested on a dataset consisting of chest X-ray images taken from Kaggle Datasets. This Dataset Consists of two image classes (i) Normal - Fig. 1a and (ii) Pneumonia - Fig. 1b. Figure 1 shows some sample images from the dataset. A Normal chest X-ray shows a clear lung and there are no irregular "Opaque" areas and the second one shows the chest X-ray images of people affected with pneumonia have increased lung density and it is depicted as whiteness in the X-ray. The lungs' most frequent alterations are consolidation, nodular shadowing, and ground glass opacities (GGO).

Table 1. Chest X-ray Image Dataset Distribution

Images	Train	Validation
Normal	1341	234
Pneumonia	3875	390

They primarily impact the bottom and periphery of the lungs. The most frequent finding on chest X-rays for GGO is lower lobe predominance in the periphery. Dataset Distribution was sufficient to train the model as in Table 1. The dataset has been shuffled and sampled while training. For Text classification, we utilized the IMDB movie review dataset with two classes (i) Positive and (ii) Negative.

3.2 Proposed Architecture

The main objective of our model is to select and train the model or predict the desired output based on the given input and problem statement. This reduces the problem of training all models with the same dataset and selecting the model which gives the best output. Instead, we could select the best model and train it or predict using it automatically based on given input and problem statement.

Our model architecture consists of two phases. Phase 1 we propose it has a Model Selection phase and Phase 2 proposes a Prediction or Training Phase as in Fig. 2a. In the Model Selection phase, we have DeepLSTM Network for selecting a model based on the problem statement and input type which has been trained over a dataset that has been generated using synthetic data generation. This has the target of choosing CNN, LSTM, FCN, or combinations of the according to the requirement of the problem. In Phase 2, we use the selected model to train or predict. Here Prediction is taken using the transfer learning concept. We have pre-trained models for CNN, such as ResNET50v2, VGG16, InceptionV3, Deep CNN, LSTM, and FCN model that is being exploited by the architecture.

To train we set an attribute prediction as FALSE so that it would go for training using the given dataset. In predictions of CNN, we predict output using all mentioned models and apply the concept of ensembling. This has been done as we would like to get a maximum vote of prediction and choose the most probable output. This maximum vote helps us in reducing the effect minimum validation accuracy as the model sees new data, thus, trying to output the desired output.

Flow of Proposed Method. As in Fig. 2b, model takes Input as the problem statement P, input data D, classes of prediction C, and input type I. Model Selection Phase *(DLN)* - (Phase 1): Train the *DeepLSTM* Network *(DLN)* on synthetic data, S. Determine the

---

Algorithm 1. Model Selection and Training/Prediction

Require:
1: P: Problem statement
2: D: Input data
3: C: Classes of prediction
4: I: Input type
5: f: Boolean indicating whether models already exist (true for existing models, false for non-existing models)
6: n: Number of classes defined already
7: η: Number of epochs for training
8: β: Batch size for training
9: μ: Step size for training
10: ϕ: Model architecture ($\phi \in \{$CNN, LSTM, FCN$\}$)
11: θ : Transfer Learning model ($\theta \in \{$ResNet50, VGG19, VGG16, InceptionV3,XLNet … $\}$)
12: $\theta \subseteq \phi$
13: **procedure** MODELSELECTIONPHASE(S,ϕ,P,I)
14:     Train the DeepLSTM Network (DLN) on synthetic data S.
15:     Determine the suitable model architecture ϕ_j based on P and I using DLN.
16:     I is fed into Model Architecture ϕ_j.
17:     **return** ϕ_j
18: **end procedure**
19: **procedure** PREDICTIONORTRAININGPHASE($\phi_j,f,D,\eta,\beta,\mu$)
20:     **if** f is **false then**
21:         **Training Phase**
22:         Train the models ϕ_j on D with η epochs, β batch size, and μ step size.
23:         TRAINABLEPHASE(ϕ_j,D,η,β,μ)
24:     **else**
25:         **Direct Prediction**
26:         Perform Predictions with Trained Transfer Learning Models θ_j.
27:         TRANSFERLEARNINGBLOCK(θ_j,D)
28:     **end if**
29: **end procedure**
30: **procedure** TRANSFERLEARNINGBLOCK(θ_j,D)
31:     **Use pre-trained model**
32:     Use the selected pre-trained model architecture θ_j for predictions on D.
33:     PREDICTIONPHASE(f,ϕ_j,θ_j,D,n)
34: **end procedure**
35: **procedure** TRAINABLEPHASE(ϕ_j,D,η,β,μ)
36:     **Train the models**
37:     Train the models ϕ_j on D with η epochs, β batch size, and μ step size.
38:     PREDICTIONPHASE(f,ϕ_j,θ_j,D,n)
39: **end procedure**
40: **procedure** PREDICTIONPHASE(f,ϕ_j,θ_j,D,n)
41:     **if** n is not **None then**
42:         **if** f is **false then**
43:             **Go for prediction using n classes defined already**
44:             **for** each sample d_i in D **do**
45:                 Use model ϕ_j to predict the class of d_i for the defined n classes.
46:             **end for**
47:         **else**
48:             **Go for prediction using n classes defined already**
49:             **for** each sample d_i in D **do**
50:                 Use model θ_j to predict the class of d_i for the defined n classes.
51:             **end for**
52:         **end if**
53:     **end if**
54: **end procedure**
55: **Main Algorithm**
56: MODELSELECTIONPHASE(S,ϕ,P,I)
57: PREDICTIONORTRAININGPHASE($\phi_j,f,D,\eta,\beta,\mu$)

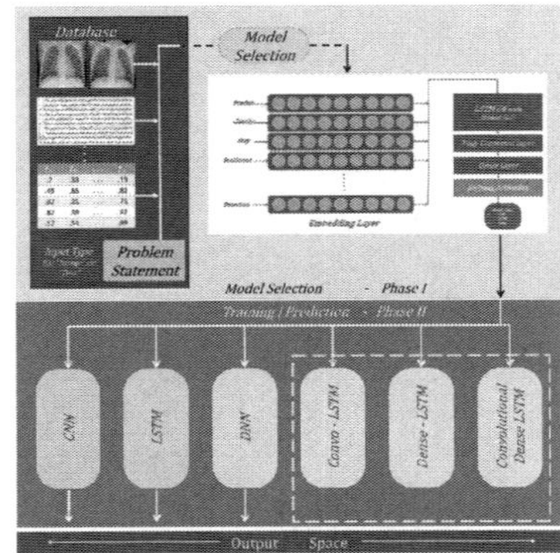

(a) Architecture of Multi-Model Deep
Neural Network for Multi-Type
Dataset (MMD)

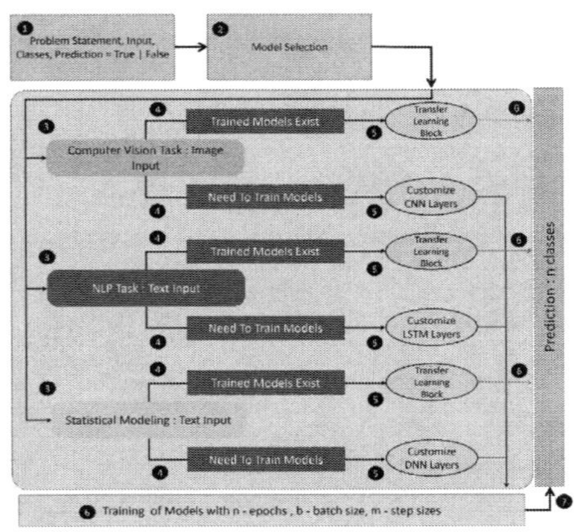

(b) WorkFlow of MMD Architecture

Fig. 2. Proposed Methodology

suitable model architecture ϕ based on P & I using the *(DLN)* is fed into Model Architecture ϕ. Prediction or Training Phase (Phase 2): If the need is to train models (i.e., f is false), go for training. Otherwise, go for further process. If models already exist (i.e., f is true), do prediction. Transfer Learning Block / Customizable Models (Phase 2): Use the selected pre-trained model architecture θ for predictions on D if f is true. Otherwise, do further process. Customize the respective models ϕ to train models if f is false & go for the trainable phase. Trainable Phase(Phase 2): Go for prediction using n classes defined already. Otherwise, go for further process. Train the models ϕ on D with η epochs, β batch size, & μ step size. Direct Prediction: Perform Predictions with Trained Model ϕ / Transfer Learning Models θ.

3.3 Transfer Learning Models

Residual Network. Deep neural network design known as Residual Networks, or ResNets for short, was first developed in 2015. Vanishing gradients are a typical issue in deep neural networks with several layers, although ResNets can resolve it. The network finds it challenging to learn from the data when gradients are so small that they are effectively zero. This condition is known as the vanishing gradient problem. By utilizing skip connections [42], which let the network bypass some layers and send input straight to a later layer, ResNets can address this issue.

InceptionV3. Google unveiled InceptionV3 in 2015, a deep neural network architecture for image recognition. The InceptionV3 model is a variant of the Inception architecture, which aims to be highly accurate while being computationally efficient. The ImageNet Large Scale Visual Recognition Challenge (ILSVRC) and the Microsoft Common Objects in Context (COCO) dataset are two image recognition benchmarks where the InceptionV3 [43] model has demonstrated state-of-the-art performance.

Visual Geometry Group. With 19 layers, comprising 16 convolutional layers and 3 fully connected layers, VGG19 is a deep convolutional neural network (CNN) architecture. In contrast to earlier architectures like AlexNet, it uses modest 3×3 convolutional filters consistently across the network to create a deeper network. VGG19 can accurately categorize photos into several categories by learning hierarchical features from raw pixel data. In the 2014 ImageNet Large Scale Visual Recognition Challenge (ILSVRC) [44], it demonstrated outstanding performance on image recognition tasks including object localization and picture classification. Because of its success, deeper networks are crucial for drawing out meaningful representations from pictures.

Xception. Xception is a CNN architecture built on depthwise separable convolutions [45]. In order to facilitate fast computing, it suggests utilizing depthwise separable convolutions to decouple cross-channels and spatial correlations. The 36 convolutional layers of the network are arranged into 14 modules with linear residual connections. The classic Inception modules are replaced with depthwise separable convolutions as part of the "Extreme Inception" idea. Although it uses parameters more effectively than Inception V3, it has a comparable number of parameters. Convergence requires residual connections. In depthwise separable convolutions, non-linearity between pointwise and depthwise operations slows convergence and degrades performance. Future research will examine the spectrum's transitional regions between normal convolutions and depthwise separable convolutions.

MobileNet. Using depth-wise separable convolutions as its foundation, MobileNet is a powerful model architecture. It employs two distinct convolutional layers: a depthwise convolution layer for spatial filtering and a pointwise convolution [46] layer for cross-channel filtering. By doing this, accuracy is maintained while reducing processing complexity. In order to regulate model size and latency, MobileNets use width multipliers and resolution multipliers.

3.4 Model Selection Phase I

This section describes how the Phase I actually functions and how it employs the technique of predicting a suitable model (Fig. 3) for the respective input. Initially the problem statement and input type go in as a concatenated vector into a word embedding layer that gives out a context vector into the LSTM layer and further a n classification *softmax* layer gives the probability of which model to utilize for the given inputs.

3.5 Image Classification Model Phase II

For the Image classification task, Phase II puts forward the notion of stacking the models that perform well with particular problems and input. By taking maximum voting, it is biased to give a more appropriate prediction with fewer deviations. This is an experimental analysis for ImagNet models which also be employed for other tasks like Text classification and predictions by stacking various models of the respective arena they belong to.

Maximum Voting, sometimes known as majority voting, is a popular assembly method in machine learning. It is used to produce a final forecast by combining the predictions of numerous different models as in Fig. 4a. The underlying notion is that the final forecast will be decided by a majority vote among the various models. Assume we have N distinct models, each of which predicts a class label for a given input. Maximum voting aggregates these N guesses and chooses the most frequent forecast as the outcome. In other words, the class with the most votes from the individual models is picked as the final forecast.

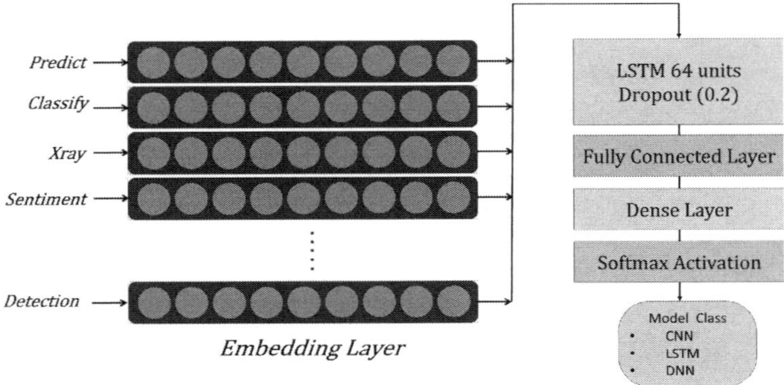

Fig. 3. Architecture of Phase I - Model Selection

Let M be the set of models denoted by M_i, where each model M_i makes a prediction y_i for a given input x. The set of predictions made by all models for input x is denoted as $Y = \{y_1, y_2, \ldots, y_m\}$, where m is the total number of models in the ensemble. The predictions Y should be one of the classes where $C = \{c_1, c_2, \ldots, c_n\}$; n denotes number of classes. $Y \in C$ stays true always as predictions always fall under particular defined classes.

The maximum voting ensemble method selects the prediction with the highest occurrence in the set Y as the final prediction for the input x. This can be represented as follows:

$$y_{\text{final}} = \underset{\substack{y_j \in Y \\ c_i \in C}}{\arg\max} \left(\text{Count} \left(\sum_{\substack{i=1,2,\ldots,n \\ j=1,2,\ldots,m \\ i \neq j}} (c_i == y_j) \right) \right) \tag{1}$$

where count (y_j) represents the number of occurrences of prediction y_j among all the predictions made by the models in the ensemble. The final prediction y_{final} is the one that appears most frequently among all the predictions. If there is a tie in the counts, the argmax function will return any of the tied predictions.

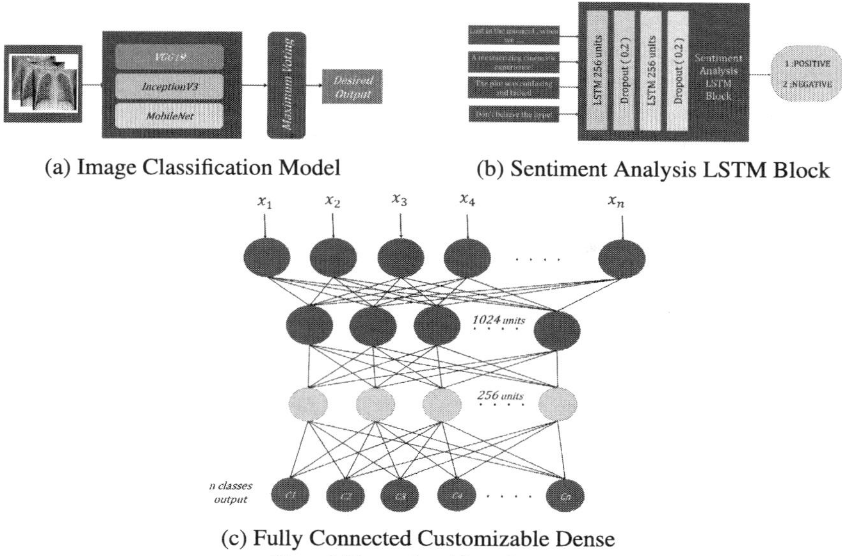

(a) Image Classification Model   (b) Sentiment Analysis LSTM Block

(c) Fully Connected Customizable Dense
Neural Network with n classes

Fig. 4. Proposed Methodology

3.6   Text Classification Model Phase II

The practice of automatically categorizing or labeling a particular text document based
on its content is referred to as text classification, also known as text categorization. It
is a key task in natural language processing (NLP) and has several uses, including document categorization, sentiment analysis, spam filtering, and topic modeling. Feature
extraction and classification are the two primary processes in the text classification process (Fig. 4b). In the feature extraction stage, pertinent features or attributes, such as
word frequencies, n-grams, or word embeddings, are extracted from the text data. The
numerical representation of these features is then changed so that it may be fed into a
machine-learning system. A machine learning system is trained on a labeled dataset in
the classification step to anticipate the category or label of a novel, unexplored text item.
Text classification includes the subfield of sentiment analysis. It entails the automatic
classification of the sentiment polarity (positive, negative, or neutral) of a certain written document, such as a product review, social media post, or movie review. Traditional
machine learning techniques like Naive Bayes, Support Vector Machines (SVMs), and
Decision Trees, as well as deep learning models like Convolutional Neural Networks
(CNNs) or Recurrent Neural Networks (RNNs), can be used to analyze sentiment. Text
classification spans a number of subfields, including sentiment analysis, topic modeling, document categorization, and spam filtering, among others. These subfields are all
concerned with the automatic labeling or categorization of text documents according to
their content.

3.7   Dense Neural Network Phase II

A Dense Neural Network is a form of artificial neural network (ANN) that has several hidden layers between the input and output layers and a Fully Connected; so-called Fully-connected Neural Network (FCN) in Fig. 4c. These hidden layers enable the network to learn and represent increasingly complicated data patterns. FCNs are widely employed in a wide range of applications, including computer vision, natural language processing, speech recognition, and many more.

An FCN's architecture generally comprises the following layers: Input Layer, Hidden Layers and an Output Layer. Diabetes develops when the body is unable to efficiently use or generate enough insulin, resulting in elevated blood sugar levels. Over time, this could harm the body's systems. There are various forms of diabetes, including reversible disorders like gestational diabetes and prediabetes, as well as chronic conditions like type 1 and type 2 diabetes. In healthcare, notably in the identification and prognostication of diseases, AI and machine learning are being employed more and more. Deep learning in particular has seen success in learning intricate patterns from vast volumes of data, increasing classification accuracy.

We utilize this model for predicting diabetes as implementation with 3 classes (i) No Diabetes (ii) Pre-Diabetes (iii) Diabetes. This Dense Neural Network is trained with enough data samples and achieves good accuracy. But as for this proposal, we are more concentrating and image and text classification. Further more models and problems can be solved by stacking up more models according to needs like image generation, object detection and so on which requires models like Generative and Adversarial networks. In the next section, we will discuss the model performances.

Table 2. Performances of All Models

Base	Models	Training Accuracy	Testing Accuracy	Training Time (s)
CNN + LSTM	ModelSelection	81.28%	**76.29%**	157
CNN	VGG19 [44]	98.37%	**91.51%**	259
	InceptionV3 [43]	99.69%	**91.35%**	296
	MoblieNet [46]	96.65%	**91.02%**	55.88
	ResNet50 [42]	98.11%	90.33%	154
	Xception [45]	91.82%	89.22%	207.92
	DenseNet121 [47]	95.38%	86.44%	149.32
	MobileNetV2 [48]	96.22%	86.11%	81.12
	Deep CNN	97.53%	85.11%	185
	VGG16 [44]	98.86%	84.26%	204
	DenseNet169 [47]	96.41%	83.44%	157.30
LSTM	Sentiment Classifier	94.12%	**90.00%**	293
FCN	Diabetes Classifier	84.28%	**84.10%**	189

4 Results and Discussion

In the 1st Phase of our model, we achieved 76.29 % of accuracy for Deep LSTM architecture that predicts which model to be selected for the training or prediction. To predict, NLP concepts like embedding, and tokenization are used to vectorize the problem statement and input type. The data has been augmented using the synthetic data generation concept. These techniques have a direct effect on the accuracy of the whole architecture as this phase is crucial and core of our proposed model. In Fig. 5, we can see the models have been trained over pneumonia chest X-ray images for classification and validation of all models seem to downperform. Similarly, LSTM for IMDB Sentiment classification and Fully connected neural network for Diabetes classification. As a result, we chose to ensemble the image models and get a maximum output as discussed earlier. Now these models can be trained over lots of other classes and they can be made generic.

4.1 Accuracy Comparison of Various Models

$$Accuracy = \frac{TN + TP}{TN + TP + FN + FP} \tag{2}$$

$$Precision = \frac{TP}{TP + FP} \tag{3}$$

$$Specificity = \frac{TN}{TN + FP} \tag{4}$$

$$Sensitivity = \frac{TP}{TP + FN} \tag{5}$$

$$F_1\ Score = 2 \times \frac{Precision \times Recall}{Precision + Recall} \tag{6}$$

Metrics for measuring performance are crucial for assessing the effectiveness of deep learning categorization models. Following the training phase, the effectiveness of each model on the test data set was assessed and compared using ten performance metrics, including accuracy, precision, sensitivity or recall, and F1-score.

These metrics are derived from the True Positive (TP), True Negative (TN), False Positive (FP), and False Negative (FN) parameters of the confusion matrix.

The notations TP, TN, FP, and FN stand for the number of normal images that were mistakenly identified as pneumonia images, normal images that were incorrectly identified as pneumonia images, and pneumonia images that were mistakenly identified as normal.

In Table 2, we give the model performances over training and validation accuracy and time taken for training the dataset over different models. Training Accuracy of all models seems to perform better than validation. As in other Multi-Model architectures, we didn't train all models with the same data instead, in the proposed model we train a particular model with a specific dataset and when only required which saves us the cost of training over all models. These results have shown that it could be a better architecture of deep neural networks which selects a model on its own to predict.

Table 3. Comparison of Performance Measures of Best Models

Base	Models	Precision	Recall	F_1 Score	Training Time (s)
CNN	VGG19 [44]	91.64%	91.51%	91.38%	259
	InceptionV3 [43]	91.33%	91.35%	91.28%	296
	MoblieNet [46]	90.99%	91.02%	91%	55.88
	Ensemble Model	**92.17%**	**92.15%**	**92.08%**	86
LSTM		**93%**	**89%**	**90%**	293
FCN		**91%**	**83%**	**88%**	189

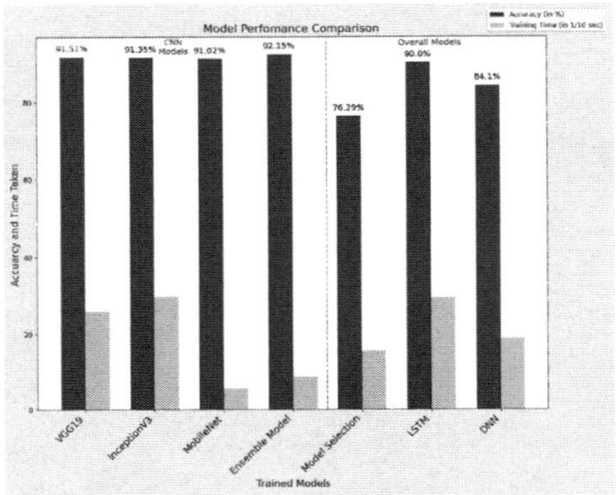

Fig. 5. Accuracy-Time Comparison of Best Models

4.2 Model Selection and Classification Performance

Table 3 shows the best 5 models of CNN, the Overall performance of the Ensemble Model, LSTM, and FCN as our models for the ensembling of the CNN and others. These models are used for prediction as their Testing accuracy seems to outperform others and also takes less time if they exhibit the same accuracy. Even though Deep CNN, VGG16 shows good training accuracy compared to Xception, MobileNet-like models, it fails to give high Testing accuracy. So this architecture is more flexible and versatile to the problems and datasets that we want to solve and train. When testing accuracy is closer, we consider training time to choose a better model. When employing the ensemble technique to best-performing models, it gives an enhanced model that assists in prediction. This proposal is a beginning of a new kind of deep learning technique to solve multiple problems with a single architecture and ensembling best performing trained-available models such as in our case VGG19, InceptionV3 and MobilNet. This paper shows an example of how we can ensemble models and train them to predict desired outputs. Here we concentrated more on CNN models for Image classification. Text summarization, classification with ensembling, NLP techniques, Object detection, and More Models related to Numerical Data using Dense Neural Networks can be expected in future work.

5 Conclusion

Multitype Model architecture is a deep neural network approach designed to select an optimal model for a given problem statement and input type. Unlike conventional multi-model approaches that apply ensembling across many model architectures, our method applies ensembling inside the selected category after intelligently choosing the best architecture based on the input type. This preserves high prediction accuracy while drastically lowering computational overhead. Our tests on diabetes prediction, sentiment analysis, and pneumonia classification show the model's versatility and efficacy with a range of data formats. There are numerous real-world instances in which the suggested adaptive model selection technique can be used. By choosing the optimal model automatically for various patient data formats, including X-ray pictures, text reports, and numerical health indicators, it can expedite diagnosis in the medical industry. It has the ability to dynamically select between classification models and time-series models for market trend analysis in financial applications. Furthermore, this framework can be used to efficiently analyze multimodal data in businesses that deal with multimedia information, such social media analysis and autonomous driving.

Limitations. The suggested strategy has certain drawbacks despite its benefits. A pre-trained DeepLSTM network is used in the model selection procedure, which may not generalize effectively to completely new problem domains without additional fine-tuning. Second, although the method presumes a definite separation of various data types (numerical, text, and image), real-world datasets frequently contain mixed or unclear data, necessitating further preprocessing. Third, even though it has improved, computational efficiency is still an issue for large-scale applications, especially those that need real-time processing. Further investigation into more adaptable and flexible model selection techniques would be necessary to overcome these constraints.

Future Research Directions. This framework can be improved in a number of ways in future research. Using reinforcement learning approaches to improve the model selection process could enable the architecture to dynamically adjust to new datasets. Furthermore, performance while working with highly interdependent data sources may be enhanced by extending the framework to accommodate multi-task learning. Lastly, incorporating more sophisticated ensembling techniques, including attention-based fusion mechanisms, may improve prediction accuracyin a variety of domains.

Declarations
Ethical Approval. This article does not contain any studies with human participants or animals performed by any of the authors.

Conflicts of Interest. The authors declare that there is no conflict of interest.

References

1. Jabeen, S., Li, X., Amin, MS., Bourahla, O., Li, S., Jabbar, A.: A review on methods and applications in multimodal deep learning. ACM Trans. Multimedia Comput. Commun. Appl. **19**(2s), 1–41 (2023).https://doi.org/10.1145/3545572
2. Baltrušaitis, T., Ahuja, C., Morency, LP.: Multimodal machine learning: a survey and taxonomy. arXiv (Cornell University) 41: 423–443 (2017). arXiv Version Number: 2. https://doi.org/10.48550/ARXIV.1705.09406
3. Summaira, J., Li, X., Shoib, AM., Li, S., Abdul, J.: Recent advances and trends in multimodal deep learning: a review (2021). https://doi.org/10.48550/ARXIV.2105.11087
4. Heidarysafa, M., Kowsari, K., Brown, D.E., Meimandi, K.J., Barnes, L.E.: An improvement of data classification using random multimodel deep learning (RMDL). Int. J. Mach. Learn. Comput. **8**(4) (2018), https://doi.org/10.18178/ijmlc.2018.8.4.703, http://www.ijml.org/index.php?m=content&c=index&a=show&catid=79&id=823
5. Kowsari, K., Heidarysafa, M., Brown, DE., Meimandi, K.J., Barnes, L.E.: RMDL: random multimodel deep learning for classification. In: Proceedings of the 2nd International Conference on Information System and Data Mining, Lakeland, FL, USA, vol. abs/1805.01890, pp. 19–28. ACM (2018). https://doi.org/10.1145/3206098.3206111
6. Sohn, K., Shang, W., Lee, H.: Improved multimodal deep learning with variation of information. In: Neural Information Processing Systems, vol. 27, pp. 2141–2149 (2014). https://papers.nips.cc/paper/5279-improved-multimodal-deep-learning-with-variation-of-information.pdf
7. Umer, M., Ashraf, I., Ullah, S., Mehmood, A., Choi, G.S.: COVINet: a convolutional neural network approach for predicting COVID-19 from chest X-ray images. J. Ambient Intell. Humanized Comput. **13**(1), 535–547 (2022). https://doi.org/10.1007/s12652-021-02917-3, https://link.springer.com/10.1007/s12652-021-02917-3
8. Hira, S., Bai, A., Hira, S.: An automatic approach based on CNN architecture to detect Covid-19 disease from chest X-ray images. Appl. Intell. **51**(5), 2864–2889 (2021). https://doi.org/10.1007/s10489-020-02010-w, https://link.springer.com/10.1007/s10489-020-02010-w
9. Kc, K., Yin, Z., Wu, M., Wu, Z.: Evaluation of deep learning-based approaches for COVID-19 classification based on chest X-ray images. Sig. Image Video Process. **15**(5), 959–966 (2021). https://doi.org/10.1007/s11760-020-01820-2, https://link.springer.com/10.1007/s11760-020-01820-2
10. Gupta, V., et al.: Improved COVID-19 detection with chest X-ray images using deep learning. Multimedia Tools Appl. **81**(26), 37657–37680 (2022). https://doi.org/10.1007/s11042-022-13509-4, https://link.springer.com/10.1007/s11042-022-13509-4
11. Hilmizen, N., Bustamam, A., Sarwinda, D.: The multimodal deep learning for diagnosing COVID-19 pneumonia from chest CT-scan and X-ray images. In: 2020 3rd International Seminar on Research of Information Technology and Intelligent Systems (ISRITI), Yogyakarta, Indonesia, pp 26–31. IEEE (2020). https://doi.org/10.1109/ISRITI51436.2020.9315478, https://ieeexplore.ieee.org/document/9315478/
12. Wang, Z., Dong, J., Zhang, J.: Multi-model ensemble deep learning method to diagnose COVID-19 using chest computed tomography images. J. Shanghai Jiaotong Univ. (Sci.) **27**(1), 70–80 (2022). https://doi.org/10.1007/s12204-021-2392-3, https://link.springer.com/10.1007/s12204-021-2392-3
13. Israel, S.A., et al.: Generative adversarial networks for classification. In: 2017 IEEE Applied Imagery Pattern Recognition Workshop (AIPR), Washington, DC, pp. 1–4. IEEE (2017). https://doi.org/10.1109/AIPR.2017.8457952, https://ieeexplore.ieee.org/document/8457952/

14. Arun Prakash, J., Asswin, C., Ravi, V., Sowmya, V., Soman, K.: Pediatric pneumonia diagnosis using stacked ensemble learning on multi-model deep CNN architectures. Multimedia Tools Appl. **82**(14), 21311–21351 (2023). https://doi.org/10.1007/s11042-022-13844-6, https://link.springer.com/10.1007/s11042-022-13844-6
15. Uppal, S., et al.: Multimodal research in vision and language: a review of current and emerging trends. Inf. Fus. **77**, 149–171 (2022). https://doi.org/10.1016/j.inffus.2021.07.009, https://linkinghub.elsevier.com/retrieve/pii/S1566253521001512
16. Tembhurne, J.V., Diwan, T.: Sentiment analysis in textual, visual and multimodal inputs using recurrent neural networks. Multimedia Tools Appl. **80**(5), 6871–6910 (2021). https://doi.org/10.1007/s11042-020-10037-x, https://link.springer.com/10.1007/s11042-020-10037-x
17. Dwarakanath, B., Latha, M., Annamalai, R., Kallimani J.S., Walia, R., Belete, B.: A novel feature selection with hybrid deep learning based heart disease detection and classification in the e-healthcare environment. Comput. Intell. Neurosci. **2022**, 1–12 (2022). https://doi.org/10.1155/2022/1167494, https://www.hindawi.com/journals/cin/2022/1167494/
18. Ngiam, J., Khosla, A., Kim, M., Nam, J., Lee, H., Ng, A.Y.: Multimodal deep learning. In: International Conference on Machine Learning, pp. 689–696 (2011). https://doi.org/10.48550/arxiv.2301.04856, https://ai.stanford.edu/~ang/papers/icml11-MultimodalDeepLearning.pdf
19. Stahlschmidt, S.R., Ulfenborg, B., Synnergren, J.: Multimodal deep learning for biomedical data fusion: a review. Brief. Bioinf. **23**(2), bbab569 (2022). https://doi.org/10.1093/bib/bbab569, https://academic.oup.com/bib/article/doi/10.1093/bib/bbab569/6516346
20. Kline, A., et al.: Multimodal machine learning in precision health: a scoping review. npj Digit. Med. **5**(1), 171 (2022). https://doi.org/10.1038/s41746-022-00712-8, https://www.nature.com/articles/s41746-022-00712-8
21. Abdu, S.A., Yousef, A.H., Salem, A.: Multimodal video sentiment analysis using deep learning approaches, a survey. Inf. Fus. **76**, 204–226 (2021). https://doi.org/10.1016/j.inffus.2021.06.003, https://linkinghub.elsevier.com/retrieve/pii/S1566253521001299
22. Kundid Vasić, M., Papić, V.: Multimodel deep learning for person detection in aerial images. Electronics **9**(9), 1459 (2020). https://doi.org/10.3390/electronics9091459, https://www.mdpi.com/2079-9292/9/9/1459
23. Liu, W., Zheng, W.L., Lu, B.L.: Multimodal emotion recognition using multimodal deep learning. Cornell University arXiv:1602.08225 (2016). https://doi.org/10.48550/ARXIV.1602.08225
24. Hong, D., et al.: More diverse means better: multimodal deep learning meets remote-sensing imagery classification. IEEE Trans. Geosci. Remote Sens. **59**(5), 4340–4354 (2021). https://doi.org/10.1109/TGRS.2020.3016820, https://ieeexplore.ieee.org/document/9174822/
25. Venugopalan, J., Tong, L., Hassanzadeh, H.R., Wang, M.D.: Multimodal deep learning models for early detection of Alzheimer's disease stage. Sci. Rep. **11**(1), 3254 (2021). https://doi.org/10.1038/s41598-020-74399-w, https://www.nature.com/articles/s41598-020-74399-w
26. Annamalai, R., Nedunchelian, R.: Diabetes Mellitus prediction and severity level estimation using OWDANN algorithm. Comput. Intell. Neurosci. **2021**, 1–11 (2021). https://doi.org/10.1155/2021/5573179, https://www.hindawi.com/journals/cin/2021/5573179/
27. Zargar, O.S., Baghat, A., Teli, T.A.: A DNN model for diabetes mellitus prediction on PIMA dataset **21**(2) (2024)
28. Fujimori, N., Endo, R., Kawai, Y., Mochizuki, T.: Modality-specific learning rate control for multimodal classification. In: Palaiahnakote, S., Sanniti di Baja, G., Wang, L., Yan, W.Q. (eds.) ACPR 2019. LNCS, vol. 12047, pp. 412–422. Springer, Cham (2020). https://doi.org/10.1007/978-3-030-41299-9_32

29. Gayathri, J.L., Abraham, B., Sujarani, M.S., Nair, M.S.: A computer-aided diagnosis system for the classification of COVID-19 and non-COVID-19 pneumonia on chest X-ray images by integrating CNN with sparse autoencoder and feed forward neural network. Comput. Biol. Med. **141**, 105134 (2022). https://doi.org/10.1016/j.compbiomed.2021.105134, https://linkinghub.elsevier.com/retrieve/pii/S0010482521009288

30. Sudharson, S., Kokil, P.: An ensemble of deep neural networks for kidney ultrasound image classification. Comput. Meth. Programs Biomed. **197**, 105709 (2020). https://doi.org/10.1016/j.cmpb.2020.105709, https://linkinghub.elsevier.com/retrieve/pii/S016926072031542X

31. Mahadar, A., Mangukiya, P., Baraskar, T.: Comparison and evaluation of CNN architectures for classification of Covid-19 and pneumonia. In: 2021 Sixth International Conference on Image Information Processing (ICIIP), IEEE, Shimla, India, vol. v2, pp. 110–115 (2021). https://doi.org/10.1109/ICIIP53038.2021.9702676, https://ieeexplore.ieee.org/document/9702676/

32. Guefrechi, S., Jabra, M.B., Ammar, A., Koubaa, A., Hamam, H.: Deep learning based detection of COVID-19 from chest X-ray images. Multimedia Tools Appl. **80**(21–23), 31803–31820 (2021). https://doi.org/10.1007/s11042-021-11192-5, https://link.springer.com/10.1007/s11042-021-11192-5

33. Saha, P., Neogy, S.: Concat_cnn: a model to detect COVID-19 from chest X-ray images with deep learning. SN Comput. Sci. **3**(4), 305 (2022). https://doi.org/10.1007/s42979-022-01182-1, https://link.springer.com/10.1007/s42979-022-01182-1

34. Mukhi, S.E., Varshini, R.T., Sherley, S.E.F.: Diagnosis of COVID-19 from multimodal imaging data using optimized deep learning techniques. SN Comput. Sci. **4**(3), 212 (2023). https://doi.org/10.1007/s42979-022-01653-5, https://link.springer.com/10.1007/s42979-022-01653-5

35. Hammad, M., et al.: Efficient multimodal deep-learning-based COVID-19 diagnostic system for noisy and corrupted images. J. King Saud Univ. Sci. **34**(3), 101898 (2022). https://doi.org/10.1016/j.jksus.2022.101898, https://linkinghub.elsevier.com/retrieve/pii/S1018364722000799

36. Farhat, H.J., Sakr, G.E., Kilany, R., Smayra, T., Mallak, I.: Pneumonia and COVID-19 classification in chest X-rays using faster region-based convolutional neural networks (faster r-CNN), preprint (2022, in review). https://doi.org/10.21203/rs.3.rs-1285679/v1, https://www.researchsquare.com/article/rs-1285679/v1

37. Kumar, A., Garg, G.: Sentiment analysis of multimodal Twitter data. Multimedia Tools Appl. **78**(17), 24103–24119 (2019). https://doi.org/10.1007/s11042-019-7390-1, http://link.springer.com/10.1007/s11042-019-7390-1

38. Rithani, M., Kumar, R.P., Doss, S.: A review on big data based on deep neural network approaches. Artif. Intell. Rev. **56**(12), 14765–14801 (2023). https://doi.org/10.1007/s10462-023-10512-5, https://link.springer.com/10.1007/s10462-023-10512-5

39. Yadav, A., Vishwakarma, D.K.: Sentiment analysis using deep learning architectures: a review. Artif. Intell. Rev. **53**(6), 4335–4385 (2020). https://doi.org/10.1007/s10462-019-09794-5, http://link.springer.com/10.1007/s10462-019-09794-5

40. Kumar, A., Srinivasan, K., Cheng, W.H., Zomaya, A.Y.: Hybrid context enriched deep learning model for fine-grained sentiment analysis in textual and visual semiotic modality social data. Inf. Process. Manage. **57**(1), 102141 (2020). https://doi.org/10.1016/j.ipm.2019.102141, https://linkinghub.elsevier.com/retrieve/pii/S0306457319306934

41. Tan, K.L., Lee, C.P., Lim, K.M., Anbananthen, K.S.M.: Sentiment analysis with ensemble hybrid deep learning model. IEEE Access **10**, 103694–103704 (2022). https://doi.org/10.1109/ACCESS.2022.3210182, https://ieeexplore.ieee.org/document/9903622/

42. He, K., Zhang, X., Ren, S., Sun, J.: Deep residual learning for image recognition (2015). https://doi.org/10.1109/cvpr.2016.90, https://arxiv.org/abs/1512.03385

43. Szegedy, C., Vanhoucke, V., Ioffe, S., Shlens, J., Wojna, Z.: Rethinking the inception architecture for computer vision (2015). https://doi.org/10.1109/cvpr.2016.308, https://arxiv.org/pdf/1512.00567.pdf
44. Simonyan, K., Zisserman, A.: Very deep convolutional networks for large-scale image recognition. arXiv arXiv:1409.1556 (2015). https://cir.nii.ac.jp/ja/crid/1371977243859268618
45. Chollet, F.: Xception: deep learning with depthwise separable convolutions. In: Proceedings of the IEEE Conference on Computer Vision and Pattern Recognition (CVPR), pp 1800–1807. IEEE Computer Society (2017). https://doi.org/10.1109/cvpr.2017.195, https://arxiv.org/pdf/1610.02357
46. Howard, A.G., et al.: MobileNets: efficient convolutional neural networks for mobile vision applications (2017). https://doi.org/10.48550/arxiv.1704.04861, https://arxiv.org/abs/1704.04861
47. Huang, G., Liu, Z., van der Maaten, L., Weinberger, K.Q.: Densely connected convolutional networks. arXiv arXiv:1608.06993 (2018)
48. Sandler, M., Howard, A., Zhu, M., Zhmoginov, A., Chen, L.C.: MobileNetV2: inverted residuals and linear bottlenecks. arXiv arXiv:1801.04381 (2019)

Beyond Classification: Understanding Why URLs Are Malicious with Transparent Convex Optimization and Interpretable XAI

Yi Anson Lam[✉], Kam-Pui Chow, and Siu-Ming Yiu

The University of Hong Kong, Hong Kong, Hong Kong, Special Administrative Region of China
`yiansonlam@connect.hku.hk, {chow,smyiu}@cs.hku.hk`

Abstract. The detection of malicious URLs is a critical task in cybersecurity, as they are often used to distribute malware, steal sensitive information, and conduct phishing attacks. Traditional machine learning models for malicious URL detection, while effective, often lack interpretability, making it difficult to justify decisions in legal or investigative contexts. In this study, we propose a complementary framework that integrates Explainable AI (XAI) techniques to enhance trust, transparency, and interpretability in malicious URL detection, thereby facilitating audits and adherence to standards in cybersecurity practices.

We employ convex optimization, valued for its global interpretability, to classify URLs based on lexical features such as URL length, special character count, and domain information. This approach not only improves the comprehensibility of the model's decisions but also aligns with industry standards for accountability in AI systems. To supplement this global interpretability, we apply Local Interpretable Model-agnostic Explanations (LIME) to provide local, instance-specific explanations for individual predictions. This dual-layered interpretability ensures that stakeholders can confidently assess model outputs, thus meeting regulatory requirements and enhancing the overall robustness of malicious URL detection processes.

Contrary to our initial hypothesis, our findings reveal that local explanations provided by LIME do not always align with the global feature importance derived from convex optimization. Instead, the two methods offer distinct yet complementary insights. This highlights the need for a two-stage framework, where convex optimization provides global trends, and LIME offers granular, instance-specific explanations. This parallel approach addresses both global and local interpretability requirements, enhancing the overall transparency and reliability of malicious URL detection systems.

The models are evaluated using standard metrics such as accuracy, precision, recall, and F1-score. Our results demonstrate the effectiveness of the proposed framework in balancing global and local explainability, making it a robust and interpretable solution for cybersecurity applications. This work contributes to the field of explainable AI in cybersecurity by offering a transparent and accountable approach to detecting

S. Goel et al. (Eds.): AICON 2025, LNICST 672, pp. 70–84, 2026.
https://doi.org/10.1007/978-3-032-14805-6_5

malicious URLs and integrating global and local perspectives on interpretability.

Keywords: XAI · Malicious URL · Convex Optimaization · Auditable · machine learning · LIME · Cyber Secuirity · Interpretability

1   Introduction

Malicious URLs pose a significant threat to cybersecurity, as they are frequently used to distribute malware, conduct phishing attacks, and deface websites. Traditional approaches to detecting malicious URLs often rely on black-box machine learning models, which, while effective, lack interpretability. This lack of transparency can hinder trust in the model's predictions and make it difficult to justify why a URL is classified as malicious. Explainable AI (XAI) techniques, such as Local Interpretable Model-agnostic Explanations (LIME), offer a potential solution by providing interpretable, instance-specific explanations for model predictions.

In this study, we address the challenge of interpreting machine learning models for malicious URL detection by proposing a complementary framework that integrates global and local interpretability. Specifically, we employ convex optimization, known for its inherent global interpretability, as the primary model for detecting malicious URLs based on lexical features. Lexical features—derived directly from the URL string—are particularly advantageous as they are easy to extract and do not require external information. These features include URL length, special character count, and domain information. To complement the global insights provided by convex optimization, we apply LIME to generate local explanations for individual predictions, offering instance-specific interpretability.

Contrary to our initial hypothesis that local explanations from LIME would closely align with the global feature importance derived from convex optimization, our findings reveal a divergence between global and local interpretability. This unexpected outcome suggests that global interpretability cannot always validate local explanations. Instead, the two approaches provide distinct but complementary insights into the model's behavior. This highlights the need for a two-stage framework where convex optimization and LIME are used in parallel to supplement each other, addressing both global and local explainability requirements.

The key contribution of this work lies in proposing a two-stage complementary framework that leverages the strengths of both convex optimization and LIME. This framework enhances the transparency and trustworthiness of malicious URL detection systems by combining global trends with instance-specific insights. By treating global and local interpretability as distinct yet complementary perspectives, this study advances the field of explainable AI in cybersecurity, offering a robust and interpretable framework to strengthen defenses against malicious URLs.

2 Objective of the Study

The primary objective of this study is to develop a complementary framework for malicious URL detection by integrating convex optimization and Explainable AI (XAI). Specifically, we aim to:

- Leverage convex optimization, renowned for its global interpretability, to identify malicious URLs based on a comprehensive set of lexical features, including URL length, special character count, and domain information.
- Apply local interpretable model-agnostic explanations (LIME) as a tool for local interpretability, offering granular insights into individual URL classifications.
- Investigate the relationship between global and local interpretability, analyzing whether LIME's local explanations align with the global feature importance derived from convex optimization.
- Propose a two-stage complementary framework, where convex optimization and LIME are used in parallel to provide both global and local explanations for malicious URL detection, supplementing each other to enhance overall transparency and reliability.

By achieving these objectives, this study highlights the importance of treating global and local interpretability as distinct but complementary perspectives. It contributes to advancing the field of explainable AI in cybersecurity by offering a framework that balances global trends and instance-specific insights, ensuring an interpretable and trustworthy system for malicious URL detection.

3 Related Work

Detecting malicious URLs is a critical research area in cybersecurity, addressing the growing sophistication of phishing, malware attacks, and other cyber threats. This section reviews related works on malicious URL detection, advancements in machine learning, and explainable AI (XAI) to enhance model interpretability.

3.1 Malicious URL Detection

Early works focused on rule-based and blacklist-based approaches. However, these methods became less effective due to the rapid generation of new malicious URLs. Ma et al. [2] introduced one of the earliest machine learning-based approaches for malicious URL detection, leveraging features like URL length and special character counts. Canali et al. [3] proposed Prophiler, which combined lexical analysis and heuristics to detect malicious web pages.

More recent works have explored advanced machine learning and deep learning methods. Raja et al. [4] used lexical features and machine learning models like Random Forest to classify URLs as benign or malicious. Similarly, Patil et al. [10] used decision trees for binary classification of URLs. Deep learning-based approaches have also gained traction, as demonstrated by Le et al. [7], who developed the URLNet model for learning URL representations.

In 2023 and 2024, researchers adopted modern techniques like transformers and graph neural networks. Chen et al. [19] proposed transformer-based models for URL detection, while Singh et al. [20] leveraged graph neural networks (GNNs) to model relationships between URL components. These approaches improve detection accuracy by capturing more complex feature interactions.

3.2 Explainable AI in Cybersecurity

Explainable AI (XAI) has become a vital tool for improving the interpretability of machine learning models in cybersecurity. Ribeiro et al. [5] introduced LIME, one of the first frameworks to explain individual predictions. Poddar et al. [15] applied XAI techniques like Accumulated Local Effects (ALE) to explain the impact of 21 URL features on classification results, addressing the black-box nature of ensemble models.

Recent works have extended XAI applications. Kumar et al. [16] used SHAP and LIME to explain predictions in phishing URL detection systems. Chen et al. [19] combined transformer-based architectures with SHAP to identify critical features influencing malicious URL classifications.

3.3 Real-Time and Federated Learning Approaches

The need for real-time malicious URL detection has driven the adoption of federated learning (FL). Ali et al. [18] presented a federated learning framework that ensures privacy while achieving high detection accuracy. This approach is particularly relevant for large-scale, distributed systems.

3.4 Contributions of This Work

Existing works demonstrate the effectiveness of machine learning and lexical features in malicious URL detection but lack focus on interpretability. Black-box models hinder trust and transparency, while integrating domain knowledge into explainable AI remains underexplored. Our approach uses LIME for interpretable explanations and combines lexical features with domain knowledge for enhanced feature extraction. Unlike global methods like ALE or PDPs, which provide generalized insights, LIME offers instance-specific explanations by approximating model behavior around individual URLs. This shift aids in explaining why a URL is malicious, crucial for enforcement officers or prosecutors during investigations.

4 Methodology

The proposed methodology for detecting malicious URLs begins with the preparation of a labeled dataset, named `malicious_phish (dataset).csv`, which

Table 1. Summary of Extracted Lexical Features for URL Classification

No.	Feature Name	Description
1	URL Length	Total number of characters in the URL.
2	Number of Dots	Count of dots ('.') in the URL.
3	Number of Digits	Count of numeric digits in the URL.
4	Number of Special Characters	Count of special characters such as '-', '_', '%', '?', and '='.
5	Count of 'http'	Number of times 'http' appears in the URL.
6	Count of 'www'	Number of times 'www' appears in the URL.
7	Subdomain Count	Number of subdomains in the URL.
8	Domain Length	Length of the domain name.
9	TLD Count	Number of top-level domains (TLDs) in the URL.
10	Path Length	Length of the path in the URL.
11	Query Parameter Count	Number of query parameters in the URL.
12	Consecutive Character Count	Count of consecutive identical characters in the URL.
13	URL Entropy	Measure of randomness in the URL (Shannon entropy).
14	Uses HTTPS	Binary feature indicating if the URL uses HTTPS.
15	IP Address Usage	Binary feature indicating if the URL uses an IP address instead of a domain.
16	Suspicious Port Usage	Binary feature indicating use of non-standard ports in the URL.
17	Brand Name Similarity	Binary feature indicating similarity of the URL to known brand names.
18	Country Code Detection	Binary feature indicating if the URL ends with a country code domain (ccTLD).
19	URL Encoding	Binary feature indicating if URL-encoded characters (e.g., '%20') are present.
20	Ratio of Alphabet to Characters	Ratio of alphabetic characters to the total number of characters in the URL.
21	Ratio of Numeric to Characters	Ratio of numeric characters to the total number of characters in the URL.

was obtained from the popular open-source dataset platform Kaggle [21]. This dataset categorizes URLs into two classes: malicious (e.g., *phishing*, *defacement*, *malware*) and benign. Malicious URLs are labeled as 1, while benign URLs are labeled as 0. To ensure the robustness of the analysis, the dataset was preprocessed to achieve a balanced class distribution.

Next, lexical features were engineered to transform each URL into a numerical representation. A total of 21 features were extracted, as summarized in Table 1. These features form the foundation for the classification process, enabling the differentiation between malicious and benign URLs.

5 Convex Optimization Models

In this study, three convex optimization models were trained using the extracted features to classify URLs as malicious or benign. These models were chosen for their interpretability, prioritizing understanding *why* a URL is classified as malicious rather than simply identifying *what* is malicious. This emphasis on explainability ensures that the decision-making process is transparent and actionable, which is crucial in cybersecurity applications.

5.1 Logistic Regression

- A generalized linear model for binary classification was trained to minimize log-loss.
- Logistic regression was chosen for its simplicity and transparency, as the learned coefficients directly indicate the contribution of individual features to the classification.
- The `LogisticRegression` implementation from `scikit-learn` was used with the default solver.

5.2 Lasso Regression

- Lasso regression introduced L1 regularization to enforce sparsity in the coefficients, identifying the most influential features while reducing overfitting.
- By promoting sparsity, lasso regression not only improves interpretability but also highlights *why* certain features contribute to the classification decision.
- The regularization parameter was set to $\alpha = 0.1$.

5.3 Gradient Descent

- A custom implementation of gradient descent was used to minimize binary cross-entropy loss.
- This iterative approach provided flexibility in optimizing the model while maintaining transparency in the optimization process.
- Key hyperparameters:
  - Learning rate: 0.01
  - Maximum iterations: 1000
  - Tolerance: 10^{-6}
- Early stopping was employed when the loss difference between iterations fell below the tolerance threshold, ensuring convergence without unnecessary complexity.

6   Primary Model Findings

The models were evaluated on the test dataset using accuracy, precision, recall, and F1-score metrics. The results are summarized in Table 2.

- **Logistic Regression** achieved the highest accuracy (**91.44%**) and balanced performance across precision, recall, and F1-score. It is the most effective model for detecting malicious URLs.
- **Gradient Descent** performed comparably to the accuracy of Logistic Regression (**90.98%**), demonstrating the flexibility of custom optimization techniques.
- **Lasso Regression** The finding of this convex model underperformed due to L1 regularization (**83.46%**), which likely removed important features, leading to reduced accuracy and recall.

These findings highlight that, while all three convex optimization approaches are viable, Logistic Regression offers the best trade-off between simplicity and performance. Gradient Descent serves as a strong alternative, especially for custom implementations. Logistic Regression achieved the highest accuracy, demonstrating its effectiveness in utilizing the extracted features to predict malicious URLs.

To further validate the interpretability of the model, we visualize the learned parameters (coefficients) from Logistic Regression. These coefficients reveal the contribution of each feature in determining whether a URL is malicious or benign. Furthermore, we compare these insights with a model-agnostic explainer, such as LIME (Local Interpretable Model-agnostic Explanations), to ensure the reliability and consistency of the model's predictions. This comparison is crucial, as validating the interpretability of the model aligns with the primary goal of this study.

Table 2. Model Performance Comparison

Model	Accuracy	Precision	Recall	F1-Score
Logistic Regression	91.44%	90%	84%	87%
Lasso Regression	83.46%	80%	69%	74%
Gradient Descent	90.98%	89%	85%	87%

Figure 1 illustrates the feature importance in the Logistic Regression model based on the coefficient values for each feature. Features with positive coefficients (bars extending to the right) increase the likelihood of a URL being classified as malicious, while those with negative coefficients (bars extending to the left) decrease this likelihood. The magnitude of the bars represents the strength of each feature's influence on the classification decision.

From the graph, we can observe that the most influential features for predicting malicious URLs are the Count of 'http', Count of 'www', and URL Length,

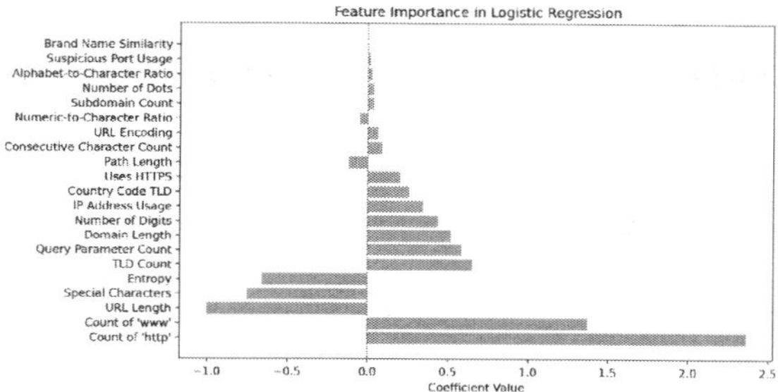

Fig. 1. Feature importance from a relatively interpretable convex optimatization model

all of which have strong positive coefficients, indicating that higher values for these features are associated with malicious URLs. Entropy and TLD Count also moderately contribute to the likelihood of maliciousness. On the other hand, features like Brand Name Similarity and Suspicious Port Usage have negative coefficients, suggesting they are more indicative of benign URLs.

Less impactful features, such as Subdomain Count, URL Encoding, and Uses HTTPS, exhibit smaller coefficients, playing a relatively minor role in the classification. Overall, the model relies heavily on structural characteristics of the URL, such as length and the frequency of specific components, to distinguish between malicious and benign URLs. This graph provides insights into how the Logistic Regression model makes its decisions, highlighting which features are most influential in its predictions.

7   Application XAI LIME

The application of Explainable Artificial Intelligence (XAI) tools like LIME (Local Interpretable Model-Agnostic Explanations) is crucial in understanding the decision-making process of machine learning models, particularly in sensitive domains like cybersecurity. In this case, LIME is used to explain predictions made by a Logistic Regression model to classify URLs as malicious or benign. By analyzing individual predictions, LIME identifies the contribution of each feature (e.g., URL length, special characters, entropy, etc.) to the final decision, offering a clear and interpretable explanation of why a specific URL is flagged as malicious. This transparency is essential for debugging models, improving feature engineering, and building trust in automated systems.

Moreover, LIME enables security analysts to understand the patterns associated with malicious URLs, such as frequent use of "http," high entropy, or excessive subdomains, which are common in phishing or malware links. By aggregating explanations across multiple URLs, analysts can uncover trends in malicious behavior, providing actionable insights for building better defenses against cyber threats. The ability to visualize and quantify feature importance empowers organizations to validate and refine their models, ensuring that automated systems align with domain knowledge and make decisions that are both accurate and explainable. This makes LIME a powerful tool for enhancing the interpretability and reliability of machine learning systems in cybersecurity.

8   Graphical Representation of XAI Outputs

The figures below illustrate the graphical outputs generated by XAI (LIME) for explaining model decisions regarding malicious URLs (Fig. 2 and 3).

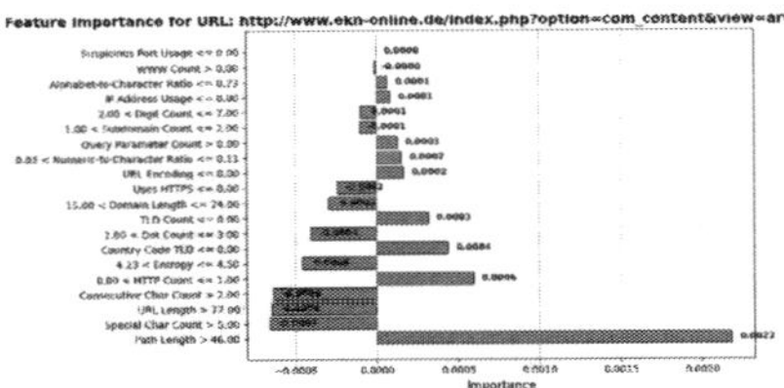

(a) Feature importance for URL 1

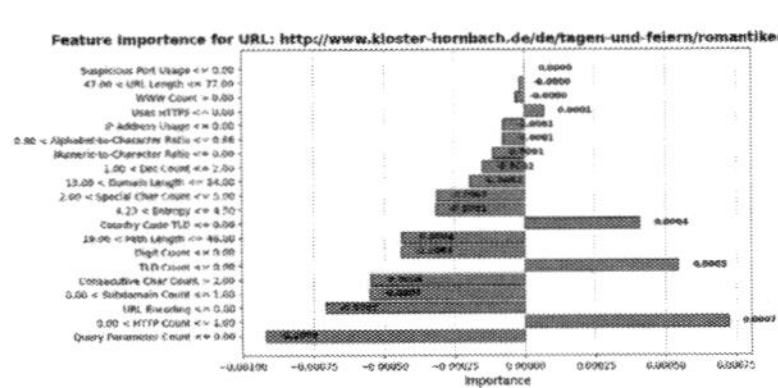

(b) Feature importance for URL 2

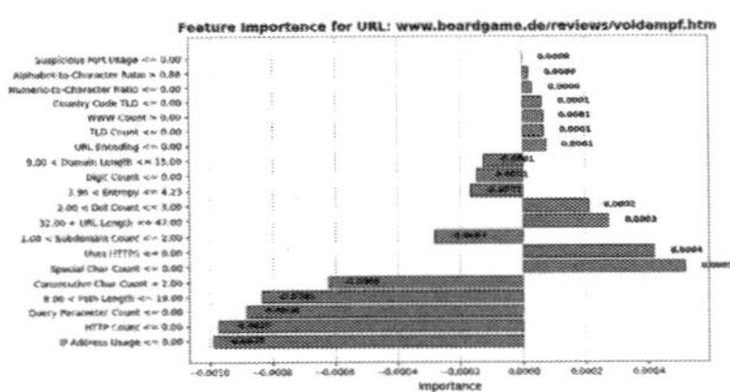

(c) Feature importance for URL 3

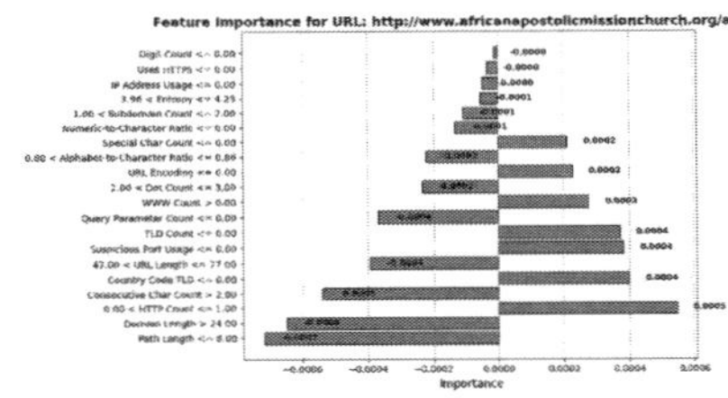

(d) Feature importance for URL 4

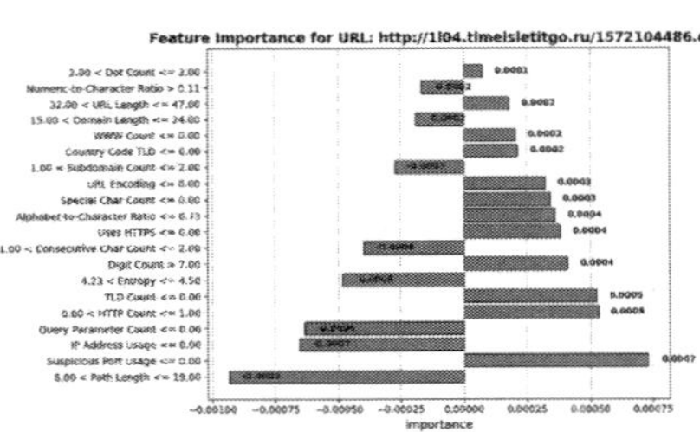

(e) Feature importance for URL 5

Fig. 2. Visualization of feature importance for the first five URLs using LIME. Each plot highlights how features influence the classification of the URL as malicious or benign.

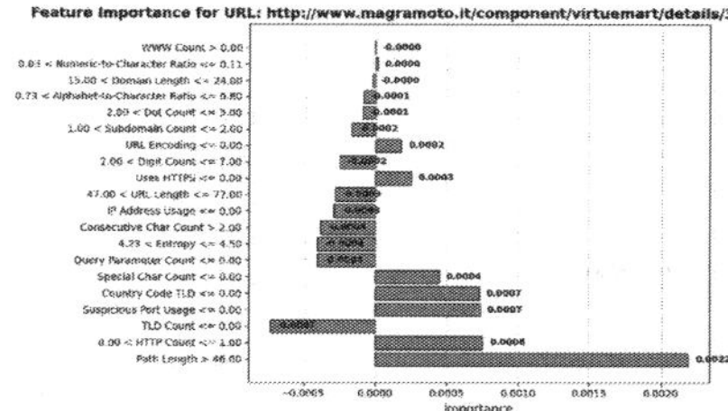

(a) Feature importance for URL 6

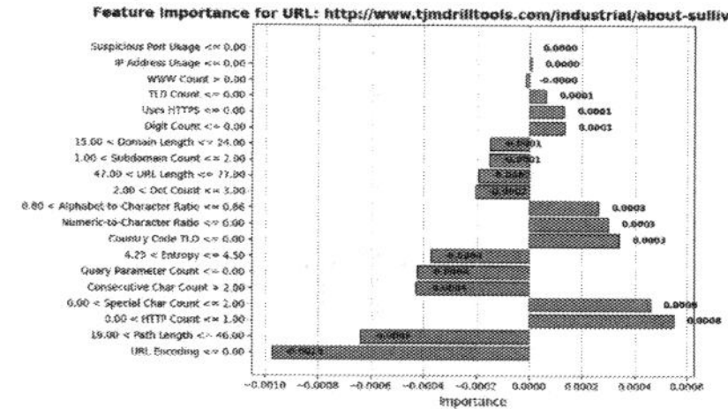

(b) Feature importance for URL 7

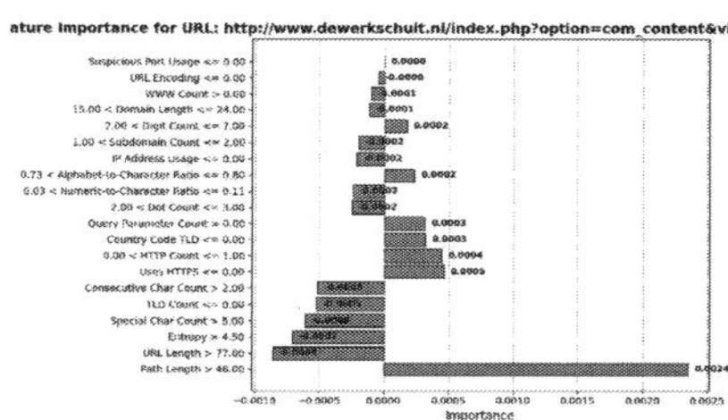

(c) Feature importance for URL 8

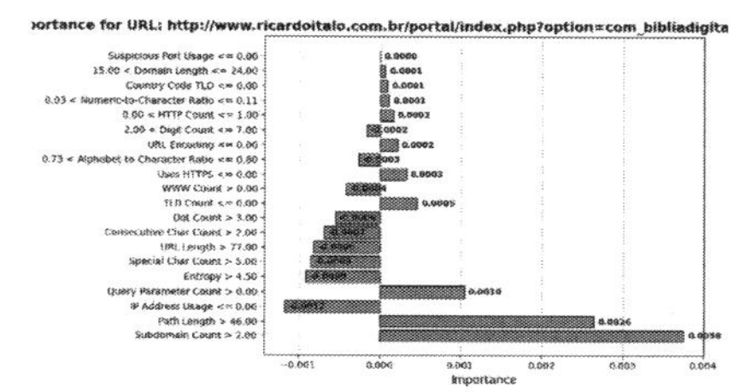

(d) Feature importance for URL 9

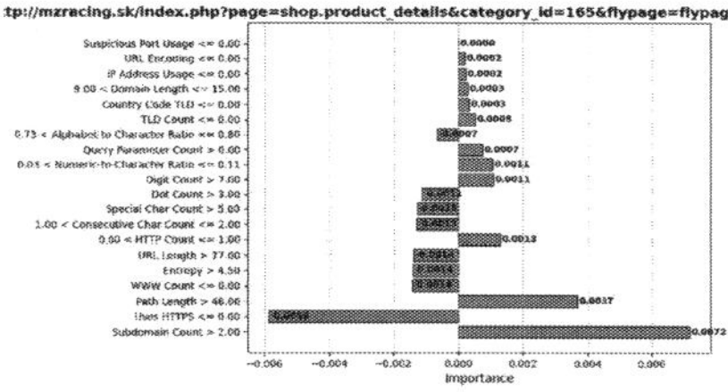

(e) Feature importance for URL 10

Fig. 3. Visualization of feature importance for the next five URLs using LIME. Each plot highlights how features influence the classification of the URL as malicious or benign.

9 Comparison Between Logistic Regression and XAI-LIME Outputs

Understanding the behavior of machine learning models is critical, especially in sensitive domains like cybersecurity. The blue bar chart generated by Logistic Regression provides a **global view** of feature importance, showing how different features contribute to the classification of URLs as malicious or benign across the entire dataset. On the other hand, the green bar charts generated by XAI-LIME offer **local explanations** for individual URLs, revealing how specific features influence the classification decision for each instance. This section breaks down the comparison into several aspects, highlighting their differences, similarities, and use cases.

10   Discussion

10.1   Global vs. Local Perspectives

The Logistic Regression output (blue bar) provides a **global perspective** on feature importance. It shows the overall influence of each feature on the model's predictions across the entire dataset. Features like *Count of 'http'*, *Count of 'www'*, and *URL Length* have the largest coefficients, indicating their consistent significance in determining whether a URL is classified as malicious. This global view is useful for understanding the general behavior of the model and the relative importance of features used during training.

In contrast, the XAI-LIME graphs (green bars) provide **local explanations**, focusing on how features impact the classification of a specific URL. For example, while *Path Length* may generally be important in the dataset, its contribution can vary significantly for individual URLs. This instance-specific insight allows for a deeper understanding of why a particular URL is flagged as malicious or benign.

10.2   Feature Importance Magnitude

The magnitude of feature importance differs between the global and local explanations. In the Logistic Regression output, features such as *Count of 'http'* and *URL Length* dominate with large positive coefficients, indicating their strong influence across the dataset. Features like *URL Encoding* or *Subdomain Count* have much smaller coefficients, suggesting they have a minimal impact globally.

However, in the XAI-LIME outputs, the importance of features varies significantly for each URL. For instance, *Path Length* is a highly influential feature for most URLs but may play a smaller role in specific cases. Similarly, features like *Special Char Count* or *Subdomain Count*, which are globally less important, become critical for certain URLs. For example, in the analysis of http:// mzracing.sk, *Subdomain Count* and *Special Char Count* are among the most influential features.

10.3   Dataset-Wide Trends vs. Instance-Specific Insights

The Logistic Regression output is ideal for identifying **dataset-wide trends**. It helps analysts understand the general patterns that distinguish malicious URLs from benign ones. For example, longer URLs with more occurrences of *http* and *www* are more likely to be classified as malicious. This global understanding is valuable for optimizing the model, selecting features, and understanding the general behavior of the dataset.

On the other hand, XAI-LIME provides **instance-specific insights**, offering a fine-grained explanation of individual predictions. This is particularly useful in cybersecurity, where decisions must often be justified for a specific URL. For example, the analysis of http://www.ekn-online.de shows that *Path Length* and *Count of 'http'* are the most influential features, while for http://www. ricardoitalo.com.br, *Query Parameter Count* and *Path Length* are more significant. This variability underscores the value of XAI in debugging and validating specific predictions.

10.4   Consistency Between Global and Local Explanations

Despite their differences, both the Logistic Regression and XAI-LIME outputs exhibit some consistency in identifying key features. Features like *Path Length*, *Count of 'http'*, and *URL Length* are consistently important across both global and local perspectives. This alignment reinforces the reliability of the Logistic Regression model, as the most influential features globally also play a significant role in local predictions.

However, there are cases where globally less important features, such as *Special Char Count* or *Subdomain Count*, become critical in local explanations. This highlights the value of XAI-LIME in providing context-specific explanations that the global view cannot offer.

10.5   Use Cases for Global and Local Explanations

The Logistic Regression (blue bar) output is best suited for **high-level analysis**. It helps identify the most important features across the dataset, which can guide model refinement and feature engineering. This global view is particularly useful for understanding general patterns in malicious URLs, such as the tendency of attackers to use long paths, multiple occurrences of *http*, and excessive subdomains.

The XAI-LIME (green bars) outputs, on the other hand, excel in providing **detailed, instance-specific explanations**. They are invaluable for investigating individual predictions, debugging misclassifications, and building trust in the model. For example, security analysts reviewing a flagged URL can use LIME's explanations to understand why the URL was classified as malicious, enabling them to take informed actions.

Interestingly, the original hypothesis of this study was that the explanations provided by the XAI tool, LIME, would largely align with the global feature importance derived from Logistic Regression or the convex optimization model. It was assumed that the inherently interpretable nature of the convex optimization model could serve as a means to validate the local interpretability of LIME. However, the findings show certain divergence between global and local interpretations, challenging this hypothesis.

10.6   Mismatch Between Global and Local Interpretations

While convex optimization and Logistic Regression offer consistent global feature importance rankings (e.g., features like URL length or character counts having high influence), the local explanations provided by LIME often highlight different features as critical for individual predictions. For example, features deemed globally insignificant (such as subdomain count or query parameters) were occasionally identified as the most impactful for specific URLs. This discrepancy indicates that local interpretability does not always align with global trends.

10.7   Disproving the Hypothesis

The results suggest that using a globally interpretable convex optimization model to validate LIME's local explanations may not always be feasible. Instead, the two methods reveal complementary insights: convex optimization captures dataset-wide trends, while LIME explains instance-specific decisions. This finding disproves the hypothesis that a globally interpretable model can reliably validate local explanations in this use case.

10.8   Implications for the Proposed Framework

The divergence between global and local interpretations highlights the value of using a two-stage stacked framework, where the convex optimization model and the XAI-LIME explainer are used in parallel rather than as a validation mechanism for one another. This parallel approach allows the framework to leverage the strengths of both methods:

- **Global Interpretability:** Convex optimization provides a clear understanding of dataset-wide feature importance, which is useful for model refinement, feature selection, and understanding general patterns.
- **Local Interpretability:** LIME offers granular insights into individual predictions, making it valuable for debugging, anomaly detection, and justifying specific decisions.

10.9   Use Cases for the Framework

This complementary framework is particularly suited for applications where both global and local explainability are required:

- **For Security Analysts:** Global insights can guide general strategies for identifying malicious URLs, while local explanations can justify specific flagged instances.
- **For Model Debugging:** Discrepancies between global and local interpretations can help identify edge cases, dataset biases, or unexpected model behavior.

10.10   Broader Insights

The findings challenge the assumption that local interpretability frameworks like LIME should always align with global interpretations. Instead, they highlight the importance of treating global and local explainability as distinct but complementary perspectives. This insight underscores the need for multi-faceted explainability frameworks in sensitive domains like cybersecurity.

The Logistic Regression (blue bar) output and XAI-LIME (green bar) graphs provide complementary insights into the model's behavior. While the global view offers an understanding of dataset-wide trends and feature importance, the local explanations reveal how features contribute to individual predictions. Together, these perspectives enable a comprehensive understanding of the model, making it more interpretable, reliable, and actionable for cybersecurity applications.

11   Conclusion

In this study, we proposed a complementary framework for detecting malicious URLs by combining the global interpretability of convex optimization with the local explanations provided by LIME under the Explainable AI (XAI) paradigm. The methodology involved preparing and analyzing a labeled dataset, engineering 21 lexical features from URLs, and leveraging these features for classification. Convex optimization was utilized despite achieving slightly lower accuracy compared to black-box machine learning models, as it offers unparalleled interpretability and transparency, which are critical for understanding why a URL is classified as malicious rather than merely identifying it as such. This interpretability enables cybersecurity practitioners to gain deeper insights into the underlying factors contributing to malicious behaviors, fostering better-informed decision-making and trust in the model.

LIME complemented the global insights of convex optimization by providing instance-specific explanations, further enhancing the explainability of individual predictions. The results demonstrate that this hybrid approach not only achieves effective detection of malicious URLs but also prioritizes interpretability, which is essential for real-world cybersecurity applications where understanding the "why" is often more important than simply knowing the "what."

By addressing both global and local perspectives of explainability, this framework bridges the gap between model performance and the need for actionable insights. Future work will explore extending this approach to other domains, integrating additional XAI techniques, and improving the trade-off between accuracy and interpretability to further refine the framework's utility and robustness.

References

1. Sheng, S., Holbrook, M., Kumaraguru, P., Cranor, L.F., Downs, J.S.: An empirical analysis of phishing blacklists. In: Proceedings of the Sixth Conference on Email and Anti-Spam (CEAS) (2009)

2. Ma, J., Saul, L.K., Savage, S., Voelker, G.M.: Learning to detect malicious URLs. In: Proceedings of the IEEE International Conference on Communications (ICC), pp. 1–6. IEEE (2011)

3. Canali, D., Cova, M., Vigna, G., Kruegel, C.: Prophiler: a system for detecting malicious web pages. In: Proceedings of the IEEE International Conference on Communications (ICC), pp. 1–6. IEEE (2011)

4. Raja, K., Anwar, S., Khan, A.: Lexical features-based malicious URL detection using machine learning techniques. Int. J. Comput. Sci. Netw. Secur. **19**(2), 150–159 (2019)

5. Ribeiro, M.T., Singh, S., Guestrin, C.: Should you trust this classification? Explaining individual classifications. In: Proceedings of the 22nd ACM SIGKDD International Conference on Knowledge Discovery and Data Mining, pp. 1135–1144. ACM (2016)

6. Sahoo, D., Liu, C., Hoi, S.C.H.: Malicious URL detection using ensemble learning. J. Inf. Secur. Appl. **34**, 1–10 (2017)

7. Le, T.H., Alzahrani, M.Y., Alfarraj, O., et al.: URLNet: a deep learning approach for malicious URL detection. IEEE Access **6**, 1–10 (2018)

8. Symantec: Internet Security Threat Report. Symantec Corporation (2019). https://www.symantec.com

9. Choi, J., Lee, H., Kim, H.: Domain-specific features for phishing detection. Comput. Secur. **87**, 101–115 (2019)

10. Patil, S., Deshmukh, R.: Detecting malicious URLs using decision trees. Int. J. Adv. Res. Comput. Eng. Technol. **9**(3), 212–218 (2020)

11. Hou, S., Chen, Y., Zhang, Z.: Malicious web content detection using machine learning. J. Web Secur. Priv. **12**(4), 101–120 (2020)

12. Wang, Y., Li, H., Xu, J.: Domain-aware feature extraction for malicious URL detection. J. Cybersecur. Priv. **1**(1), 1–20 (2020)

13. Ghaleb, M., Al-Hadhrami, T., Hussain, S.: Threat detection using ensemble learning. J. Cybersecur. Res. **8**(1), 45–60 (2021)

14. Zhang, Y., Wang, X., Li, Q.: A transformer-based model for malicious URL detection. IEEE Trans. Netw. Serv. Manage. **18**(2), 1–15 (2021)

15. Poddar, S., Chowdhury, D., Dwivedi, A.D., Mukkamala, R.R.: Data-driven based malicious URL detection using explainable AI. In: IEEE International Conference on Trust, Security and Privacy in Computing and Communications (TrustCom), pp. 1–7. IEEE (2022). https://doi.org/10.1109/TrustCom56396.2022.00176

16. Kumar, A., Mehta, R., Singh, T.: Explainable AI for cybersecurity: a case study on phishing URL detection. Comput. Secur. **123**, 102956 (2023)

17. Verma, A., Sharma, P., Raj, K.: Detection of malicious URLs using hybrid machine learning models. Cybersecur. Priv. J. **3**(1), 1–19 (2023)

18. Ali, S., Khan, M., Rehman, F.: Real-time malicious URL detection using federated learning. IEEE Access **11**, 10234–10245 (2023)

19. Chen, J., Li, Y., Zhang, H.: Enhancing URL detection with transformer models and explainable AI. IEEE Trans. Inf. Forensics Secur. **19**(4), 1452–1463 (2024)

20. Singh, R., Gupta, A., Sharma, V.: Leveraging graph neural networks for malicious URL detection. Neural Comput. Appl. (2024)

21. Malicious and Benign URLs Dataset. Kaggle (2023). https://www.kaggle.com/datasets/sid321axn/malicious-urls-dataset. Accessed 30 Mar 2025

Forecasting Cyber Vulnerabilities: A Critical Analysis of ARIMA Models' Efficacy and Efficiency

N. H. M. Arafat and Weiqing Sun[✉]

The University of Toledo, Toledo, OH 43606, USA
`nhm.arafat@rockets.utoledo.edu, weiqing.sun@utoledo.edu`

Abstract. Given the increasing intricacy of cyber attacks, it is crucial to anticipate security vulnerabilities to implement proactive defensive tactics precisely. This study provides a comprehensive examination of the efficacy and efficiency of the Autoregressive Integrated Moving Average (ARIMA) model for forecasting trends in security vulnerabilities. The objective of this research is not to propose or present revolutionary solutions but to contribute a rigorous evaluation of ARIMA's applicability in this domain. The data is sourced from an open-access Common Vulnerabilities and Exposures (CVE) dataset, encompassing nearly a decade of information. Our analysis focuses on 16 specific vulnerabilities using Common Weakness Enumeration (CWE) keywords, including SQL injection, cross-site scripting (XSS), and buffer overflow, with an emphasis on tracking and forecasting their occurrences. We rigorously evaluate the accuracy of the ARIMA model's predictions by comparing them with actual observed data from 2023. The evaluation primarily assesses the model's capacity to predict each type of vulnerability's incidence rate, highlighting its strengths and limitations. Our findings illustrate the correlation between expected and actual events, demonstrating the model's ability to capture the dynamic nature of cybersecurity vulnerabilities. This paper contributes to the field by providing empirical evidence of the efficacy of statistical model-based time-series forecasting in cybersecurity. It also suggests improvements for predictive models and advocates for integrating predictive analytics into cybersecurity strategies.

Keywords: Cybersecurity · Vulnerabilities · ARIMA Model · Time-Series Forecasting · Predictive Analytics · CVE dataset · OSINT

1 Introduction

1.1 Background Information

With the growing reliance on digital technology globally, security concerns are also on the rise [9,19]. The range of risks includes both fundamental vulnerabilities that might jeopardize personal data and advanced exploits that can destroy

Master's Programs in Cyber Security, College of Engineering, The University of Toledo.

S. Goel et al. (Eds.): AICON 2025, LNICST 672, pp. 85–107, 2026.
https://doi.org/10.1007/978-3-032-14805-6_6

company and government networks [8]. Cybersecurity experts and researchers use the Common Vulnerabilities and Exposures (CVE) database to understand and reduce risks. This database is a publicly available record of security flaws and exposures. An investigation of CVE data can uncover significant trends and patterns that are crucial for the formulation of defensive solutions [59]. However, the large number and complexity of vulnerabilities present a rising challenge to traditional analysis methods, hence requiring predictive models that can anticipate threats before they occur. The Autoregressive Integrated Moving Average (ARIMA) model is highly effective in time series research and forecasting because it can leverage past patterns to create accurate models and predictions [15]. However, there is a notable lack of significant research addressing real-time prediction of issues associated with the 16 known vulnerabilities simultaneously, as identified by Common Weakness Enumeration (CWE) keywords. This study aims to assess the efficacy of ARIMA in forecasting cybersecurity vulnerabilities in a constantly changing digital threat landscape.

The 16 vulnerabilities we are discussing from the CVE dataset using the CWE keywords are overflow, Memory Corruption, SQL Injection, Cross-Site Scripting (XSS), Directory Traversal, File Inclusion, Cross-Site Request Forgery (CSRF), XML External Entity (XXE), Server-Side Request Forgery (SSRF), Open Redirect, Input Validation, Code Execution, Bypass, Privilege Escalation, Denial of Service (DoS), and Information Leak.

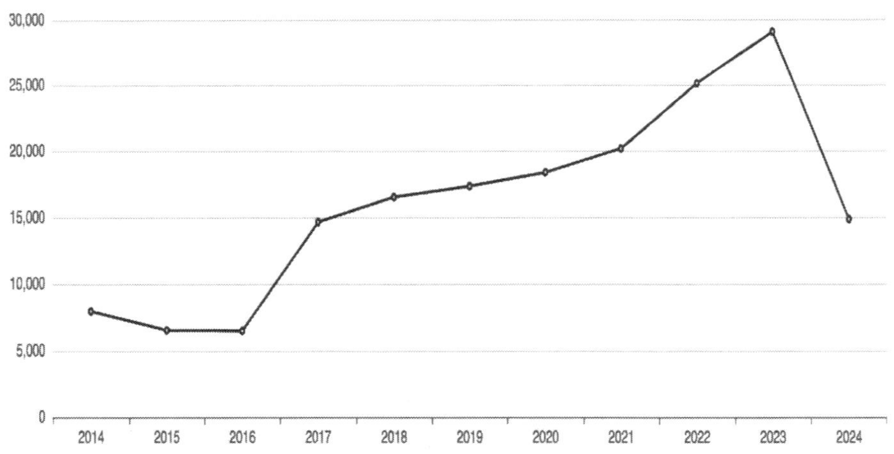

Fig. 1. An Overall Picture of Vulnerabilities Increment by Year

The illustration presents a thorough overview of cybersecurity vulnerabilities monitored from 2014 to the first quarter of 2024, which facilitates clear observation of changes across the decade in Fig. 1 [21].

In general, there is a steady rise in the overall number of vulnerabilities, starting from slightly over 5,000 in 2014 to about 30,000 in 2023. It is important to acknowledge that the significant decline to approximately 15,000 in 2024 is based solely on the data from the first quarter. This indicates that it is not a whole year count but rather a partial glimpse into the situation. If it increases for the rest of the months at the same pace, there is a high possibility of crossing the total number of occurrences in 2023.

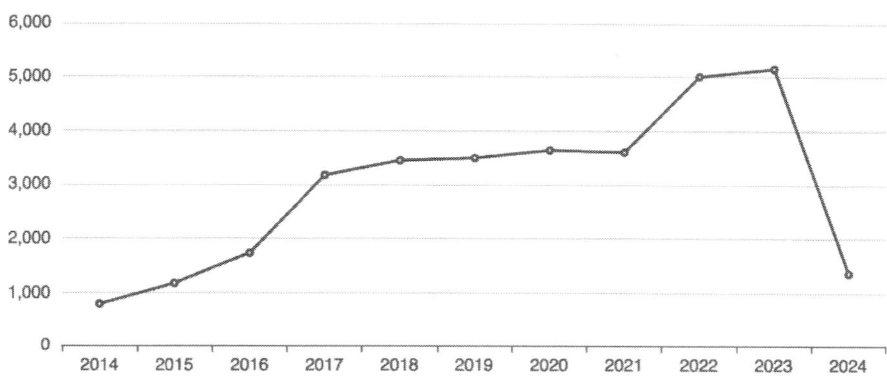

Fig. 2. An Overall Picture of Vulnerabilities with CVSS (9–10)

The provided Fig. 2 offers a comprehensive examination of cybersecurity vulnerabilities, organized according to their maximum Common Vulnerability Scoring System (CVSS) base ratings, spanning from 2014 to the first quarter of 2024 [20]. The CVSS values span from 0 to 10, with higher scores denoting a more severe vulnerability.

Commencing in 2014, the graph displays a rather small quantity of significant vulnerabilities (scoring 9–10), commencing at around 500 instances. During the course of the decade, there has been a considerable rise in high-severity vulnerabilities, reaching their highest point in 2023 with more than 5,000 reported occurrences. This increase indicates a concerning pattern in the appearance of extremely severe vulnerabilities that present substantial dangers.

In the first quarter of 2024, there was a significant decrease to less than 2,000 instances in the same high-severity group. Given that this decline is based on data from only a portion of the year, one should exercise caution when interpreting it. And it's still much higher than the whole year's instances of 2014. If this pattern continues for the rest of the year, it may indicate a substantial change in the cybersecurity environment.

The graphs illustrate the cybersecurity industry grappling with escalating and formidable difficulties. Over the past decade, the significant increase in high-severity vulnerabilities emphasizes security breaches' escalating intricacy and potential consequences. This trend underlines the necessity for ongoing awareness and innovation in cybersecurity measures to successfully mitigate these vulnerabilities at a high-risk level.

1.2 Research Problem

While the utility of CVE data is undisputed, the ability to forecast the emergence and progression of cyber vulnerabilities remains limited. Current predictive solutions often offer hybrid models rather than revealing or using the existing capability of existing models like ARIMA, lacking the performance of existing resources. This is partly due to the aggressive nature of predicting cyber threats, driven by human factors, technological advances, and the adaptive behavior of threat actors. The research problem thus centers on assessing ARIMA's capacity to effectively predict the trends of security vulnerabilities reported in the CVE database. It questions whether a statistical model can capture the complexities of cyber threats and translate historical data into accurate future projections.

1.3 Objectives and Scope

The objectives of this study are set against the backdrop of a pressing need for improved cybersecurity threat forecasting. The study aims to:

1. Critically evaluate the predictive power of the ARIMA model using historical CVE data.
2. Analyze trend consistency and prediction accuracy across various categories of vulnerabilities.
3. Explore the model's sensitivity to changes in threat dynamics and its adaptability to the cybersecurity context.
4. Offer recommendations for future research directions based on the rigorous evaluation of ARIMA's capabilities and shortcomings.

The study includes a dataset spanning a decade of CVE entries. The dataset was carefully selected to represent a wide range of cyber risks and ensure that the ARIMA model performs well across various vulnerability categories. This era offers a significant historical context for comprehending enduring patterns while also encompassing contemporary changes in the cyber threat environment.

1.4 Significance of Study

The importance of this work is in its capacity to transform how cyber threats are predicted and dealt with. An effective predictive model could function as a crucial instrument for cybersecurity experts, enabling them to proactively allocate resources and enhance defenses. Additionally, it has the potential to provide policymakers and stakeholders with evidence-based insights to develop well-informed cybersecurity policies and strategies. This research aims to demonstrate the effectiveness of ARIMA in predicting vulnerabilities, which could have significant implications for predictive analytics in cybersecurity. It highlights the importance of statistical models in improving digital security. This study makes a substantial contribution to the field of cyber vulnerability prediction, as, to the best of our knowledge, no prior research has utilized the ARIMA model for predicting all common vulnerabilities simultaneously based on CWE keywords within the CVE dataset. Moreover, we conducted a critical analysis of the model's limitations and provided recommendations for future research based on our findings and observations.

1.5   Structure of the Paper

The paper is organized into the following sections:

1. Section 2 reviews relevant literature on applying time-series forecasting in cybersecurity and discusses the ARIMA model's theoretical underpinnings.
2. Section 3 details the methodology adopted for data collection, preparation, and the ARIMA model's application to the CVE dataset.
3. Section 4 presents the results and discussion of the model's predictions alongside actual data from the CVE records, followed by a comprehensive analysis of the findings.
4. Section 5 concludes the work with a summary of the research contributions, limitations, and suggestions for future work in this area.

2   Related Works

2.1   Cybersecurity and Role of Predictive Model

In the field of cybersecurity, the environment is always changing as threats become increasingly intricate and advanced [31]. In order to counteract these ever-changing dangers, multiple strategies have been suggested. Predictive analytics has been recognized as a viable method in behavioral cybersecurity, assisting in creating adaptive cybersecurity mechanisms [1]. Machine learning models in cybersecurity possess the potential to learn from past data and improve their ability to detect and counter new threats, making them very flexible and adaptable [40]. Furthermore, the incorporation of artificial intelligence (AI) into cybersecurity has become a crucial area for improving the identification, reaction, and reduction of threats [38]. As firms face the difficulties of changing cyber threats, the importance of proactive and adaptable cybersecurity measures becomes crucial [50]. The Adaptive Cybersecurity Culture Model (ACCM) incorporates the principles of "Learn, Unlearn, and Relearn" to promote resilience and adaptation in response to evolving threats [25]. Moreover, the significance of elucidating machine learning in cybersecurity is underscored, emphasizing the necessity for clarity in the models employed for producing predictions [57]. To effectively manage cybersecurity risks, enterprises must quantitatively evaluate emerging threats. This involves utilizing technology and security measures to minimize the occurrence of data breaches [5]. The ever-changing nature of cybersecurity threats highlights the significance of consistently developing, being watchful, and being flexible in cybersecurity practices [45]. Furthermore, the evolving characteristics of cyber threats and their influence on political stability underscore the need for strong cybersecurity measures [39]. In order to strengthen defenses against constantly evolving and complex cyber threats, it is essential to utilize predictive analytics, artificial intelligence, machine learning, and adaptive cybersecurity models. Organizations should implement proactive and transparent cybersecurity policies to efficiently reduce risks and protect against perpetually shifting cyber threats.

2.2 Time Series Forecasting in Cybersecurity

Time series forecasting in cybersecurity is an essential field that employs diverse computing approaches and models to anticipate future patterns in cyber events. Scientists have investigated many methods to improve the precision of prediction models.

Several studies have explored various predictive models to enhance cybersecurity measures. One such study [10] employed Seasonal ARIMA (SARIMA) to analyze threats within a university network, achieving superior prediction accuracy as evidenced by a reduced Root Mean Squared Error (RMSE) value. Other researches [24,28] focused on deep learning techniques, developing models using Time Series, Multilayer Perceptron (MLP), Convolutional Neural Network (CNN), Long Short-Term Memory (LSTM), Convolutional LSTM (ConvLSTM), and CNN-LSTM.

A closely related study [24] applied the ARIMA model using the keyword "Android" in conjunction with deep learning methods, which differs from our focus on CWE keywords. Additionally, their model exhibited an error rate of 18.449. In another relevant study [32], common vulnerabilities were predicted using the same dataset (CVE dataset); however, unlike our approach, which utilizes a statistical model-based time-series forecasting (ARIMA), they employed supervised predictive algorithms.

In a scholarly work [56], researchers utilized attack data from Hackmageddon to forecast cyber threats. Their tool outperformed naïve forecasting methods by 14.1% when predicting attacks of any type and by up to 21.2% for specific attack types. Another study [44] developed a predictive analytic model using a time series approach for three popular desktop operating systems—Windows 7, Mac OS X, and Linux Kernel—based on reported vulnerabilities from the National Vulnerability Database (NVD).

Hybridized forecasting methods have also been investigated, such as the combination of ARIMA models and Bayesian Networks (BN) [55], ARIMA supplemented with additional metrics [33], and bi-directional recurrent neural networks with long short-term memory (BRNN-LSTM) [23]. Furthermore, research has addressed specific attacks on particular networks, including DDoS attacks in SIP networks [48] and DDoS threats using ARIMA and ETS forecasting techniques [22].

A research [16] utilized Koopman's approach and the Dynamic Mode Decomposition (DMD) algorithm to consolidate and forecast cybersecurity incident reports in the field of cybersecurity incident reports. This method emphasizes the importance of utilizing sophisticated algorithms to process cybersecurity data to make accurate predictions.

In addition, researchers [51] proposed the Cybersecurity Granger Causality (CGC) framework to analyze and use Granger causality in time series data of cyber attack rates for predictive purposes. This paradigm provides a systematic method for assessing causal correlations in cybersecurity data, improving forecasts' accuracy.

In addition, a research was incorporated into an intuitionistic fuzzy time series forecasting model, resulting in enhanced predicting accuracy as compared to conventional models [3]. This integration showcases the capacity to merge various methodologies to improve the accuracy of prediction.

A research [29] established a model selection framework for time series forecasting models. They used Convolutional Neural Networks (CNN) and data augmentation techniques to handle small sample data. The study highlights the significance of choosing suitable forecasting methods to achieve accurate forecasts. This methodology facilitates identifying the optimal approach for forecasting cybersecurity time series.

Combining these sources emphasizes the significance of utilizing sophisticated computational techniques, algorithmic methodologies, and model selection procedures to improve the accuracy of time series forecasting in cybersecurity.

2.3   ARIMA Model in Trend Prediction

The Autoregressive Integrated Moving Average (ARIMA) model is renowned for its simplicity, structured framework, and reliable forecasting capabilities, contributing to its widespread adoption as a prominent method for time series forecasting [17]. The ARIMA model has been utilized by researchers in diverse domains such as epidemiology, infectious disease prediction, and stock price forecasting [11,63,64]. The ARIMA model has proven to be highly valuable in forecasting patterns associated with infectious diseases such as COVID-19, mortality rates of colorectal cancer, and the occurrence of scarlet fever [6,26].

Although the ARIMA model has demonstrated efficacy in forecasting patterns for different phenomena, several researchers have highlighted its shortcomings, particularly in addressing non-linear correlations in intricate and evolving issues such as the transmission of COVID-19 [2]. Nevertheless, the ARIMA model has effectively been integrated with other models, such as neural networks, to improve predictive abilities in domains like pollution prediction and error compensation [62]. In addition, the ARIMA model has been employed alongside machine learning methods to predict the demand for medical services [27,61].

The ARIMA model demonstrates its versatility by successfully predicting trends in diverse fields, including agriculture, environmental forecasting, and GDP forecasting for nations such as Nigeria [52,54]. The model's capacity to effectively manage both upward and downward trends in time series data and auto-correlations renders it a desirable tool for forecasting [18].

A research [54] showed that the ARIMA-ERNN model was more effective than the classic ARIMA model in forecasting pertussis incidence in mainland China. In a similar vein, [62] discovered that a hybrid model combining ARIMA and neural network techniques outperformed the standalone ARIMA model when it came to forecasting cases of human brucellosis. These studies emphasize the possibility of improving prediction accuracy by combining ARIMA with other models.

In addition, [35] highlighted the superiority of the ARIMA with exogenous variables (ARIMAX) model in accurately predicting the occurrence of pulmonary tuberculosis by including extra components. These findings indicate that the inclusion of external variables can enhance the predicted accuracy of the ARIMA model.

Although the ARIMA model has demonstrated efficacy in several applications, it is crucial to consider its constraints. According to [58], the ARIMA model may not be appropriate for predicting time series data that include non-linear properties, such as forecasting the air quality index. This highlights the significance of comprehending the characteristics of the data while choosing a predictive model.

In cybersecurity, evaluating prediction models is essential for foreseeing and minimizing potential dangers. The ARIMA model has been widely used in many domains for forecasting various events. Research has indicated that the effectiveness of the ARIMA model can be improved by integrating supplementary techniques or models.

The ARIMA model continues to be an important tool for forecasting time series data, particularly in cybersecurity. Hence, we anticipate its projected forecast outcomes.

2.4   Utilization of the CVE for Prediction

The Common Vulnerabilities and Exposures (CVE) database is an essential cybersecurity tool, offering organized and quantifiable severity data for known vulnerabilities [47]. The models trained using historical CVE data have demonstrated a high F1 score in accurately predicting the absence of crucial elements in vulnerability descriptions [34]. Moreover, characteristics and measurements extracted from CVE entries can be employed to train vulnerability predictors using conventional machine learning and deep learning models [12,49].

Vulnerability databases such as CVE and the National Vulnerability Database (NVD) play a vital role in Cyber Threat Intelligence and are widely used in security solutions worldwide [53]. These databases facilitate the use of quantitative tools to prioritize insights and conduct predictive analysis in security processes [30]. The CVE database has crucial data, including descriptions, Common Vulnerability Scoring System (CVSS) scores, vulnerable product configurations, and weakness categorizations for each vulnerability [42].

Studies have shown that CVE data can be used to forecast upcoming susceptible libraries and accelerate the distribution of patches in software repositories [36,43]. In addition, the CVE database has been utilized in several research domains, such as applying Convolutional Neural Networks (CNNs) to forecast vulnerability severity [41]. The CVE database is widely acknowledged as a prominent and extensive repository of software and hardware vulnerability data that is accessible to the public [13].

The CVE database is a fundamental resource for managing, predicting, and analyzing vulnerabilities in cybersecurity. The structured information and historical data provided by this database enable the successful construction of models, prediction of missing components in vulnerability descriptions, and enhancement of security practices.

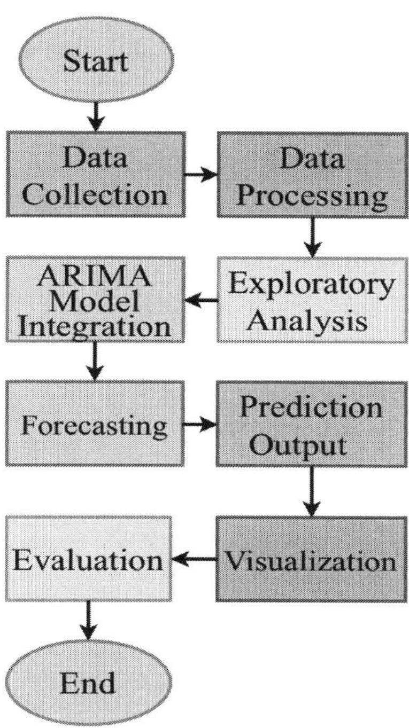

Fig. 3. Simplified Methodology

3   Methodology

3.1   Research Design

This study utilizes a quantitative research design to analyze and anticipate vulnerabilities. It specifically focuses on leveraging historical data from the CVE dataset. The research is divided into two primary phases: (1) doing an exploratory analysis of CVE entries to uncover patterns and historical trends in vulnerabilities, and (2) evaluating the effectiveness of the ARIMA predictive model in anticipating future vulnerabilities. This approach allows for a thorough comprehension of historical and current susceptibility patterns, which in turn enables the creation of precise predictive models. A simplified methodology of this work is presented in Fig. 3.

To clarify for readers, since this research conducts a critical analysis of the ARIMA model's capabilities and shortcomings in predicting vulnerabilities, we are not introducing any novel solutions to vulnerability trend prediction. Therefore, no machine learning or other statistical learning models have been utilized in this paper to enhance the ARIMA model's performance against the discovered shortcomings. We have proposals for that at the end of the paper.

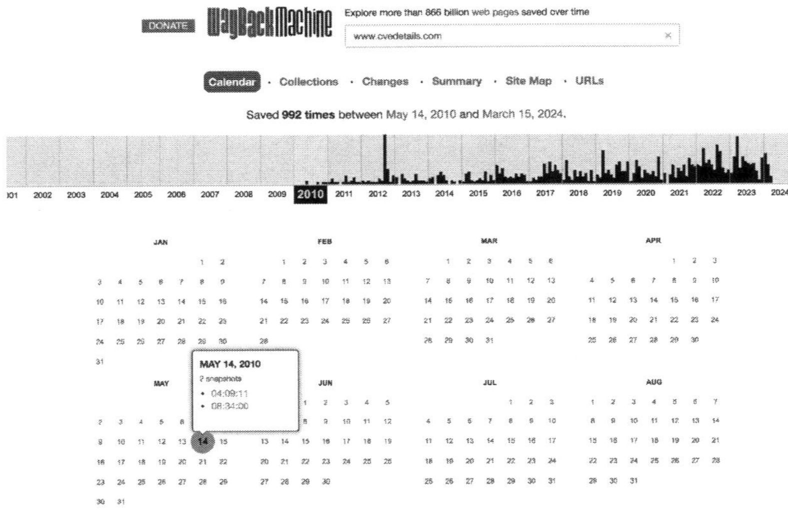

Fig. 4. Authenticity Check 1: Wayback Machine

3.2   Data Collection

The National Vulnerability Database (NVD) provides the CVE dataset, which is the main data source for this study. The latest version we used of the dataset was from https://cve.mitre.org/data/downloads/index.html on March 26, 2024 (CVE Version 20061101). The dataset is directly downloadable from the link. The dataset contains comprehensive explanations, references, assignment dates, and more metadata about every vulnerability entry. Data collection entails the retrieval of CVE records from the last ten years, with a specific emphasis on vulnerabilities. This time period offers a comprehensive set of data to comprehend past patterns and determine the efficacy and efficiency of the ARIMA forecasting model.

Due to the extensive descriptions contained in the directly downloadable dataset, it is not conducive to effective common vulnerability prediction. To support our main dataset, we used data from a third-party website, https://www.cvedetails.com/vulnerabilities-by-types.php, as of March 21, 2024. This website assigns types or categories to vulnerabilities using Common Weakness

Enumeration (CWE) ids and keywords. Each type of vulnerability was tracked over a period from 2014 to 2023, with data points representing the number of incidents recorded annually.

3.3   Authenticity Check

We standardized the data by cross-checking using Open Source Intelligence (OSINT) techniques for that particular website in 3 steps to ensure authenticity and correctness to ensure useablity.

Fig. 5. Authenticity Check 2: Domain Name Age Checker

1. **Way Back Machine:** The Wayback Machine, created by the Internet Archive, is a digital repository of the World Wide Web that enables users to see past versions of web pages, making it valuable for confirming a website's validity and historical accuracy [7,46]. We applied the link to the WayBack Machine (Fig. 4) to check the historical footprints of the website to make sure that it has good track records. And we found at least 264 achieved data footprints for the website from Way Back Machine since 2010.
2. **Domain Name Age Checker:** A Domain Name Age Checker is a tool utilized to ascertain a domain's registration date and age. This information is crucial in evaluating the genuineness and reliability of a website, as older domains are commonly seen as more dependable [14,37]. We checked the domain age (Fig. 5) besides the previous action mentioned. The website has been serving for around 14 years, and the service is promising.
3. **WhoIs Lookup:** A WhoIs Lookup is a protocol used to retrieve a domain's registration information. It is important to confirm the validity of a website since it provides details about the domain owner, registration dates, and

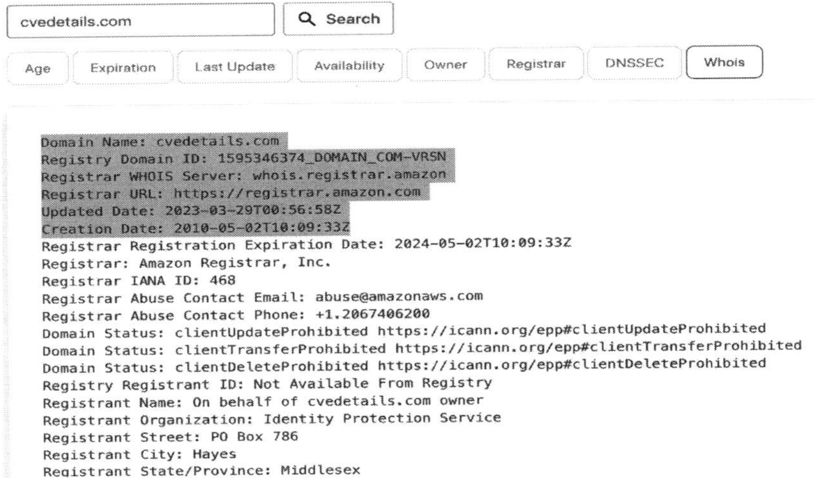

Fig. 6. Authenticity Check 3: Whois Lookup

contact information [4,60]. We tried to know to whom the website is registered and if they updated the registration regularly. In this stage, the website passed our test successfully because it is registered with Amazon and updated very recently (Fig. 6).

Overall, no complaint was found against the website on which we collected the supporting data. Besides, by doing OSINT, we found clear historical footprints. Therefore, we relied on the data provided by the website.

3.4   Time Series Analysis

ARIMA Model Integration: We chose the ARIMA model for its effectiveness in handling time series data, where data points are chronologically ordered. The ARIMA model parameters autoregression (p), differencing (d), and moving average (q) − (p, d, q) were set to do initial tests which suggested this configuration provided the best balance between complexity and forecasting accuracy.

Model Fitting: We imported ARIMA from "statsmodels.tsa.arima.model" to accomplish our task, and in the function, we provided different p, d, q values like $(0, 1, 1)$, $(1, 1, 1)$, $(2, 1, 1)$, $(0, 0, 1)$, $(0, 2, 1)$, $(0, 1, 0)$, and $(0, 1, 2)$ gradually to test the parameters which helped to judge this configuration provided the best balance between complexity and forecasting accuracy.

3.5   Forecasting

Using the fitted model, we forecasted the number of incidents for the year following the last data point (2023). This prediction helped us estimate the trend—

whether a particular type of vulnerability was expected to increase or decrease in frequency.

3.6   Prediction Output

The output of our model provided a numerical estimate of the incidents for 2023, which we compared against real-world data to validate our model's accuracy. This step was crucial for refining our model and improving future forecasts.

3.7   Visualization

We plotted the results using Matplotlib to visualize the predictions against the actual numbers for 2023, from where we could see the most and the least successful predictions. These visual representations helped in easily comparing forecasted data with actual data, thereby assessing the performance of our predictive models.

3.8   Evaluation

Finally, we calculated the prediction success rates and displayed these as tables to evaluate the overall effectiveness of our forecasts. We also used line graphs to juxtapose the predicted values against the actual values for each vulnerability, providing a clear and visual format to assess model performance.

4   Results and Discussion

4.1   Real VS Predicted Results

The results are visually represented through line graphs. Predictions are shown in blue lines in the line graph, while the actual 2023 figures are displayed in orange. The line graph complements this data by connecting annual figures, facilitating trend visualization and comparison between predicted and actual data.

Furthermore, the Tables 1 and 2 present a thorough analysis of actual and projected outcomes for several cybersecurity vulnerabilities in 2023, utilizing distinct ARIMA (AutoRegressive Integrated Moving Average) models. This comprehensive comparison facilitates the assessment of the prediction capacities of these models for various categories of vulnerabilities.

The first table, labeled as Table 1, presents the factual recorded data for several categories of vulnerabilities in the year 2023. Additionally, it includes the projected values created by three separate ARIMA models. The columns are structured as follows: the initial column displays the categories of vulnerabilities, the second column exhibits the actual values for 2023, and the subsequent columns showcase the forecasts generated by ARIMA models with parameters (0,1,1), (1,1,1), and (2,1,1).

As an example, in the context of "Memory Corruption," the precise count of documented occurrences in the year 2023 is 2813. The ARIMA (0,1,1) model

Table 1. Real VS Predicted Results (part 1) for 2023

Vulnerabilities	Real 2023	ARIMA (0,1,1)	ARIMA (1,1,1)	ARIMA (2,1,1)
Overflow	1724	1912	1711	1650
Memory Corruption	2813	3636	3739	4376
Sql Injection	2159	2245	2030	2098
XSS	5179	3573	3556	3529
Directory Traversal	808	821	834	743
File Inclusion	137	100	99	96
CSRF	1398	798	754	738
XXE	138	128	139	123
SSRF	248	245	245	257
Open Redirect	188	142	153	156
Input Validation	786	871	798	884
Code Execution	2581	2048	2169	2137
Bypass	1059	983	976	965
Privilege Escalation	1525	1482	1636	1546
Denial of Service	2559	2069	2211	2144
Information Leak	1545	1186	1144	1192

Table 2. Real VS Predicted Results (part 2) for 2023

Vulnerabilities	ARIMA (0,0,1)	ARIMA (0,2,1)	ARIMA (0,1,0)	ARIMA (0,1,2)
Overflow	1639	2037	1886	1684
Memory Corruption	2457	3772	3420	4257
Sql Injection	1391	2793	1790	2006
XSS	2444	3707	3407	3542
Directory Traversal	626	801	735	799
File Inclusion	85	113	101	98
CSRF	576	832	769	752
XXE	128	135	127	136
SSRF	176	265	235	245
Open Redirect	106	159	147	145
Input Validation	867	863	823	897
Code Execution	1726	2204	2067	2079
Bypass	793	1041	944	972
Privilege Escalation	1438	1693	1527	1439
Denial of Service	2191	2599	2437	2145
Information Leak	1082	1245	1145	1237

forecasts 3636 occurrences, the ARIMA (1,1,1) model forecasts 3739, and the ARIMA (2,1,1) model forecasts 4376. The considerable discrepancy in forecasts highlights the difficulties and intricacies of effectively predicting these vulnerabilities.

Similarly, the documented value for "XSS" vulnerabilities is 5179. The models' forecasts vary between 3529 and 3573, suggesting that all of them significantly underestimated the actual value. This implies that the models might require further modification or extra data to enhance their accuracy for this specific vulnerability.

The table additionally presents forecasts for other vulnerabilities, including "SQL Injection," "Directory Traversal," and "Denial of Service," with differing levels of accuracy observed among the different ARIMA models. As an illustration, the actual number for "SQL Injection" is 2159, whereas the model's predictions range from 2030 to 2245, indicating a higher level of similarity compared to other vulnerabilities.

The second table, labeled as Table 2, expands upon the analysis by providing forecasts from four distinct ARIMA models. These models have the following parameter values: (0,0,1), (0,2,1), (0,1,0), and (0,1,2). This table excludes the actual recorded data for 2023 and instead presents the expected values from each model.

The ARIMA models anticipate the following number of occurrences for "Overflow" vulnerabilities: 1639 for the ARIMA (0,0,1) model, 2037 for the ARIMA (0,2,1) model, 1886 for the ARIMA (0,1,0) model, and 1684 for the ARIMA (0,1,2) model. These forecasts exhibit a broad spectrum, indicating varying model sensitivity to the underlying data trends.

Regarding "Memory Corruption," the forecasts exhibit much greater variability. The ARIMA (0,0,1) model forecasts 2457 events, whereas the ARIMA (0,2,1) model predicts a significantly higher value of 3772. The ARIMA (0,1,0) model forecasts a value of 3420, while the ARIMA (0,1,2) model predicts a value of 4257. The extensive variety of parameters demonstrates the substantial influence they can exert on the prediction results.

Additional vulnerabilities, such as "XSS" and "SQL Injection," exhibit comparable patterns of unpredictability. The projections for "XSS" vary from 2444 to 3707, suggesting that certain models may greatly overestimate or underestimate the actual incidence rates.

Both tables offer useful data regarding the performance of different ARIMA models in forecasting cybersecurity vulnerabilities. The comparison emphasizes the significance of choosing suitable model parameters and the difficulties associated with effectively predicting such intricate and ever-changing data. Through the examination of disparities between actual and projected values, it is possible to determine the models that are more dependable for particular vulnerabilities, thereby providing guidance for enhancing predictive analytics in the field of cybersecurity.

4.2   Comprehensive Comparison

Table 3 comprehensively compares forecast errors among several ARIMA models. The errors are classified into four specific ranges: 0–2%, 3–5%, 6–10%, and over 10%. In addition, it displays the overall percentage of forecasts with an error range of less than 10% for each ARIMA model, offering a holistic perspective on the predictive accuracy of the models.

Table 3. Models, Number of vulnerabilities within error range, and Overall Success

Models	0–2%	3–5%	6–10%	>10%	<10% overall error(%)
ARIMA (0,1,1)	4	4	5	3	81.25
ARIMA (1,1,1)	6	2	3	5	68.75
ARIMA (2,1,1)	4	4	5	3	81.25
ARIMA (0,0,1)	4	3	7	2	87.5
ARIMA (0,2,1)	5	3	5	3	81.25
ARIMA (0,1,0)	4	4	6	2	87.5
ARIMA (0,1,2)	5	3	5	3	81.25

When using the ARIMA (0,1,1) model, we find that it has relatively good accuracy, with 81.25% of its forecasts having an error rate of less than 10%. Most of its mistakes lie within the 0–2% and 3–5% intervals, suggesting that

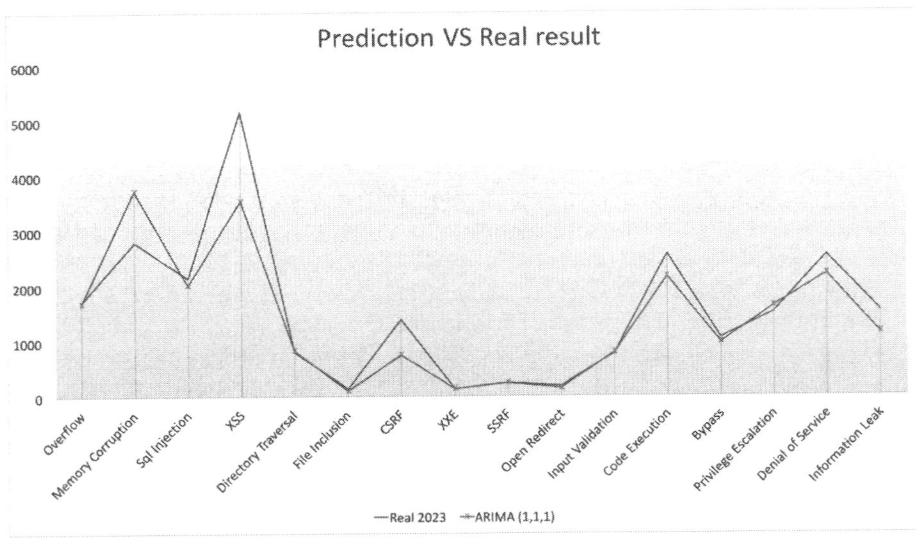

Fig. 7. Overall least successful, but most successful in 0–2% error category

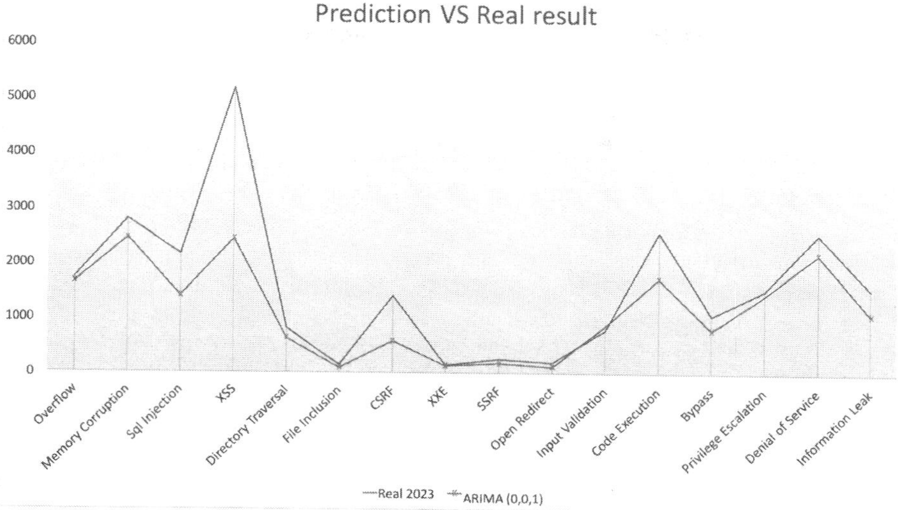

Fig. 8. One of the most successful predictions (1)

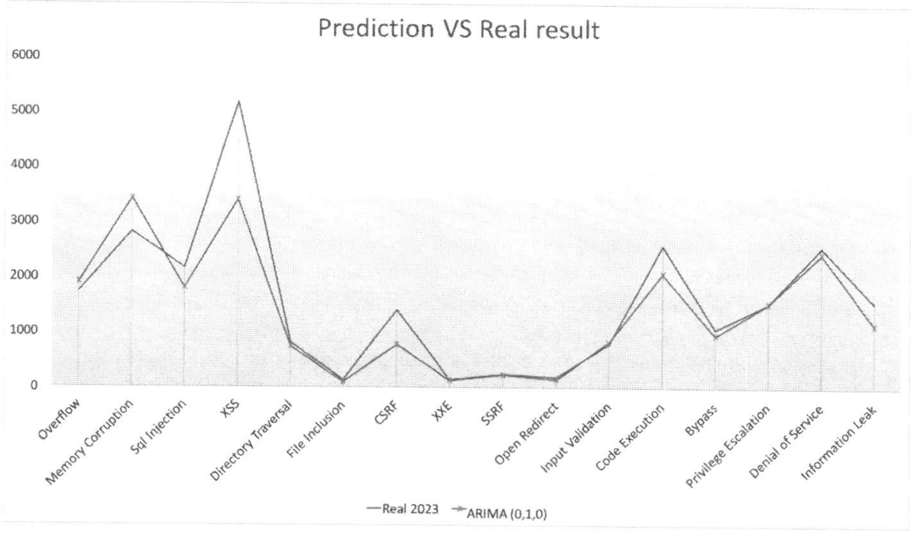

Fig. 9. One of the most successful predictions (2)

this model has a propensity for making accurate predictions. Nevertheless, there are still significant inaccuracies, with three forecasts surpassing a 10% margin of error, indicating specific areas where the model's precision may be enhanced.

On the other hand, the ARIMA (1,1,1) model has the lowest percentage of success compared to the other models mentioned. Only 68.75% of its predictions are within the error range of less than 10%. Although this model has the biggest number of forecasts inside the 0–2% error range, it also has a substantial number of predictions that exceed a 10% inaccuracy. This suggests that although the ARIMA (1,1,1) model can be quite precise in certain situations, it is also susceptible to significant mistakes, necessitating additional improvement. A line graph is provided in Fig. 7 to support a clearer understanding of the results.

The ARIMA (2,1,1) model has a comparable success record to ARIMA (0,1,1), with 81.25% of its predictions falling into an error range of less than 10%. The distribution of mistakes is similar, with the majority of errors focused within the 0–2% and 3–5% intervals. The consistent performance of the ARIMA (2,1,1) model indicates its reliability, while there is still potential for enhancement, particularly in lowering forecasts with errors exceeding 10

The ARIMA (0,0,1) model demonstrates a notable level of effectiveness, as 87.5% of its forecasts exhibit an error rate below 10%. The majority of its errors fall between the range of 6–10%, and it has a relatively small number of predictions that have an error surpassing 10%. This model exhibits significant predictive skills, highlighting its resilience and dependability in forecasting cybersecurity vulnerabilities. To improve understanding, we visualized the data using a line graph in Fig. 8.

The ARIMA (0,2,1) model, together with the ARIMA (0,1,1) and (2,1,1) models, achieves a success rate of 81.25% for forecasts with an error rate of less than 10%. The errors have a rather uniform distribution over the 0–2%, 3–5%, and 6–10% intervals, suggesting that the model routinely generates pretty correct predictions, but with occasional notable deviations.

The ARIMA (0,1,0) model has a high success rate, with 87.5% of predictions falling within an error range of less than 10% (Fig. 9). The error distribution closely resembles that of the ARIMA (0,0,1) model, with the majority of errors centered within the range of 6–10%. The performance of this model demonstrates its efficacy in delivering precise forecasts for cybersecurity vulnerabilities.

Furthermore, the ARIMA (0,1,2) model exhibits a comparable success rate of 81.25% to that observed in several other models. The mistakes are uniformly distributed among the 0–2%, 3–5%, and 6–10% intervals, suggesting continuous performance with rare notable faults. This model exhibits consistent precision, although, similar to the other models, it reveals certain aspects that should be improved to better its prediction powers.

5   Conclusion and Future Direction

5.1   Conclusion

This study critically evaluated the forecasting capabilities of various ARIMA models using historical CVE data to predict cybersecurity vulnerabilities. The findings highlight that ARIMA (0,0,1) and ARIMA (0,1,0) models achieved the highest overall accuracy, with 87.5% of their predictions falling within a 10% error margin, showcasing strong potential for reliable forecasting in cybersecurity analytics. Interestingly, although ARIMA (1,1,1) had the lowest overall success rate (68.75%), it was the most successful in the narrowest error band (02%), indicating occasional high-precision predictions despite broader inconsistency. Models like ARIMA (0,1,1), (2,1,1), (0,2,1), and (0,1,2) consistently maintained a solid performance with 81.25% of predictions under 10% error, reflecting dependable results across a range of vulnerability types. While challenges remain, particularly for vulnerabilities like XSS and Memory Corruption that exhibited larger prediction gaps, the overall results affirm the viability of ARIMA models for forecasting security threats. These insights establish a foundation for future research to incorporate hybrid models or contextual features to enhance predictive robustness in the dynamic landscape of cybersecurity.

5.2 Future Work

Future work should focus on addressing the limitations identified in this study and enhancing the predictive capabilities of ARIMA models for cybersecurity applications. Key recommendations include incorporating external variables such as economic indicators, technological advancements, and regulatory changes that may impact cybersecurity trends. Advanced modeling approaches, like machine learning algorithms and hybrid models combining ARIMA with other predictive methodologies, should be explored. Developing models that dynamically adapt to changes in threat dynamics through real-time data integration and continuous learning is crucial. Utilizing extensive and current datasets that cover the full spectrum of cybersecurity risks, including newly identified vulnerabilities and attack methods, will improve model performance. Tailoring prediction models to specific contexts and vulnerability types is essential, as a one-size-fits-all approach may not be effective for all cybersecurity risks. Implementing these recommendations can enhance the predictive accuracy and adaptability of ARIMA models, leading to more effective techniques to anticipate and mitigate cybersecurity threats.

References

1. Addae, J.H., Sun, X., Towey, D., Radenkovic, M.: Exploring user behavioral data for adaptive cybersecurity. User Model. User Adapt. Inter. **29**, 701–750 (2019)
2. Alabdulrazzaq, H., Alenezi, M.N., Rawajfih, Y., Alghannam, B.A., Al-Hassan, A.A., Al-Anzi, F.S.: On the accuracy of ARIMA based prediction of COVID-19 spread. Results Phys. **27**, 104509 (2021)
3. Alam, N.M.F., Ramli, N., Mohamed, A.S.T., Adnan, N.I.M.: Integration of 4253HT smoother with intuitionistic fuzzy time series forecasting model. Pakistan J. Stat. Oper. Res., 929–941 (2022)
4. Aldairy, T., Laverick, S., McIntyre, G.: Orthognathic surgery: is patient information on the internet valid? Eur. J. Orthod. **34**(4), 466–469 (2012)
5. Algarni, A.M., Thayananthan, V., Malaiya, Y.K.: Quantitative assessment of cybersecurity risks for mitigating data breaches in business systems. Appl. Sci. **11**(8), 3678 (2021)

6. Ali, H., Patel, P., Dahiya, D.S., Gangwani, M.K., Basuli, D., Mohan, B.P.: Prediction of early-onset colorectal cancer mortality rates in the united states using machine learning. Cancer Med. **13**(1), e6880 (2024)

7. Anthony, A., Onasoga, K., Ike, D.U., Ajayi, O.: Web archiving: techniques, challenges, and solutions. Int. J. Manage. Inf. Technol. **5**(3), 598–603 (2013)

8. Arafat, N.H.M., Pramanik, M.I., Jahan, S., Uddin, M.N., Islam, M.S., Akter, K.F.: BloSecR: a conceptual framework of identity documents' security on blockchain in refugee issues and conserving fundamental rights. In: 2022 2nd International Conference on Intelligent Technologies (CONIT), pp. 1–6. IEEE (2022)

9. Arafat, N.H.M., Pramanik, M.I., Muzahid, A.J.M., Lu, B., Jahan, S., Murad, S.A.: A conceptual anonymity model to ensure privacy for sensitive network data. In: 2021 Emerging Technology in Computing, Communication and Electronics (ETCCE), pp. 1–7. IEEE (2021)

10. Awang, N., Ganthan, A., Samy, L.N., Hassan, N.H., Maarop, N., Perumal, S.: Implementation of SARIMA algorithm in understanding cybersecurity threats in university network. J. Positive School Psychol. **6**(3), 8442–8451 (2022)

11. Benvenuto, D., Giovanetti, M., Vassallo, L., Angeletti, S., Ciccozzi, M.: Application of the ARIMA model on the COVID-2019 epidemic dataset. Data Brief **29**, 105340 (2020)

12. Bhandari, G., Naseer, A., Moonen, L.: CVEfixes: automated collection of vulnerabilities and their fixes from open-source software. In: Proceedings of the 17th International Conference on Predictive Models and Data Analytics in Software Engineering, pp. 30–39 (2021)

13. Blinowski, G.J., Piotrowski, P.: CVE based classification of vulnerable IoT systems. In: Zamojski, W., Mazurkiewicz, J., Sugier, J., Walkowiak, T., Kacprzyk, J. (eds.) DepCoS-RELCOMEX 2020. AISC, vol. 1173, pp. 82–93. Springer, Cham (2020). https://doi.org/10.1007/978-3-030-48256-5_9

14. Bojrab, D.I., Fritz, C., Babu, S., Lin, K.F.: A critical analysis of the information available online for ménière's disease. Otolaryngol. Head Neck Surg. **162**(3), 329–336 (2020)

15. Box, G.E., Jenkins, G.M., Reinsel, G.C., Ljung, G.M.: Time Series Analysis: Forecasting and Control. Wiley (2015)

16. Carriegos, M.V., Castañeda, Á.L.M., Trobajo, M.T., De Zaballa, D.A.: On aggregation and prediction of cybersecurity incident reports. IEEE Access **9**, 102636–102648 (2021)

17. Ceylan, Z.: Estimation of covid-19 prevalence in Italy, Spain, and France. Sci. Total Environ. **729**, 138817 (2020)

18. Claris, S., Delson, C.: Predicting south Africa's daily COVID-19 cases using ARIMA forecasting model: 6 March to 6 July 2020 (2021)

19. Craigen, D., Diakun-Thibault, N., Purse, R.: Defining cybersecurity. Technol. Innov. Manage. Rev. **4**(10) (2014)

20. CVE Details: CVSS score distribution chart (2024). https://www.cvedetails.com/cvss-score-charts.php. Accessed 08 May 2024

21. CVE Details: Vulnerabilities by types (2024). https://www.cvedetails.com/vulnerabilities-by-types.php. Accessed 08 May 2024

22. Falowo, O.I., Abdo, J.B.: 2019–2023 in review: projecting DDoS threats with ARIMA and ETS forecasting techniques. IEEE Access **12**, 26759–26772 (2024)

23. Fang, X., Xu, M., Xu, S., Zhao, P.: A deep learning framework for predicting cyber attacks rates. EURASIP J. Inf. Secur. **2019**, 1–11 (2019)

24. Gencer, K., Başçiftçi, F.: Time series forecast modeling of vulnerabilities in the android operating system using ARIMA and deep learning methods. Sustain. Comput. Inform. Syst. **30**, 100515 (2021)
25. Gundu, T.: Learn, unlearn and relearn: adaptive cybersecurity culture model. In: International Conference on Cyber Warfare and Security, vol. 19, pp. 95–102 (2024)
26. Guo, H., Chen, S., Xing, Z., Li, X., Bai, Y., Sun, J.: Detecting and augmenting missing key aspects in vulnerability descriptions. ACM Trans. Softw. Eng. Methodol. (TOSEM) **31**(3), 1–27 (2022)
27. Huang, Y., Xu, C., Ji, M., Xiang, W., He, D.: Medical service demand forecasting using a hybrid model based on ARIMA and self-adaptive filtering method. BMC Med. Inform. Decis. Mak. **20**, 1–14 (2020)
28. Islam, M.S., Hasan, M.M., Abdullah, S., Akbar, J.U.M., Arafat, N.H.M., Murad, S.A.: A deep spatio-temporal network for vision-based sexual harassment detection. In: 2021 Emerging Technology in Computing, Communication and Electronics (ETCCE), pp. 1–6. IEEE (2021)
29. Jiang, W., Ling, L., Zhang, D., Lin, R., Zeng, L.: A time series forecasting model selection framework using CNN and data augmentation for small sample data. Neural Process. Lett. **55**(5), 5783–5810 (2023)
30. Jiang, Y., Jeusfeld, M., Ding, J.: Evaluating the data inconsistency of open-source vulnerability repositories. In: Proceedings of the 16th International Conference on Availability, Reliability and Security, pp. 1–10 (2021)
31. Kaur, R., Gabrijelčič, D., Klobučar, T.: Artificial intelligence for cybersecurity: literature review and future research directions. Inf. Fus., 101804 (2023)
32. Kia, A.N., Murphy, F., Sheehan, B., Shannon, D.: A cyber risk prediction model using common vulnerabilities and exposures. Exp. Syst. Appl. **237**, 121599 (2024)
33. Kohlrausch, J., Brin, E.A.: Arima supplemented security metrics for quality assurance and situational awareness. Digit. Threat. Res. Pract. **1**(1), 1–21 (2020)
34. Li, Y., Zhou, L., et al.: Time series analysis and prediction of scarlet fever incidence trends in Jiangsu province, China: using ARIMA and TBATS models (2022)
35. Li, Z.Q., Pan, H.Q., Liu, Q., Song, H., Wang, J.M.: Comparing the performance of time series models with or without meteorological factors in predicting incident Pulmonary Tuberculosis in Eastern China. Infect. Dis. Poverty **9**, 1–11 (2020)
36. Machiry, A., Redini, N., Camellini, E., Kruegel, C., Vigna, G.: Spider: enabling fast patch propagation in related software repositories. In: 2020 IEEE Symposium on Security and Privacy (SP), pp. 1562–1579. IEEE (2020)
37. Meade, M., Dreyer, C.: An assessment of the treatment information contained within the websites of direct-to-consumer orthodontic aligner providers. Aust. Dent. J. **66**(1), 77–84 (2021)
38. MohanaKrishnan, M., et al.: Artificial intelligence in cyber security. In: Handbook of Research on Deep Learning Techniques for Cloud-Based Industrial IoT, pp. 366–385. IGI Global (2023)
39. Nadeem, M.A., Hashmi, S., Khan, M.A.: Exploring the interplay of cybersecurity and cybercrime in Pakistan's digital landscape. Contemp. Issues Soc. Sci. Manage. Pract. **2**(4), 207–222 (2023)
40. Oh, S.H., Jeong, M.K., Kim, H.C., Park, J.: Applying reinforcement learning for enhanced cybersecurity against adversarial simulation. Sensors **23**(6), 3000 (2023)
41. Palacio, D.N., McCrystal, D., Moran, K., Bernal-Cárdenas, C., Poshyvanyk, D., Shenefiel, C.: Learning to identify security-related issues using convolutional neural networks. In: 2019 IEEE International Conference on Software Maintenance and Evolution (ICSME), pp. 140–144. IEEE (2019)

42. Panda, S., Rass, S., Moschoyiannis, S., Liang, K., Loukas, G., Panaousis, E.: Honey-Car: a framework to configure honeypot vulnerabilities on the internet of vehicles. IEEE Access **10**, 104671–104685 (2022)

43. Pekaric, I., Felderer, M., Steinmüller, P.: VULNERLIZER: cross-analysis between vulnerabilities and software libraries. arXiv preprint arXiv:2309.09649 (2023)

44. Pokhrel, N.R., Rodrigo, H., Tsokos, C.P.: Cybersecurity: time series predictive modeling of vulnerabilities of desktop operating system using linear and non-linear approach. J. Inf. Secur. (2017)

45. Raheman, F.: The future of cybersecurity in the age of quantum computers. Fut. Internet **14**(11), 335 (2022)

46. Rockembach, M., Serrano, A.: Climate change and web archives: an Ibero-American study based on the Portuguese and Brazilian contexts. Rec. Manag. J. **31**(3), 222–239 (2021)

47. Ruohonen, J.: A look at the time delays in CVSS vulnerability scoring. Appl. Comput. Inform. **15**(2), 129–135 (2019)

48. Semerci, M., Cemgil, A.T., Sankur, B.: An intelligent cyber security system against DDoS attacks in sip networks. Comput. Netw. **136**, 137–154 (2018)

49. Tang, M., Alazab, M., Luo, Y., Donlon, M.: Disclosure of cyber security vulnerabilities: time series modelling. Int. J. Electron. Secur. Digit. Forensics **10**(3), 255–275 (2018)

50. Thomas, G., Sule, M.J.: A service lens on cybersecurity continuity and management for organizations' subsistence and growth. Organ. Cybersecur. J. Pract. Process People **3**(1), 18–40 (2023)

51. Trieu-Do, V., Garcia-Lebron, R., Xu, M., Xu, S., Feng, Y.: Characterizing and leveraging granger causality in cybersecurity: framework and case study. ICST Trans. Secur. Saf. **7**(25) (2021)

52. Ugoh, C.I., Echebiri, U.V., Temisan, G.O., Iwuchukwu, J.K., Guobadia, E.K., et al.: On forecasting Nigeria's GDP: a comparative performance of regression with ARIMA errors and ARIMA method. Int. J. Math. Stat. Stud. **10**(4), 48–64 (2022)

53. Vishnu, P., Vinod, P., Yerima, S.Y.: A deep learning approach for classifying vulnerability descriptions using self attention based neural network. J. Netw. Syst. Manage. **30**(1), 9 (2022)

54. Wang, M., et al.: ARIMA and ARIMA-ERNN models for prediction of pertussis incidence in mainland China from 2004 to 2021. BMC Pub. Health **22**(1), 1447 (2022)

55. Werner, G., Okutan, A., Yang, S., McConky, K.: Forecasting cyberattacks as time series with different aggregation granularity. In: 2018 IEEE International Symposium on Technologies for Homeland Security (HST), pp. 1–7. IEEE (2018)

56. Werner, G., Yang, S., McConky, K.: Time series forecasting of cyber attack intensity. In: Proceedings of the 12th Annual Conference on Cyber and Information Security Research, pp. 1–3 (2017)

57. Yan, F., Wen, S., Nepal, S., Paris, C., Xiang, Y.: Explainable machine learning in cybersecurity: a survey. Int. J. Intell. Syst. **37**(12), 12305–12334 (2022)

58. Yan, L., Xu, X., Meng, Y.: Daily air quality index forecasting based on a mixture of ensemble empirical mode decomposition and ARIMA model. In: Second International Conference on Electronic Information Engineering, Big Data, and Computer Technology, EIBDCT 2023, vol. 12642, pp. 124–129. SPIE (2023)

59. Yosifova, V., Tasheva, A., Trifonov, R.: Predicting vulnerability type in common vulnerabilities and exposures (CVE) database with machine learning classifiers.

In: 2021 12th National Conference with International Participation (ELECTRON-ICA), pp. 1–6. IEEE (2021)

60. Yousif, H., Al-saedi, K.H., Al-Hassani, M.D.: Mobile phishing websites detection and prevention using data mining techniques. iJIM **13**(10), 205 (2019)

61. Yu, L., Wu, C., Xiong, N.N.: An intelligent data analysis system combining ARIMA and LSTM for persistent organic pollutants concentration prediction. Electronics **11**(4), 652 (2022)

62. Zhai, M., et al.: Research on the predictive effect of a combined model of ARIMA and neural networks on human brucellosis in Shanxi province, China: a time series predictive analysis. BMC Infect. Dis. **21**, 1–12 (2021)

63. Zheng, Y., Zhang, L., Zhu, X., Guo, G.: A comparative study of two methods to predict the incidence of hepatitis b in Guangxi, China. PLoS ONE **15**(6), e0234660 (2020)

64. Zhu, Z.: Trend prediction of rubella incidence based on ARIMA model and holt-winters multiplicative model. In: Third International Conference on Biological Engineering and Medical Science, ICBioMed 2023, vol. 12924, pp. 709–716. SPIE (2024)

Watchguard: Real Time Women Safety Detection System

Seema Srinivas[1], B. C. Divakara[2], C. R. Nagarathna[3](✉), G. Nandini[4], M. Ramya[5], R. B. Suchithra[5], and T. Suchithra[5]

[1] Electronics and Communication, Global Academy of Technology, Bangalore, Karntaka, India
[2] Electronics and Communication Engineering, Global Academy of Technology, Bangalore, Karnataka, India
[3] Deptartment of Artificial Intelligence and Machine Learning, BNM Institute of Technology, Bengaluru, India
Nagarathna.binu@gmail.com
[4] Deptartment of Information Science and Engineering, BNM Institute of Technology, Bengaluru, India
[5] Artificial Intelligence and Machine Learning, BNM Institute of Technology, Bengaluru, India

Abstract. The increasing concern for the safety of women in public places, therefore, demands intelligent safety solutions that must be calculated rather than reactive. This work is intended to build an intelligent based system that will provide real- time detection and prevention of threats. The proposed solution at present incorporates AI&ML, Convolutional Neural Network (CNN) and Computer Vision (CV) technologies for analysis of video feeds, identification of abnormal behaviours, and recognition of distress patterns. A notification system ensures immediate alerts to law enforcement and nearby individuals, while Safe Space Identification provides users with guidance to nearby safe locations based on their current position. The system is equipped with functions in multiple languages to improve accessibility to a wide spectrum of potential users and hotspot identification functions utilising historical data analysis to identify areas at high risk.

Keywords: Handwritten text recognition · digitization · deep learning · CNN · RNN · spell- check · preprocessing · document automation

1 Introduction

Women's safety in public spaces remains significant concern, with traditional surveillance systems being reactive and unable to prevent incidents in real time. Current approaches fail to detect potential threats like harassment or distress gestures, leaving women vulnerable and limiting timely interventions by law enforcement.

This project is focused on using Artificial Intelligence (AI) and video analytics to help improve women's safety in public spaces. As we know, safety is a huge concern, especially for women, who often face threats like harassment and violence when walking

S. Goel et al. (Eds.): AICON 2025, LNICST 672, pp. 108–115, 2026.
https://doi.org/10.1007/978-3-032-14805-6_7

alone at night or in isolated areas. Even though many public spaces have CCTV cameras installed, these systems are usually reactive, meaning they only provide footage after an incident has already happened. So, the problem with these traditional systems is that they don't stop incidents from occurring, they just help with investigation afterward. Our project aims to take a more proactive approach to public safety.

Once the system detects a threat, it will immediately send alerts to law enforcement or security personnel, enabling them to intervene before an incident occurs. This system can act as a powerful tool to prevent crimes and protect women in real time, creating a safer environment. The goal of the project is to combine AI- driven video monitoring with real-time alerting to ensure that women can feel safer when navigating public spaces. The system's ability to detect threats early and notify authorities instantly can make a big difference in ensuring public safety. Beyond just recording what happens, it's designed to actively prevent dangerous situations from escalating. In summary, this project represents a step forward in creating smart, proactive surveillance systems that use the latest technologies to keep women safe. By focusing on real-time threat detection, we aim to transform how public safety is managed, making public spaces more secure for everyone, especially women.

2 Objectives

To achieve the goal of enhancing women's safety in public spaces, this project focuses on addressing key objectives that ensure real-time detection, effective intervention, and improved public safety measures. Real-Time Threat Detection: Develop a system that continuously monitors public spaces using video analytics to identify potential threats in real time.

- Gender Classification: Implement AI-based techniques to detect and classify individuals by gender, helping assess the gender distribution in various areas.
- Anomaly Detection: Identify unusual or suspicious behaviors, such as a lone woman in a risky area, a woman surrounded by a group of men, or other potentially dangerous situations.
- Gesture Recognition: Use machine learning models to detect distress gestures (e.g., waving or other SOS signals) that could indicate someone is in danger.
- Real-Time Alerts: Enable the system to generate immediate alerts and notifications for law enforcement or security personnel, allowing them to intervene quickly and prevent incidents.
- Hotspot Identification: Analyze historical data to identify high-risk areas or "hotspots" where incidents are more likely to occur, aiding in strategic planning for public safety.

3 Motivation

The motivation behind this project comes from the growing concerns about women's safety in public spaces. Despite various measures, incidents of harassment and violence against women continue to be a significant problem, particularly in isolated or poorly lit areas. Traditional surveillance systems often fall short because they are reactive—only useful for reviewing footage after an incident has occurred. There is a need for a more proactive approach that can detect threats in real time and help prevent incidents from happening in the first place. Additionally, advancements in AI and machine learning provide new opportunities to develop intelligent safety systems that go beyond simple monitoring. By using these technologies, we can create a solution that not only watches but also understands what is happening, making public spaces safer for everyone, especially women. The project aims to use modern technology for a social cause, contributing to community well-being and supporting gender equality by ensuring that women feel secure in their surroundings.

4   Literature Survey

Women safety detection systems have gained significant traction as technology-driven solutions to enhance safety in public and private spaces. These systems utilize advanced AI and IoT technologies to detect and mitigate potential threats in real-time. The literature survey below highlights the recent advancements, methodologies, and challenges in the field of women safety detection systems. Women safety detection systems incorporate diverse methodologies, such as IoT devices, machine learning algorithms, and real-time monitoring, to ensure user safety. These systems aim to identify unusual or potentially threatening behaviors and provide timely alerts to the user or concerned authorities. For instance, "Watch Guard: A Comprehensive Real-Time Women Safety System" [1–4] introduces an IoT- enabled wearable device that monitors biometric and environmental parameters to detect distress situations. This study emphasizes the integration of machine learning for anomaly detection and raises concerns about privacy issues and data reliability. Similarly, "An AI-Driven Women Safety Detection and Alert System" [5–9] presents a real-time application utilizing image processing and deep learning techniques for detecting suspicious activities in surveillance footage. While promising, the study highlights challenges in managing false alarms and adapting to different environments. Studies like "IoT and AI-Powered Women Safety Devices" [10–14] propose wearable devices that combine GPS tracking and accelerometer-based fall detection for emergency alerts. However, the authors note limitations in battery life and connectivity in remote areas.

Work, such as "A Comprehensive Review of Women Safety Solutions Using AI and IoT" [9, 14–16], surveys existing systems and highlights gaps in scalability and accuracy. This review underscores the need for robust algorithms that can operate seamlessly across diverse scenarios without compromising user privacy.

A. Gaps in Literature Survey and Focus of the Study

Despite significant advancements, several challenges remain in developing robust women safety systems. Scalability is a major issue, as most systems perform well in controlled environments but face difficulties in real- world, large-scale applications. Additionally, adaptability to diverse environments and individual behaviors remains limited. For instance, IoT devices may fail to detect distress signals in crowded or noisy settings.

Another challenge is the high computational cost associated with machine learning models, particularly for real-time video and audio analysis. While models like YOLO and R-CNN are effective, they require substantial computational resources, limiting their deployment on resource-constrained devices.

The focus of this study is to develop a scalable, robust, and adaptable women safety system. By integrating IoT-based wearable devices, advanced machine learning models, real-time video surveillance, and NLP techniques, the proposed system aims to enhance distress detection accuracy in diverse and challenging environments. Additionally, the study will explore cost-effective solutions to make the system accessible for widespread adoption.

5 Proposed Methodology

The methodology for this project involves a systematic approach to designing an AI-based public safety system by following several key steps and it id depicts in Fig. 1. The process begins with data collection and integration, where real-time video feeds from public surveillance cameras, IoT devices, and other sensors are gathered. Historical crime data and crowd behavior datasets are also collected to train the AI models effectively. Next, preprocessing techniques are applied to remove noise and enhance the resolution of video feeds, ensuring high-quality data for analysis. Threat detection and analysis are carried out using deep learning models such as CNNs and RNNs to identify anomalies like distress gestures, aggressive movements, or abnormal crowd formations. Gesture recognition and safe space identification are also implemented to detect distress signals and guide individuals toward safer areas.The system further employs AI-powered analytics to identify high-risk zones by overlaying historical and real-time data, producing heatmaps that visually highlight areas of danger for strategic resource deployment. Multi-channel alert mechanisms are developed to notify law enforcement and bystanders via SMS, email, or public alarms like flashing lights and sirens. These alerts are integrated with smart city platforms to enable coordinated responses. Post-detection measures include logging detected threats and system responses for evaluation, as well as providing real-time feedback to enhance detection accuracy and improve the AI models. Finally, the system is deployed in various public spaces with compatibility for existing infrastructure. It is designed to scale efficiently to larger areas through the use of cloud computing and lightweight AI models.

To ensure scalability, the system is optimized for deployment on cloud platforms and designed with lightweight AI models for efficient operation. Finally, comprehensive testing and validation are conducted to ensure compatibility with existing infrastructure, signals, while a Safe Space Identification module is created to provide users wit safe route recommendations. A Hotspot Identification system is developed using AI analytics to overlay historical and real-time data, generating heat maps that highlight high-risk areas and aid in resource allocation. Alert mechanisms are built to support multi-channel notifications, including SMS, email, and public alarms, ensuring rapid communication during emergencies. These alert systems are integrated with smart city platforms to enable a coordinated response. A logging and evaluation system is also developed to record detected threats, system actions, and user feedback for continuous improvement of the models and overall system performance.

A. Data Collection and Preprocessing

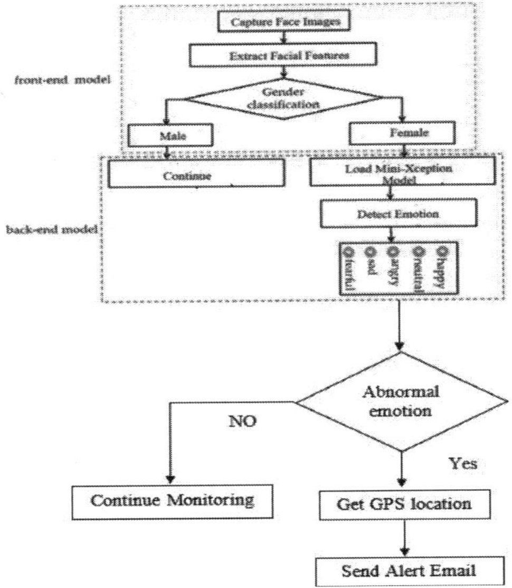

Fig. 1. System Architecture

Data collection consists of various handwritten datasets, that have samples of written text in multiple styles and conditions. Preprocessing techniques are critical to data preparation for the model. The major preprocessing steps include:

Noise Reduction: This is achieved through the use of filters or denoising techniques that remove background noises from scanned or photographed documents [17].

Image Alignment and Deskewing: Handwritten text must be properly aligned and not skewed so that its text can be read or recognized with accuracy [18].

Segmentation: Segmentation of the input image into smaller units such as lines, words, and individual characters, making recognition easier and more accurate.

Binarization: Converting the image to black-and- white for better contrast and easier processing by neural networks.

6   Benefits and Features

The AI-based public safety system offers numerous benefits and features that significantly enhance safety in public spaces. One of its primary benefits is real-time threat detection, which allows the system to identify anomalies such as distress gestures, aggressive behavior, or abnormal crowd dynamics, ensuring immediate responses to potential dangers. The system's multi-channel alert mechanism sends notifications to law enforcement, bystanders, and emergency services via SMS, email, and public alarms, enabling swift action and effective coordination.

A key feature is its Safe Space Identification, which guides individuals to nearby secure locations, such as police stations or well-lit areas, providing an added layer of safety. The system also includes hotspot identification, using AI analytics to create heatmaps of high-risk zones based on historical and real-time data, helping authorities allocate resources more strategically.

With multi-language support, the system is accessible to diverse user groups, ensuring inclusivity in multicultural environments. Additionally, its scalable architecture, powered by cloud computing and lightweight AI models, enables it to monitor vast areas efficiently. The integration of privacy-preserving techniques ensures compliance with ethical standards, protecting individual identities while maintaining high detection accuracy. These features collectively provide a comprehensive and adaptable solution for enhancing public safety in dynamic urban environments.

A. Features

The AI-based public safety system is equipped with a range of advanced features designed to enhance security and provide real-time protection. At its core is anomaly.

detection, powered by deep learning models like CNNs and RNNs, which identifies unusual behaviors such as distress gestures, aggressive movements, or abnormal crowd dynamics. The system also includes Safe Space Identification, guiding users to nearby secure locations, such as police stations or well-lit public areas, ensuring immediate safety during emergencies.

A standout feature is its multi-channel alert system, which sends instant notifications to law enforcement, emergency contacts, and bystanders via SMS, email, and public alarms such as sirens or flashing lights. The system also leverages hotspot identification using AI analytics, which overlays historical and real-time data to generate heatmaps of high-risk zones, aiding authorities in targeted resource deployment.

Furthermore, the system offers multi-language support, making it accessible to diverse user groups in multicultural environments. It is built on a scalable architecture, allowing for seamless integration into cloud platforms and efficient monitoring across large areas. Privacy-preserving mechanisms, such as data anonymization, ensure ethical use of surveillance data while maintaining high accuracy in threat detection. These comprehensive features make the system robust, inclusive, and well-suited for ensuring public safety in dynamic urban spaces.

7 Challenges

The implementation of an AI-based public safety system comes with several challenges that must be addressed to ensure its effectiveness and reliability. One of the primary challenges is handling false positives, where normal behaviors may be incorrectly flagged as threats, leading to unnecessary alerts and reduced user trust. Another significant issue is scalability, as the system must process vast amounts of real-time data from multiple locations without compromising accuracy or speed.

Connectivity limitations in remote or poorly connected areas can hinder the system's ability to function seamlessly, especially for IoT-based components and real-time alerting mechanisms. Additionally, the high computational requirements of deep learning models, such as CNNs and RNNs, pose challenges in resource- constrained environments, requiring optimization to balance performance and efficiency.

Ensuring privacy and ethical compliance is also a critical challenge, as the system processes sensitive data, such as video feeds and personal information, which must be anonymized and secured against misuse. Finally, adapting the system to diverse environments and cultural variations can be complex, as behavioral patterns and social norms differ widely across regions. Addressing these challenges is essential to develop a robust, scalable, and universally applicable safety solution.

8 Conclusion

In conclusion, the AI-based public safety system represents a significant advancement in ensuring the safety and security of individuals in public spaces. By integrating cutting-edge technologies such as IoT, deep learning, and Computer Vision, the system provides real-time detection of threats, proactive alerts, and actionable insights to law enforcement and emergency responders. Features like Safe Space Identification, multi-channel alerts, and hotspot detection enhance its ability to respond effectively to diverse scenarios while ensuring inclusivity and scalability.

Despite challenges such as handling false positives, scalability, and privacy concerns, the system demonstrates immense potential for improving public safety when these issues are addressed through optimization and ethical considerations. Its adaptability across different environments and robust architecture positions it as a reliable solution for modern urban safety challenges. This system not only empowers individuals by providing real-time protection but also contributes to creating safer, more inclusive communities.

References

1. Gupta, P., Garg, A.: Mobile app for women safety with emergency alerts. In: Proceedings of the International Conference on Smart Cities, pp. 103–108 (2020)
2. Bansal, M., et al.: Real-time women safety detection using machine learning and IoT. J. Comput. Vis. Pattern Recogn. **25**(4), 457–463 (2019)
3. Kumar, R., et al.: AI-powered women safety device with real-time monitoring. IEEE Trans. Internet of Things **17**(1), 89–98 (2020)
4. Yadav, S., et al.: Implementation of a women safety surveillance system using CNN. J. Artifi. Intell. Res. **39**(6), 1147–1157 (2021)
5. Nair, S., Thomas, R.: Women safety framework using artificial intelligence and IoT. In: Proceedings of the International Conference on Advanced Technologies, pp. 204–212 (2021)
6. Agarwal, P., et al.: Enhancing women safety in public transport using computer vision. Inter. J. Mach. Learn. Data Mining **10**(3), 249–255 (2023)
7. Ali, T., et al.: Women safety application: a comprehensive study of IoT integration. Sens. Actuators, A **302**(4), 123–130 (2023)
8. Mahanthesha, U., Tejaswini, R.M., Nagarathna, C.R., Ravikumar, Y.T.: Face recognition using MTCNN, inception - Resnet with ensemble approach. In: 2025 International Conference on Intelligent and Innovative Technologies in Computing, Electrical and Electronics (IITCEE), Bangalore, India, pp. 1–6 (2025). https://doi.org/10.1109/IITCEE64140.2025.109 15271

9. Nagarathna, C.R., Chinnaswamy, C.N.: The technique to detect and avoid the denial of service attacks in wireless sensor networks. Inter. J. Res. Eng. Technol. (IJRET) **3**(05) (2014)

10. Chandana, S., Nagarathna, C.R., Amrutha, A., Jayasri, A.: Detection of image forgery using error level analysis. In 2024 International Conference on Intelligent and Innovative Technologies in Computing, Electrical and Electronics (IITCEE), pp. 1–5. IEEE (January 2024)

11. Jain, D., Kulkarni, R.: Deep learning solutions for real-time women safety monitoring. IEEE Access **20**(5), 3240–3248 (2022)

12. Nagarathna, C.R., Kusuma, M.M.: Early detection of Alzheimer's Disease using MRI images and deep learning techniques. Alzheimers Dement. **19**, e062076 (2023)

13. Reddy, V., et al.: AI-based public safety system for women: a review. J. Smart Cities Artifi. Intell. **12**(1), 15–23 (2024)

14. Bhavyashree, H.L., Nagarathna, C.R., Preetham, A.,Priyanka, R.: Modified cluster based certificate blocking of misbehaving node in MANETS. In 2019 1st international conference on advanced technologies in intelligent control, environment, computing & communication engineering (ICATIECE), pp. 155- 161. IEEE (March 2019)

15. Nagarathna, C.R., Kusuma, M.: Comparative study of detection and classification of Alzheimer's disease using Hybrid model and CNN. In: 2021 International Conference on Disruptive Technologies for Multi-Disciplinary Research and Applications (CENTCON), vol. 1, pp. 43–46. IEEE (November 2021)

16. Debnath, S., Preetham, A., Vuppu, S., Kumar, S.N.P.: Optimal weighted GAN and U-Net based segmentation for phenotypic trait estimation of crops using Taylor Coot algorithm. Appl. Soft Comput. **144**, 110396 (2023)

17. Preetham, A., et al.: Instinctive recognition of pathogens in rice using reformed fractional differential segmentation and innovative fuzzy logic-based probabilistic neural network. J. Food Qual. **2022**(1), 8662254 (2022)

18. Rao, A., Kulkarni, S.B.: An improved technique of plant leaf classification using hybrid feature modeling. In 2017 International Conference on Innovative Mechanisms for Industry Applications (ICIMIA), pp. 5–9. IEEE (February 2017)

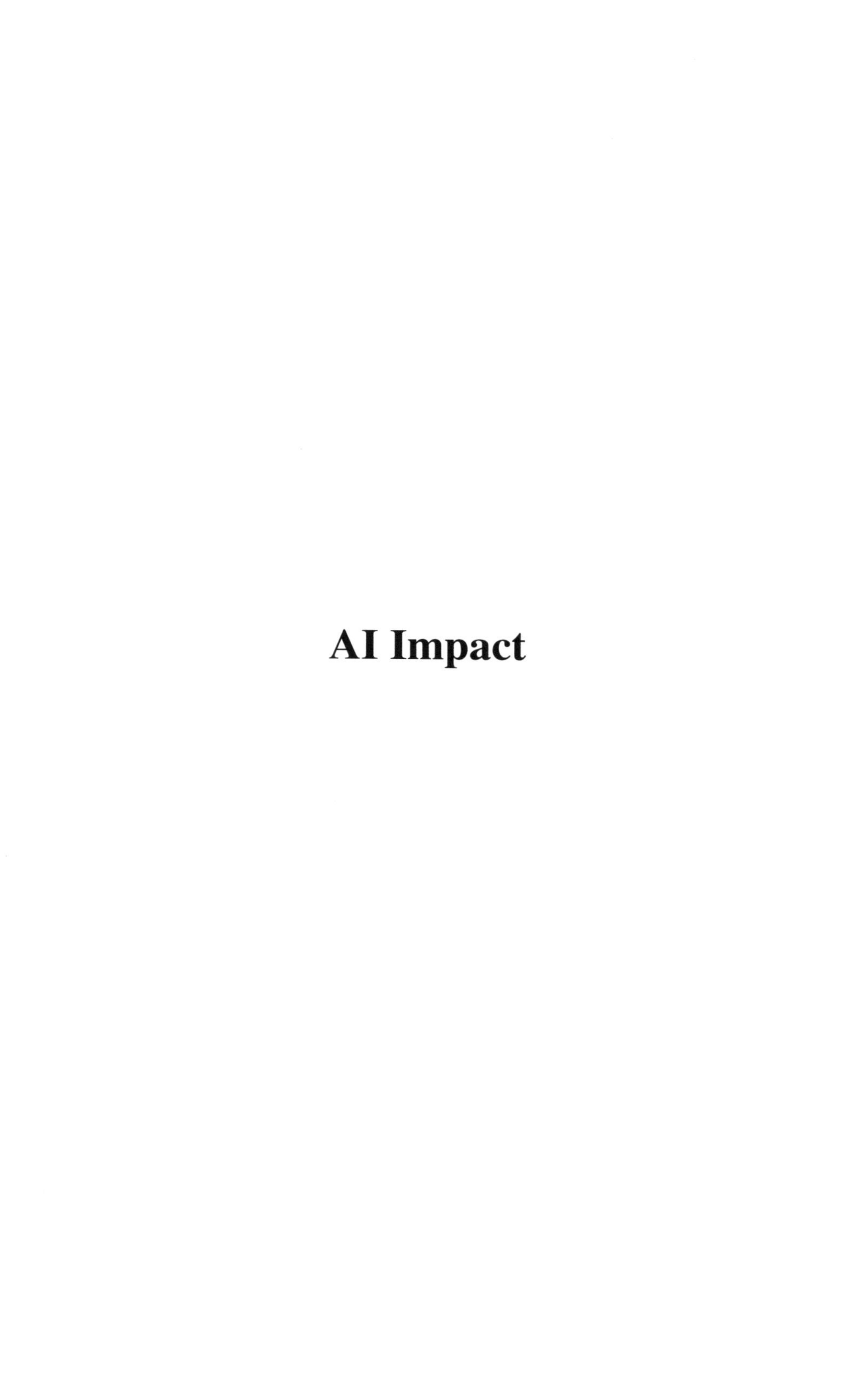

AI Impact

A Survey of AI-Enhanced Augmented Reality in Phobia Treatment: Innovations, Challenges, and Societal Impacts

M. Abinaya$^{(\boxtimes)}$ and G. Vadivu

Department of Data Science and Business Systems, School of Computing, SRM Institute of Science and Technology, Kattankulathur, Chennai 603203, India
{am0150,vadivug}@srmist.edu.in

Abstract. Phobia is a major mental health issue, faced by people and affects their everyday functioning and general well-being. In the traditional method, for treating Phobia Conventional therapeutic approaches, like cognitive-behavioural therapies and exposure therapy, are frequently used by the patients because of their acceptability, adherence, and accessibility. In this research, there is a possibility of using immersive technology for treatment like Augmented Reality (AR) technology for creating the immersive, interactive kind of therapy for exposure method and desensitization, and it gives the best alternative to traditional phobia treatment methods. This paper elaborates on the extensive use of AR in Phobia treatment so far and the further research in AR-based phobia therapy research, by giving a detailed review of the essential discoveries, useful implications, and future possibilities. In this study, we examine a thorough foundation for AR therapy, practical implementation, future considerations in clinical settings, and example case studies by giving the demonstration of effective interventions through AR Therapy. At the end of the paper, a limitation, as well as a future gap, is discussed with the help of incorporating immersive cutting-edge AR technology in the therapeutic of phobia treatment along with artificial intelligence and machine learning.

Keywords: Artificial Intelligence · Augmented Reality · Clinical Measures · Immersive Environment · Social Phobia · Phobia Treatment

1 Introduction

Phobias are characterized by the avoidance and the fear of specific things ,objects , activities and the situations in intense that leads to distress and prohibit from doing their day to day life [1] . There are many phobias one such common phobias are fear of spider(Arachnophobia), Fear of Heights (Acrophobia) and Fear of Social situations(Social Phobia) [2]. These Phobias affect the people quality of their daily life. Exposure Therapy , Cognitive-Behavioral Therapy(CBT), and

S. Goel et al. (Eds.): AICON 2025, LNICST 672, pp. 119–137, 2026.
https://doi.org/10.1007/978-3-032-14805-6_8

Medication are the two main traditional method for phobia. In Exposure Therapy, people are exposed to the situation of fear in a limited controlled environment to come out of fear [3]. CBT is given for the person to create and challenge the thoughts irrationally and the associated beleifs with the phobia.These traditional methods have a lot of limitations including accessibility, reluctance to exposure and to engage. Augmented Reality is the best solution for the Phobia to make the person to be immersive and interactive [4]. Even though there is an effective treatment method, there is a requirement for accessible and effective methods for the treatment of Phobia. In CBT there is a need for a person to interact face to face such kind of situations are difficult for persons in remote areas and persons with limited mobility. When it comes to creating the exact scenario of fear more realistically it costs high sometimes it may lead to inaccurate imagination stimuli or the scenario [5]. This makes the system need for effective treatment and the interest in creating innovative immersive technology, Augmented Reality(AR) for the treatment of Phobia.AR Provides a real-time scenario and allows the person to interact and engage in the scenario like the real world. By using this technique this helps the clinicians and the researchers help for the rectification of Phobia [6].

Augmented Reality is a new innovative technology that embeds digital information into the real world to make the persons to interact and engage in real-time and enhance their perception [7]. In AR we can able to visualize the real world as well as the digital world. AR Technology can be viewed with the help of hardware like Tablets, Head Mounted Displays, Smart Mobile Phones, AR Glasses, and Google Cardboards to view the AR content [8]. These devices have a camera, accelerometer, gyroscope, and real-time monitoring sensors for measuring the depth sensing the environment to detect the object and to place the 3D model in the real world accurately. Now a days AR is used in every industries due to the advancement in the software and the hardware facilities. AR provides the better and unique adavnatage than the traditional phobia treatment , it provides the controlled and the safe environment [9].

The objective of the paper is to identify the potential Augmented Reality technique, methods, and hardware used for the Phobia Treatment from the Previous Study and implement the new techniques based on the limitations of the previous study. Advantage of using Augmented reality is discussed in this section. With the help of the current research study and real-time evaluations, this paper deals with the efficacy of AR interventions in this field. The current research work contributes to the Phobia treatment with AR Technology and the future Phobias to address.

2   Literature Review

2.1   Review Based on Types of Phobias Treated with Augmented Reality

This section deal with different type of Specific Phobias existing in Augmented Reality

1. **Cockroach Phobia**
   A frequent phobia or anxiety disorder that many individuals experience is cockroach phobia, also known as katsaridaphobia. It is characterized by an extreme and illogical dread of cockroaches that can cause avoidance behaviors, panic attacks, and other mental and emotional symptoms [10]. Discussed the role of the brain in processing fearful stimuli. It may also provide some background on cockroach phobia in general, such as its prevalence and potential causes. The study most likely involved recruiting a group of people with varying degrees of cockroach phobia, as well as a control group of people who do not fear cockroaches. Participants would have been asked to complete a variety of tasks when having neuroimaging performed, such as PET (positron emission tomography) or the use of functional magnetic resonance imaging (fMRI), allowing the researchers to observe changes in brain activity in response to the presentation of cockroach-related stimuli. The researchers may have used statistical techniques to analyze the data in order to identify

2. **Spider Phobia.** Spider phobia, also known as arachnophobia, is an intense and persistent fear of spiders. It is an irrational fear that can cause significant distress and interfere with daily life. People who are afraid of spiders may avoid activities or situations where they might come into contact with them, such as going outside or cleaning the house. Spider phobia is relatively common, with some estimates claiming that up to 50% of women and 10% of men are afraid of spiders the Characteristics of Spider Phobia are detail discussed by [11].

Figure 1 depicts a list of phobias we have discussed thus far, with spider and cockroach phobias being the most researched areas using Augmented Reality. In this survey, 48% of the articles focused on spider phobia and 52% on cockroach phobia. Table 1 depicts different kinds of phobias , treatment methods used in Augmented Reality and the hardwares used in the previous research. A therapeutic lamp projection-based system is a device that uses light projection to provide therapeutic benefits to patients. The system typically includes a lamp that emits light onto a surface and a projector that projects images or patterns onto that surface. The projected images or patterns can be used to create a soothing or calming environment, reduce stress, improve mood, or provide other therapeutic benefits [12]. Used Therapeutic Lamp Projection Based Augmented Reality to treat Cockroach Phobia. ARET is a type of exposure therapy that employs augmented reality technology to help people overcome their fears and anxieties. ARET makes use of a head-mounted display to superimpose computer-generated images in the real world, resulting in an augmented environment. The therapist can tailor the virtual environment to the needs of the individual and gradually expose them to the situation or object that they are afraid of. ARET has several advantages over traditional exposure therapy, including the ability to create a safe and controlled environment that can be tailored to the individual's needs. Because of its remote location and lack of exposure to actual situations, ARET may be more convenient and cost-effective than traditional exposure therapy. Used Augmented Reality Exposure Therapy for Spider and

Cockroach Phobia Treatment [13]. Anxiety disorders, phobias, and other mental health conditions are treated with in vivo exposure therapy, a sort of behavioral therapy. Therapy entails controlled, gradual exposure to and confrontation with feared situations or objects under the supervision of a mental health professional. A person receives in vivo exposure therapy in a supportive and safe environment, in which they are gradually exposed to the things or situations they are afraid of. A person who is afraid of spiders, for example, might first look at images of spiders before watching videos of them and finally handling live spiders [14]. In-vivo exposure therapy was evaluated by against t Augmented Reality Exposure treatment. Used a therapeutic lamp to conduct his experiment, and 12 exercises were provided for subsequent sessions based on the Clinical trial. With 9 participants (8 female and 1 male) and a mean age of 30.6, used AR Exposure Therapy for therapeutic purposes during one capture and visualization system session; follow-up sessions were not specified. With 20 participants, an average age of 26.40, and 12 observation sessions, used both in-vivo exposure therapy and augmented reality exposure therapy, based on a variety of inclusion criteria. All 20 participants were allowed to participate in both the therapy and the three-stage interview process conducted by the three therapists and the therapeutic assistant. This technique discusses collaboration between the client and the therapist. choose 24 participants, conducted a clinical trial, and compared the visible marker system to the invisible marker system. They concluded that the invisible marker system is best for patients who are afraid of small animals. Conducted a spider phobia trial with 66 randomly selected participants. The trial lasted 30 min, during which time the participants' behavior and the discomfort scale were assessed. They came to the conclusion that AR is critical for reducing fear. Conducted an experiment with a 25-year-old participant to address their cockroach phobia [15,16]. They discovered that augmented reality exposure therapy and practical mobile interaction reduced participant anxiety. The results of treatment for cockroach phobia, which used a projection-based system and a follow-up session lasting 3 to 12 months, demonstrated that this therapy does not require a head-mounted display. Used a haptic mobile system of augmented therapy, immersive augmented reality exposure therapy, non-immersive augmented reality exposure therapy, and in-vivo experimentation to treat spider phobia in 230 people. They concluded that the HARET method makes it simple to complete the assigned tasks. They conclude that anxiety does not differ significantly for people who are not familiar with the realism of the animal, and the ARET will be improved in future research for spider phobia after discussing it with 108 participants aged 17 to 20 and measuring behavior. The topic of Clinical Sample is discussed. Used the Hololens and an augmented reality smartphone app to treat spider phobia in 65 participants with an average age of 19.05. The findings revealed that the virtual spider could have a real-world impact, and that smartphone usage is more adaptable than HoloLens [17–20]. According to their findings, VRET and ARET are more effective than iVET techniques, with ARET being more effective and cost-effective than the other two. Investigated Augmented Reality Exposure Therapy with 32 participants and a mean age group of 31.03 for Spider and Cockroach Phobia, as well as various participants for In-vivo Exposure Therapy and Virtual Reality Exposure Therapy.

Table 1. Phobias and their Corresponding Treatments in Augmented Reality done so for

Paper ID	Phobia Type	Treatment	Augmented Reality Hardware Used
[12]	Cockroach Phobia	Therapeutic Lamp Projection-based Augmented Reality	head-mounted displays Optoma EX610SP projector Kinecttype camera (ASUS XP)
[13]	Spiders Cockroach Phobia	AR exposure session	Creative NX-Ultra camera
[14]	Spiders Cockroach Phobia	Augmented Reality Exposure Therapy (ARET) In Vivo Exposure Therapy (IVET)	Head Mounted Display (HMD)
[15]	Cockroach Phobia	Invisible marker-tracking system	Head Mounted Display
[16]	Spider Phobia	Subjective Units of Distress Scale Behavioural Approach Test (BAT)	smartphone Unity3D Photoshop
[17]	Cockroach phobia	AR Exposure	Java 2 Mobile Edition
[18]	Cockroach Phobia	A Projection-Base System	projector and ASUS XPro camera
[19]	spider phobia	Haptic Augmented Reality In Vivo Exposure Therapy Direct and Indirect	Android 4.0+ operating system
[20]	Spider Phobia	Exposure Therapy	injamock tool Android operating system
[21]	Spider,Cockroach	Behavioral Analysis Test	Smart Phone
[22]	Spider	HoloLens 2 Augmented Reality Augmented Reality Treatment	Microsoft HoloLens
[4]	All Phobias Systematic Review	-	-
[23]	Cockroach Spider	Narrative Review	-
[24]	Spider and Cockroach	Augmented Reality Exposure Therapy	5DT Head-Mounted Display
[25]	Cockroach	Augmented Reality Exposure Therapy	-
[26]	Spider	Cognitive behavioral therapy	-

2.2 Review Based on Clinical Measures Used in Augmented Reality Therapy

Figure 2 shows the most frequently used clinical measures that have been mentioned so far in the survey papers.

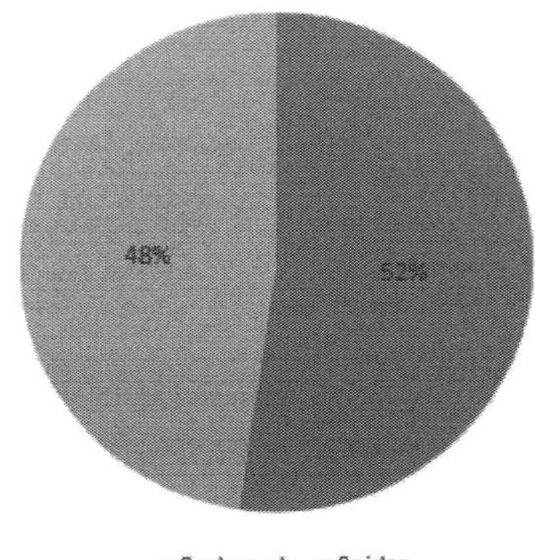

Fig. 1. Types of Phobias discussed so far through Augmented Reality

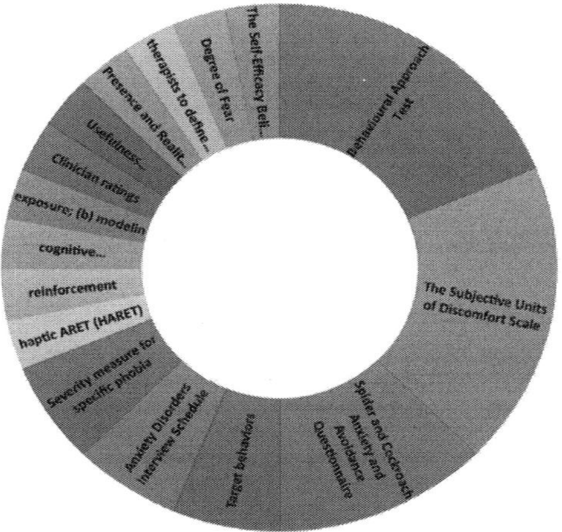

Fig. 2. Types of Clinical measures used thus for through AR Technology

1. **Subjective Units of Distress Scale.** When utilizing immersive technology, a user can use a Subjective Units of Distress Scale (SUDS; also referred to as a Subjective Units of Disturbance Scale) to measure their own subjective level of disturbance or distress when using immersive technology on a scale from 0 to 100. It is widely used by therapists to gauge a patient's level of anxiety.

2. **Behavioral Approach Test.** The BAT entails exposing an individual to the object or circumstance they are frightened of in small doses in a secure setting while imparting them to utilize coping mechanisms that decrease their anxiety [21]. A harmless replica of the feared circumstance or object could be introduced to the patient at first, with the severity of the exposure being gradually increased until the patient can manage the real-life situation without feeling overwhelmed. As part of the BAT, the therapist may employ a

variety of strategies to assist the patient in controlling their anxiety, including deep breathing, gradual muscular relaxation, or encouraging self-talk. The ultimate objective of the BAT is to assist the individual in desensitizing to the dreaded circumstance or item and learning how to control their anxiety in everyday circumstances are adapted and assessed by followed by that used BAT for assessing the Participants Behavior during the Particular Phobic Situation.

3. **Spider and Cockroach Anxiety and Avoidance Questionaries.** The Spider and Cockroach Anxiety and Avoidance Questionnaires are self-report assessments of Fear of and aversion to spiders and cockroaches Clinical and research contexts utilize these questionnaires to diagnose and assess certain phobias. The 31-item self-report Spider Anxiety and Disgust Scale (SADS) measures spider-related anxiety and disgust. Between 0 (not at all) and 4 (extremely), there are five possible scores., respondents are asked to rate their level of dread and revulsion for spider-orientedsituations, such as spotting a spider in the room or unexpectedly running into one. The 29-item self-report Cockroach Avoidance and Disgust Scale (CADS) measures cockroach avoidance and disgust. The questionnaire asks respondents to rank their fear and avoidance on a range of 0 to 4 on a 5-point scale for cockroach-related incidents such as suddenly meeting a cockroach or seeing one in public [4, 22]. Both surveys are reliable and accurate and can measure spider and cockroach fears. And studied this. These surveys help guide treatment decisions and evaluate spider and cockroach phobia therapy.

4. **Self Efficacy Beleive Questionarrie.** Self-report questionnaires are a useful tool for measuring self-efficacy beliefs. These surveys often ask participants to assess, on a scale from 1 to 10, how confident they are in their abilities to carry out a certain job. These surveys are used extensively in academic and therapeutic contexts to examine individuals' views about their own levels of self-efficacy and to create treatments intended to improve such beliefs. Increasing an individual's sense of self-efficacy may have substantial ramifications for that individual's achievement in a variety of areas.used this using a Likert scale Measure and found the beliefs of the Patient for the Spider and Cockroach Phobia [23, 24].

5. **Anxiety Disorder Interview Schedule.** To evaluate how severe an anxiety condition is, clinicians conduct interviews using the Anxiety Disorders Interview Schedule (ADIS). Social anxiety disorder, generalized anxiety disorder, panic disorder, agoraphobia, specific phobia, and post-traumatic stress disorder are just some of the anxiety disorders that the ADIS can detect. It was developed by the National Institute of Mental Health (NIMH) and is widely used by clinicians and researchers. The Anxiety Disorders Interview Schedule (ADIS) is a diagnostic interview performed by a qualified clinician, often a psychologist or psychiatrist, that covers a broad variety of anxiety symptoms and related impairments. The purpose of the in-depth interview, which may last anywhere from one to two hours, is to learn as much as possible about the individual's anxiety symptoms. Individual anxiety disorders are addressed in separate sections of the ADIS. [25, 26]. To figure out whether or

not the patient suffers from an anxiety condition, the therapist will first offer a general anxiety module. The doctor will ask a series of questions during the whole interview to gauge the patient's level of anxiety and its impacts. Questions are structured and aimed, and therapists mostly use scores to determine how seriously patients are experiencing symptoms. The doctor may also inquire about the patient's prior treatment for anxiety and any family history of anxiety disorders. A diagnosis and treatment plan will be formulated based on the information acquired during the interview [27]. Clinical trials and research studies often utilize the Anxiety Disorders Inventory (ADIS) to evaluate the success of treatments for anxiety disorders . Used this Measure in their work to access anxiety using a Likert scale measure. Figure 2 depicts the Types of Clinical measures used thus for through AR Technology

2.3   Review Based on Hardwares Used in Augmented Reality

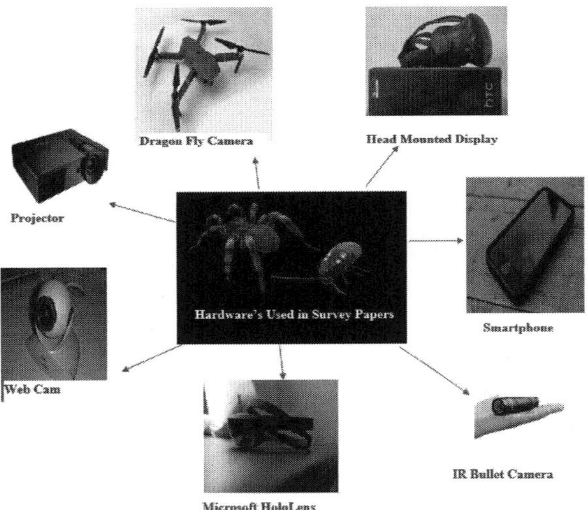

Fig. 3. Hardwares used so far with help of Augmented Reality

1. **Head Mounted Display.** In an augmented reality environment, the user's eyes and head are projected with visual and auditory information by a head-mounted display (HMD). The user dons the gadget like a pair of goggles or a helmet, and the screen faces directly in front of their eyes. Optical and video-based HMDs are the two most common varieties [28]. Video-based HMDs have tiny displays within the device, whereas optical HMDs employ lenses to project a picture directly onto the user's retina. Head-mounted displays (HMDs) can operate independently utilizing their own processing power or in

conjunction with a computer or mobile device. Due to the presence of head tracking sensors, the display on some HMDs can be modified based on the way the user's head moves. This allows for a more realistic simulation as the virtual world may now respond to the player's activities in real time. This gadget was utilised by to display spider and cockroach photos to patients [29,30].

2. **SmartPhones.** Smartphones have integrated seamlessly into our lives and are now a key component of augmented reality (AR) technology. A technique known as augmented reality projects digital data such as text, photos, and 3D models over the physical world. The technology has the ability to change how we interact with the environment around us by tracking the user's surroundings and location in real-time using computer vision, depth sensing, and other sensors. [31] The fact that smartphones come with a variety of sensors and cameras that are necessary for AR applications is one of the chief reasons. Modern smartphones, for instance, include excellent cameras, accelerometers, gyroscopes, and GPS sensors, helping them to precisely follow the user's gestures and position in real-time. This demonstrates that they can perfectly overlay digital assets on the real world to offer an AR experience that is highly immersive and this device with different versions was effectively used for the phobia treatment [32,33]. Figure 3 depicts the Hardwares used so far with help of Augmented Reality

3. **Webcam.** For augmented reality (AR) experiences on desktop and mobile devices, webcams might be crucial. AR apps may put virtual items and enable interaction with them in the user's actual environment by utilizing a surveillance device to keep an eye on the actions of the user and surroundings in real time. The input required by AR software to carry out marker-based or markerless tracking is provided via webcams. With marker-based tracking, AR material is positioned and monitored using a predetermined visual marker, such as a QR code. Markerless tracking includes identifying and following characteristics in the user's surroundings, such as the edges and corners of objects or geographical landmarks, using computer vision algorithms. In both situations, the camera records a live video feed of the user's surroundings. It feeds it to the augmented reality software, which employs image processing methods to extract pertinent data for tracking and generating virtual objects. The user may then experience augmented reality through the AR software by adding virtual things over the live video stream [34].

4. **Projector.** A projector is used in augmented reality to show digital pictures or information onto real-world surfaces or physical items. This is accomplished by overlaying digital material on top of actual items or surfaces in a manner that seems to be merged with the real world using a mix of cameras, sensors, and software to determine the position and orientation of the objects or surfaces. Projectors are used in interactive displays, which allow viewers to interact with digital material by touching or moving real-world items or surfaces. A virtual cockroach and Spider were projected onto a table using a high-resolution projector, allowing users to interact with animals [35,35].

5. **Microsoft Hololens.** The Microsoft HoloLens [36] is a mixed-reality device that combines the actual world with computer-generated imagery. Creating a secure, monitored setting for exposure therapy, has the potential to dramatically improve the treatment of phobias by
6. **IR Bullet Camera.** A surveillance camera that uses infrared light to take pictures in dim or no-light environments is referred to as an IR bullet camera or an infrared bullet camera. IR point-and-shoot camera The primary purpose of the camera in Phobia treatment using augmented reality is to be able to take pictures even when there is little to no available light. Used the camera for the treatment of Spiders and Cockroach [37–39]

2.4   Key Findings of Literature Review

Based on the review and the information about phobias from the articles [40–52]

1. Effectiveness of AR-based Therapies: Previous research has shown how well AR-based therapies work at helping people get over their fears and stuff. These therapies use immersive AR to gradually expose people to what they fear, which is called gradual desensitization making the person interact with the 3D model.
2. Benefits of AR Technology: AR technology is better than using pictures or videos to create the fear stimuli. With AR Usage we can track how people are feeling and acting, and give them feedback on their progress. This individualized approach makes therapy more accessible, effective, and tailored to each person's needs.
3. Variety of AR Hardware: Unlike other methods AR therapy uses a different variety of devices like headsets, smartphones, webcams, projectors, and Microsoft HoloLens. Each device is different, so therapists can choose the best one for each patient.
4. Need for Standardization and Long-Term Trials: AR-based therapies have been shown effective, but a lot of research is needed to check the long-term and to figure out the possible methods for Phobia Treatment. In the Previous studies only a small group of people, so it requires a large population to check this.
5. Prospects for Further Research: In the future, there's a lot of room for improvement in AR-based phobia treatment. We could compare different AR strategies, figure out how to make AR more accessible and user-friendly and study how well these therapies work over time. By tackling these challenges, we can learn more about augmented reality in therapy and how it can help people overcome their fears.

3   Methods

3.1   Review Question

A survey was done to identify the therapeutic interventions did so far for the phobia treatment using AR with the following questions

- What types of phobias might augmented reality be used to treat?
- What types of techniques have been used to treat phobias using augmented reality up to this point?
- What kinds of clinical measures have been implemented up to this point?
- What kinds of hardware are involved in the treatment of phobic disorders using augmented reality?

3.2   Review Protocal

The following set of Protocals were used

1. Did the research paper make use of augmented reality to find a solution?
2. Does the paper address the Phobia Scenario at any point?
3. Did the paper employ any of the appropriate methods?
4. Has the treatment been tried out on a person who suffers from a particular phobia?
5. Did the Paper Have Valid Results?

3.3   Strategical Search and Referred Database

A variety of academic databases, including Pub Med, Scopus, IEEE Xplore, and Google Scholar, were used to search the literature. To find pertinent studies, keywords about virtual reality, immersive technology, phobia treatment, and augmented reality were utilized. To narrow down the search and pinpoint particular literary subsets, boolean operators like "AND," "OR," and "NOT" were used.

3.4   Synthesis and Analysis of the Study

- Toderive significant findings about the effectiveness of augmented reality-based phobia treatment, the chosen papers were examined.
- To find common issues and trends, information on participant demographics, intervention protocols, outcome measures, and treatment outcomes was combined.
- The benefits and drawbacks of several augmented reality technologies, such as head-mounted displays, cellphones, cameras, projectors, and the Microsoft HoloLens, were assessed through comparative analysis.
- The goal of the investigation's analysis was to present a thorough assessment of the state of the art in the field of augmented reality-based phobia treatment and identify potential directions for further research.

4   Augmented Reality Technology

4.1   AR and Its Components

By overlaying digital content over a user's view of the real world, AR technology improves the user's perception of reality. The following are the main elements of AR technology:

1. Display Device: Head-mounted displays (HMDs), smartphones, tablets, and glasses are common display devices used to view augmented reality content. These gadgets offer a visual interface that allows digital content to be superimposed on top of the real world.
2. Sensors: By gathering data from the real world and monitoring user movements and interactions, sensors are essential to augmented reality. Cameras, gyroscopes, accelerometers, and GPS sensors are frequently found in AR devices. Accurate virtual object positioning and alignment within the user's environment is made possible by these sensors.
3. Processing Unit: ForAR applications to render digital content in real-time and seamlessly integrate it with the user's surroundings, they require powerful processing units. This processing unit may be housed inside the augmented reality gadget or it may be dependent on other computing resources, like mobile devices or cloud-based servers.
4. Software: The foundation for producing and presenting augmented experiences is provided by AR software applications, sometimes referred to as AR engines or platforms. Utilizingcomputer vision algorithms, spatial mapping methods, and gesture recognition, these software tools assess the user's surroundings and superimpose digital content appropriately.
5. Interaction Techniques: AR interfaces let users use a variety of input techniques, including touch, voice commands, gestures, and gaze tracking, to interact with virtual objects and manipulate digital content. These methods of interaction improve user engagement and make it easier for users to control AR applications intuitively.

4.2   Applications of AR in Phobia Treatment

The use of augmented reality (AR) technology in the treatment of phobias has shown promise, providing novel methods for cognitive-behavioral and exposure therapy. Key uses of AR in the treatment of phobias include:

1. Exposure therapy: With the use of augmented reality (AR), therapists can establish safe, regulated environments in which patients can progressively face their fears. With the use of digital content superimposed on the actual environment, AR exposure therapy simulates phobic stimuli to assist patients in learning coping mechanisms and desensitising to their fears.
2. Contextual Learning: By offering educational materials and details about particular phobias, AR-based phobia treatment programmes can assist patients

in comprehending the nature of their fears and the reasoning behind exposure therapy. Engaging with interactive augmented reality (AR) can provide valuable insights into the causes, manifestations, and outcomes of phobias, enabling individuals to actively participate in their own recovery.

3. Personalisation and Customisation: Using augmented reality technology, therapists can create treatment plans for phobias that are specific to the needs, interests, and degrees of severity of each patient. By matching the unique triggers and scenarios associated with each patient's phobia, virtual environments and stimuli can be tailored to improve treatment efficacy and engagement.

4. Real-time Feedback and Monitoring: During exposure therapy sessions, augmented reality (AR) systems can gather real-time data on patient responses, physiological reactions, and behavioural patterns. With the help of this feedback, therapists can ensure the best possible therapeutic results by modifying the duration and intensity of exposure by patient progress.

5. Enhanced Motivation and Engagement: Throughout the course of treatment, patients' motivation and engagement can be further bolstered by the immersive and interactive nature of augmented reality (AR) experiences. Patients' enjoyment and commitment to therapy during phobia treatment can be enhanced by the inclusion of gamification elements, rewards, and progress-tracking features.

4.3   Advantages of AR over Traditional Method

When it comes to treating phobias, augmented reality (AR) has a number of benefits over conventional techniques, including:

1. Enhanced Immersion: When compared to traditional exposure therapy, augmented reality (AR) technology offers a more engaging and productive treatment context by producing incredibly realistic and immersive environments that closely mimic the patient's real-world experiences.

2. Safe and Controlled Environment: By using AR-based exposure therapy, therapists can establish safe and controlled spaces where patients can face their fears without really running the risk of harm. By facilitating gradual desensitisation and fear extinction, this controlled exposure lowers the risk of severe anxiety or trauma.

3. Tailored and Adaptive Treatment: AR systems are capable of being tailored to meet the specific needs, preferences, and treatment objectives of each patient. This allows for the provision of adaptable and flexible treatment approaches that can be changed in real-time in response to patient feedback and progress.

4. Objective Patient Responses and Behaviours Monitoring: Augmented Reality (AR) technology allows for objective patient responses and behaviours to be recorded during therapy sessions. This data and insight can be used by therapists to plan and evaluate treatments. Treatment plan optimisation and timely adjustments are made possible by real-time feedback.

5. Accessibility and Convenience: Patients with mobility restrictions or limited access to traditional mental health services can find therapy more accessible

and convenient with AR-based phobia treatment programmes, which can be delivered remotely or in a variety of settings. This adaptability improves treatment compliance and outreach, especially for marginalised groups.

5   Real Time Usecase

5.1   Description of the Case Study

In the case study, students at a matriculation school in Thanjavur, Tamil Nadu, India, had their social anxiety treated with augmented reality (AR) technology. The purpose of the study was to evaluate how well AR-based interventions helped students with social anxiety and social interaction skills.

5.2   AR Treatment in Social Phobia

Using augmented reality (AR) technology, the study created marker- and markerless-based AR applications to augment the curriculum. Through the integration of AR applications into the curriculum, students were able to engage with digital content superimposed on top of their textbooks and the classroom environment.

Tablets or smartphones with augmented reality apps were given to the students. Students could scan particular pages in their textbooks to access more interactive material that was relevant to the lesson by using marker-based augmented reality. Conversely, marker less augmented reality (AR) made use of computer vision algorithms to identify and enhance real-world objects or scenes within the classroom setting.

5.3   Methodology

Both qualitative and quantitative techniques were used to assess the AR-based intervention's efficacy. Students' social anxiety levels and social interaction behaviors were measured through pre- and post-intervention assessments.

To learn more about students' experiences with AR technology and how it affected their symptoms of social anxiety, qualitative feedback sessions were organized. During class activities, observations of how students interacted with their peers and the augmented reality applications were also documented.

5.4   Findings

The study's findings showed that AR technology helps students with social phobias interact with others more socially and experience less social anxiety. Participants' self-reported anxiety levels significantly decreased, and their social engagement behaviours increased, according to post-intervention assessments.

Students' qualitative comments emphasizedhow the AR apps' immersive and captivating qualities promoted student participation and active learning in the classroom. Pupils who took part in group activities and interacted with their peers reported feeling more at ease and confident.

– Flexibility and Adaptability: The process of implementation brought to light how crucial these qualities are for overcoming unanticipated obstacles and modifying intervention plans as necessary. To maximise the effectiveness of the intervention and get past implementation obstacles, flexibility in the use of technology, instructional design, and administrative policies proved essential.
– Strong collaboration and engagement among stakeholders, such as educators, students, parents, and technical support teams, were essential to the implementation's success. Clear lines of communication made it easier for people to share ideas, opinions, and best practices, which created a positive atmosphere that encouraged experimentation and creativity.
– Continuous Assessment and Improvement: Determining areas for improvement and fine-tuning implementation tactics required constant assessment and contemplation. Frequent feedback loops ensured the sustainability and scalability of AR-based initiatives in educational settings by facilitating the timely identification of emerging issues and the implementation of interventions to address them.

5.5   Challenges

The study's conclusions imply that augmented reality technology has potential as a useful tool for treating social anxiety in educational settings. Teachers can simultaneously target social anxiety symptoms and give students engaging learning experiences by incorporating augmented reality (AR) applications into the curriculum.

– Technical Constraints: The technical limitations of AR technology, such as hardware compatibility issues, software bugs, and network connectivity issues, posed one of the main implementation challenges. The smooth integration of AR apps into the school's current infrastructure was hampered by these problems.
– Limited Technology Access: Many students were unable to use their own tablets or smartphones, which made it difficult for them to take part in AR-based activities. Due to the digital divide, students had different opportunities to interact with technology and gain from the intervention.
– Opposition to Change: Initially, some educators and administrators were dubious about integrating augmented reality (AR) technology into the curriculum because they were worried about upsetting established teaching techniques, lacked adequate training, and weren't sure if it would be beneficial for students' education.

6   Conclusion

AR-based phobia treatments may reduce phobic symptoms, improve therapeutic outcomes, and improve functional impairment. AR environments allow controlled exposure to phobic stimuli, enabling fear extinction through relaxing.

AR interventions have been shown to reduce anxiety, avoidance, and treatment adherence in phobic. Despite promising results, small sample sizes, methodological inconsistencies, and technological constraints require more research to determine AR-based interventions' efficacy and generalizability.Clinicians can use AR technology to improve phobia treatment efficacy and make therapy more interactive and personalized. Clinicians can use AR-based interventions to provide tailored exposure therapy in a controlled and immersive environment, improving symptom reduction and treatment outcomes. Future research should prioritise longitudinal studies to assess AR-based phobia treatment interventions' long-term efficacy and sustainability. Comparative effectiveness studies of AR modalities and treatment protocols can improve treatment guidelines and evidence-based practice. AR-based phobia treatment research and innovative interventions require interdisciplinary collaborations and patient-centered design.

7   Future Gap

AR-based phobia treatment interventions should be studied longitudinally. Tracking patients' progress and symptom remission over time will reveal treatment sustainability and relapse risk find the best AR technologies, intervention modalities, and treatment protocols for specific phobia types and patient populations, comparative studies are needed. Researchers can find best practices and optimize treatment protocols by systematically comparing outcomes across interventions is needed to determine the efficacy of AR-based interventions tailored to patient characteristics, preferences, and treatment goals. Clinicians can improve treatment outcomes and patient engagement by tailoring protocols to phobia severity, commodities, and cognitive-behavioral profiles. Advanced Sensor Technologies: Wearable bio metric sensors and eye-tracking devices may improve AR-based phobia treatment interventions. These sensors provide real-time feedback on physiological arousal, gaze patterns, and emotional responses, enabling personalizedtreatment adjustments and better outcomes VR technology with AR-based interventions can create hybrid environments that blend real-world and virtual experiences. VR's immersive nature allows clinicians to create realistic exposure scenarios and simulate difficult situations in a controlled, therapeutic setting, improving phobia exposure therapy. AR-based treatment interventions can be made more adaptable and responsive with AI-driven algorithms and machine learning. AI algorithms can identify patterns, predict treatment outcomes, and make personalized recommendations for optimizing treatment protocols and improving patient outcomes by analyzing large datasets of patient interactions AR-based phobia treatment protocols and guidelines can improve consistency, reproducible, and comparability across studies. Clear intervention design, implementation, and outcome assessment guidelines can improve collaboration, knowledge dissemination, and research rigorand quality. Encourage psychologists, psychiatrists, technologists, educators, and human-computer interaction experts to work together. Interdisciplinary collaborations can innovate, solve complex problems, and create patient-centered AR-based phobia treatments by integrating diverse perspectives and expertise. Patients' feedback, preferences, and experiences should be considered when designing interventions. Patients as co-designers and active participants in intervention design can improve treatment acceptability, engagement, and adherence, improving outcomes and patient satisfaction.

References

1. de Jong, R., Hofs, A., Lommen, M.J.J., van Hout, W.J.P.J., de Jong, P.J.D., Nauta, M.H.: Treating specific phobia in youth: a randomized controlled microtrial comparing gradual exposure in large steps to exposure in small steps. J. Anxiety Disord. **96**, 102712 (2023)
2. de Jong, R., et al.: Better together? A randomized controlled microtrial comparing different levels of therapist and parental involvement in exposure-based treatment of childhood specific phobia. J. Anxiety Disord. **100**, 102785 (2023)
3. Lin, Z., et al.: The effect of internet-based cognitive behavioral therapy on major depressive disorder: randomized controlled trial. J. Med. Internet Res. **25**, e42786 (2023)
4. Albakri, G., et al.: Phobia exposure therapy using virtual and augmented reality: a systematic review. Appl. Sci. **12**(3), 1672 (2022)
5. Giacomantonio, S.G.: Three problems with the theory of cognitive therapy. Am. J. Psychother. **66**(4), 375–390 (2012)
6. Juan, M.C., Alcaniz, M., Monserrat, C., Botella, C., Banos, R.M., Guerrero, B.: Using augmented reality to treat phobias. IEEE Comput. Graph. Appl. **25**(6), 31 (2005). Accessed 24 Apr 2024
7. Azuma, R.T.: A survey of augmented reality. Presence Teleoperators Virtual Environ. **6**(4), 355–385 (1997)
8. Carmigniani, J., Furht, B., Anisetti, M., Ceravolo, P., Damiani, E., Ivkovic, M.: Augmented reality technologies, systems and applications. Multimedia Tools Appl. **51**(1), 341–377 (2011)
9. Tatić, D., Tešić, B.: The application of augmented reality technologies for the improvement of occupational safety in an industrial environment. Comput. Ind. **85**, 1–10 (2017)
10. Rivero, F., Herrero, M., Viña, C., Álvarez-Pérez, Y., Peñate, W.: Neuroimaging in cockroach phobia: an experimental study. Int. J. Clin. Health Psychol. **17**(3), 207–215 (2017)
11. Davey, G.C.L.: Characteristics of individuals with fear of spiders. Anxiety Res. **4**(4), 299–314 (1991)
12. Wrzesien, M., et al.: The therapeutic lamp: treating small-animal phobias. IEEE Comput. Graph. Appl. **33**(1), 80–86 (2013)
13. Wrzesien, M., et al.: Treating small animal phobias using a projective-augmented reality system: a single-case study. Comput. Hum. Behav. **49**, 343–353 (2015). https://doi.org/10.1016/j.chb.2015.01.065
14. Wrzesien, M., Burkhardt, J.M., Botella, C., Alcañiz, M.: Evaluation of the quality of collaboration between the client and the therapist in phobia treatments. Interact. Comput. **24**(6), 461–471 (2012)
15. Juan, M.C., Joele, D.: A comparative study of the sense of presence and anxiety in an invisible marker versus a marker augmented reality system for the treatment of phobia towards small animals. Int. J. Hum Comput Stud. **69**(6), 440–453 (2011)

16. Zimmer, A., et al.: Effectiveness of a smartphone-based, augmented reality exposure app to reduce fear of spiders in real-life: a randomized controlled trial. J. Anxiety Disord. **82**, 102442 (2021)
17. Botella, C., et al.: Treating cockroach phobia using a serious game on a mobile phone and augmented reality exposure: a single case study. Comput. Hum. Behav. **27**(1), 217–227 (2011)
18. Lundin, R.M., Yeap, Y., Menkes, D.B.: Adverse effects of virtual and augmented reality interventions in psychiatry: systematic review. JMIR Mental Health **10**, e43240 (2023). https://doi.org/10.2196/43240
19. Ramírez-Fernández, C., Morán, A.L., Meza-Kubo, V.: A comparative study between different treatments for spider phobia. In: 8th Mexican Conference on Human-Computer Interaction (2021)
20. Ore, J., et al.: Augmented reality for the treatment of arachnophobia: exposure therapy. World J. Eng. **18**(4), 566–572 (2020)
21. De Witte, N.A.J., Scheveneels, S., Sels, R., Debard, G., Hermans, D., Van Daele, T.: Augmenting exposure therapy: mobile augmented reality for specific phobia. Front. Virtual Reality **1** (2020)
22. De Witte, N.D., et al.: Handheld or head-mounted? An experimental comparison of the potential of augmented reality for animal phobia treatment using smartphone and HoloLens 2 (2022). www.semanticscholar.org. Accessed 03 May 2023
23. Chicchi Giglioli, I.A., Pallavicini, F., Pedroli, E., Serino, S., Riva, G.: Augmented reality: a brand new challenge for the assessment and treatment of psychological disorders. Comput. Math. Methods Med. **2015**, 1–12 (2015)
24. Suso-Ribera, C., et al.: Virtual reality, augmented reality, and In Vivo exposure therapy: a preliminary comparison of treatment efficacy in small animal phobia. Cyberpsychol. Behav. Soc. Netw. **22**(1) (2019)
25. Baus, O., Bouchard, S.: Moving from virtual reality exposure-based therapy to augmented reality exposure-based therapy: a review. Front. Hum. Neurosci. **8** (2014)
26. Hinze, J., et al.: Spider phobia: neural networks informing diagnosis and (virtual/augmented reality-based) cognitive behavioral psychotherapy—a narrative review. Front. Psychiatry (2021). Accessed 03 May 2023
27. Arntz, A., Lavy, E., Van den Berg, G., Van Rijsoort, S.: Negative beliefs of spider phobics: a psychometric evaluation of the spider phobia beliefs questionnaire. Adv. Behav. Res. Ther. (1993). Accessed 03 May 2023
28. Kiyokawa, K.: Trends and vision of head mounted display in augmented reality. IEEE Xplore, 01 August 2012
29. Wolpe, J.: The practice of behavior therapy. Pergamon Press (1990). Accessed 03 May 2023
30. Öst, L.-G., Fellenius, J., Sterner, U.: Applied tension, exposure in vivo, and tension-only in the treatment of blood phobia. Behav. Res. Ther. **29**(6), 561–574 (1991)
31. Pence, H.E.: Smartphones, smart objects, and augmented reality. Ref. Libr. **52**(1–2), 136–145 (2010)
32. Öst, L.-G., Salkovskis, P.M., Hellström, K.: One-session therapist-directed exposure vs. self-exposure in the treatment of spider phobia. Behav. Ther. **22**(3), 407–422 (1991)
33. Agras, S., Sylvester, D., Oliveau, D.: The epidemiology of common fears and phobia. Compr. Psychiatr. **10**(2), 151–156 (1969)
34. Hudson, L., Rapee, R.M.: The origins of social phobia. Behav. Modif. **24**(1), 102–129 (2000)

35. Depla, M.F.I.A., ten Have, M.L., van Balkom, A.J.L.M., de Graaf, R.: Specific fears and phobias in the general population: results from The Netherlands mental health survey and incidence study. Soc. Psychiatr. Psychiatr. Epidemiol. **43**, 200–208 (2007)
36. Park, S., Bokijonov, S., Choi, Y.: Review of microsoft HoloLens applications over the past five years. Appl. Sci. **11**(16), 7259 (2021)
37. LeBeau, R.T., et al.: Specific phobia: a review of DSM-IV specific phobia and preliminary recommendations for DSM-V. Depress. Anxiety **27**(2), 148–167 (2010)
38. Boyd, J.H., et al.: Phobia: prevalence and risk factors. Soc. Psychiatry Psychiatr. Epidemiol. **25**(6), 314–323 (1990)
39. Ehlers, A., Hofmann, S.G., Herda, C.A., Roth, W.T.: Clinical characteristics of driving phobia. J. Anxiety Disord. **8**(4), 323–339 (1994)
40. McSweeney, F.K., Bierley, C.: Recent developments in classical conditioning. J. Consum. Res. **11**(2), 619 (1984)
41. Hofmann, S.G., Asnaani, A., Vonk, I.J.J., Sawyer, A.T., Fang, A.: The efficacy of cognitive behavioral therapy: a review of meta-analyses. Cogn. Ther. Res. **36**(5), 427–440 (2012)
42. Zhu, M., et al.: Haptic-feedback smart glove as a creative human-machine interface (HMI) for virtual/augmented reality applications. Sci. Adv. **6**(19) (2020)
43. Behzadan, A.H., Timm, B.W., Kamat, V.R.: General-purpose modular hardware and software framework for mobile outdoor augmented reality applications in engineering. Adv. Eng. Inform. **22**(1), 90–105 (2008)
44. Marks, I.M., Gelder, M.G.: Different ages of onset in varieties of phobia. Am. J. Psychiatry **123**(2), 218–221 (1966)
45. Kessler, R.C.: The impairments caused by social phobia in the general population: implications for intervention. Acta Psychiatr. Scand. **108**(s417), 19–27 (2003)
46. Stravynski, A., et al.: Social phobia treated as a problem in social functioning: a controlled comparison of two behavioural group approaches. Acta Psychiatr. Scand. **102**(3), 188–198 (2000)
47. Seligman, M.E.P.: Phobias and preparedness. Behav. Ther. **2**(3), 307–320 (1971)
48. McGuire, J.F., et al.: Fear conditioning and extinction in youth with obsessive-compulsive disorder. Depress. Anxiety **33**(3), 229–237 (2016)
49. Barlow, D.H.: On the relation of clinical research to clinical practice: current issues, new directions. J. Consult. Clin. Psychol. **49**(2), 147–155 (1981)
50. Tomi, A.B., Rambli, D.R.A.: An interactive mobile augmented reality magical playbook: learning number with the thirsty crow. Procedia Comput. Sci. **25**, 123–130 (2013)
51. Bentz, D., Michael, T., de Quervain, D.J.F., Wilhelm, F.H.: Enhancing exposure therapy for anxiety disorders with glucocorticoids: from basic mechanisms of emotional learning to clinical applications. J. Anxiety Disord. **24**(2), 223–230 (2010)
52. Wiederhold, M.D., Crisci, M., Patel, V., Nonaka, M., Wiederhold, B.K.: Physiological monitoring during augmented reality exercise confirms advantages to health and well-being. Cyberpsychol. Behav. Soc. Netw. **22**(2), 122–126 (2019)

Exploring Sustainability in Artificial Intelligence: Balancing Innovation and Environmental Impact?

Maria Bartekova[✉] [iD], Helena Majduchova [iD], and Anita Romanova [iD]

Bratislava University of Economics and Business, Dolnozemska cesta 1, 852 35 Bratislava, Slovakia
{maria.bartekova,helena.majduchova,anita.romanova}@euba.sk

Abstract. The rapid development of Artificial Intelligence (AI) technologies has revolutionized numerous sectors globally, but its growing computational demands raise concerns about its sustainability, particularly in relation to energy consumption and environmental impact. This paper aims to investigate the relationship between global energy consumption, the share of renewable energy sources, CO_2 emissions, and AI revenues. By employing regression analysis, we explore the extent to which AI revenues are correlated with shifts in energy consumption patterns and the associated environmental effects. Our findings provide a quantitative assessment of AI's impact on energy demand and CO_2 emissions, highlighting both the opportunities and challenges of AI's continued growth. The results offer critical insights into the role of renewable energy in mitigating the environmental footprint of AI technologies, thereby contributing to the discourse on achieving sustainability in the age of AI-driven innovation.

Keywords: Artificial Intelligence · Sustainability · Energy Consumption · Sustainable growth

1 Introduction

The rapid development of artificial intelligence (AI) technologies has brought about revolutionary innovations across industries ranging from healthcare and finance to manufacturing and transportation. However, this growth has been accompanied by serious concerns about the environmental sustainability of AI, particularly its increasing energy demands and carbon emissions. Training and deploying complex AI models – particularly deep learning systems such as large language models (LLMs), computer vision algorithms and reinforcement learning – requires significant computational power and therefore high energy consumption [1]. While the current literature mainly emphasizes how AI increases energy consumption, relatively less attention is paid to how AI itself can contribute to its optimization. AI has the potential to play a key role in sustainability through applications such as climate modeling, smart grid management, predictive maintenance and real-time energy consumption optimization [2]. These examples show

S. Goel et al. (Eds.): AICON 2025, LNICST 672, pp. 138–149, 2026.
https://doi.org/10.1007/978-3-032-14805-6_9

that AI can not only be a driver of energy consumption growth, but also a tool for its effective management and emission reduction. Furthermore, the area of regulation and governance related to energy efficiency of AI remains underdeveloped. As AI is increasingly integrated into the world's infrastructure, there is a growing need for standardized metrics to measure energy consumption, identify potential data biases, and establish standards for sustainable development [3].

This study explores the complex relationship between AI revenues, global energy consumption, renewable energy share, and CO_2 emissions. Using quantitative methods, we assess the environmental costs of AI growth as well as its potential contribution to sustainability. Importantly, we also highlight gaps in the literature – such as the need for a more detailed analysis of energy consumption across AI domains – and suggest directions for future research that see AI as part of the problem, but also as a solution on the path to sustainable innovation.

2   Literature Review

2.1   Green AI

Information Systems (IS) play a pivotal role in enabling sustainable transformations within both society and organizations. As IS usage growing, so too does the focus on developing energy-efficient IT systems to ensure that the growing demand for information and communication technologies (ICT) aligns with sustainability goals [1, 4]. This has led to the rise of the terms "Green IS" and "Green IT," which refer to IS initiatives aimed at improving efficiency and reducing the environmental impact of IT infrastructure. A key subfield of Green IS, known as Energy Informatics, specifically addresses the reduction of energy consumption through the strategic use of ICT [5].

Green IS and Energy Informatics are gaining significant attention in both academic research and real-world applications. A crucial success factor for these systems, particularly in energy-related applications, is the transparency they provide concerning historical, current, and projected energy flows [6]. This transparency, facilitated by data collected through sensors and IS, is essential for optimizing decisions around energy management. By carefully managing energy supply and demand, organizations can reduce overall energy consumption and lower emissions.

As data volumes increase, data-driven methods are becoming more prominent in energy-related research and practical implementations. These approaches are applied in areas such as predicting future energy consumption, identifying anomalies in energy usage patterns, and optimizing energy efficiency or flexibility [7, 8]. Most of these data-driven applications rely on techniques from Artificial Intelligence (AI), particularly machine learning (ML), which form the core of many AI systems. In this context, the primary objective of AI systems is to process incoming data to produce value-adding outputs in the form of actionable insights. In an AI system, ML algorithms are at the heart of this process, supported by data sources (e.g., sensors), preprocessing modules, and agents responsible for executing actions based on the processed data.

Green AI services encompass a range of applications, including green energy generation, load forecasting, load profiling, demand response, electricity pricing, storage assessment, outages, and power consumption management [2, 9]. These services collectively encourage the adoption of renewable energy sources across different sectors [2]. Various studies have explored green energy services, with some focusing on solar power generation and its applications, while others examine power generation through wind energy [10].

Load forecasting, an essential component of energy management, involves predicting power demand at different levels and over varying timeframes, such as short, medium, and long terms [11, 12]. For example, in Energy Cloud Management (ECM), load forecasting helps optimize power distribution and operational support, considering factors such as temperature, humidity, and climate variations. Studies also address load forecasting specific to renewable energy sources like solar and wind power, employing state-of-the-art techniques to improve accuracy [13].

Another critical aspect of load forecasting is load profiling, which assesses the variation in electrical load over time [14]. This helps in understanding consumption patterns and optimizing energy distribution accordingly [15–17].

ML algorithms require vast amounts of data for training, which in turn necessitates the use of powerful computer systems. These systems, often equipped with high-performance components like Graphics Processing Units (GPUs), significantly increase energy consumption [18, 19]. The issue of high energy demand has been acknowledged and highlighted by several research groups. While energy consumption measurement is becoming an increasingly important area in computer science research, it has yet to gain significant traction in Information Systems (IS) research or find widespread implementation in real-world applications [20].

Graphics processing units (GPUs), initially designed for rendering graphics, have become integral to AI due to their capacity to parallelize processing tasks and execute fast tensor operations, which are critical for AI algorithms. Table 4 illustrates NVIDIA's dominance in the AI server market, where its GPU platforms are noted for their leading computing efficiency. NVIDIA currently holds an estimated 95% market share in this sector [22].

One major challenge lies in translating the theoretical performance of GPUs into real-world performance for AI models. To maximize GPU utilization, tasks need to be inherently parallelizable, memory management must be optimized to avoid bottlenecks, and the software must be designed to ensure that all parts of the GPU are engaged, minimizing overhead and hardware limitations [23]. As a result, real-world applications often achieve GPU utilization as low as 2% to 10% [24]. However, certain AI models, such as large language models (LLMs), are better suited for high GPU utilization.

In 2023, NVIDIA is expected to have delivered around 100,000 AI server units [23]. Assuming an equal distribution between the DGX™ A100 and H100 models, this corresponds to a peak power demand of 0.84 GW for that year alone. With an ideal 100% load factor and a power usage effectiveness (PUE) of 1.12 [25], this would translate into 8.2 TWh of additional annual electricity consumption due to NVIDIA's global deliveries in 2023. By 2027, projections suggest that NVIDIA could deliver up to 1,500,000 AI server units [24]. If the newest DGX series model, the DGX™ B200, dominates the market, this could imply an additional peak capacity of 21.45 GW per year starting in 2027. If fully utilized, these servers could demand up to 210.6 TWh of electricity annually, assuming a PUE of 1.12.

2.2 Challenges and Future Directions in Decreasing AI-Related Energy Consumption

One of the primary challenges in reducing AI-related energy consumption is the enormous computational power required to train and deploy complex models, especially those based on deep learning algorithms. Training large models, such as GPT-3 or BERT, requires extensive use of graphics processing units (GPUs) and data centers that consume vast amounts of electricity. Studies have shown that training a single large-scale AI model can emit as much CO2 as five cars over their lifetime [26]. The high computational demand of these models, exacerbated by the growing complexity of AI applications, presents a substantial hurdle to reducing energy consumption.

Another significant challenge lies in the inefficient use of hardware during AI model training and deployment. Although GPUs are designed to perform parallel operations efficiently, real-world applications often fail to fully utilize these processing units, resulting in underutilization of computational resources. Research suggests that GPU utilization in AI applications can be as low as 2% to 10% due to bottlenecks in memory management and software design [1]. Achieving high GPU utilization requires optimization of both software and hardware, but such optimization is complex and time-consuming.

Data centres, which house the servers and computational infrastructure necessary to run AI applications, are responsible for a large portion of AI's overall energy consumption. These data centres often rely on non-renewable energy sources, contributing to CO_2 emissions and exacerbating the environmental impact of AI. While some companies have shifted towards using renewable energy sources, many data centres around the world still depend heavily on fossil fuels, further complicating efforts to decrease the energy consumption of AI systems [27].

One of the critical barriers to addressing AI-related energy consumption is the lack of standardized metrics and methods to measure energy use. Currently, there is no widely accepted standard for quantifying the energy consumption of AI models across different platforms and applications. This makes it difficult to track improvements, benchmark energy efficiency, or develop guidelines for more sustainable AI practices. Researchers have called for the development of standardized energy consumption metrics to facilitate comparisons across models, datasets, and training environments [28].

To address the inefficiencies in hardware utilization, the future of AI energy reduction will likely involve advancements in specialized hardware design. Innovations such as neuromorphic computing, which mimics the structure and function of the human brain, offer the potential to drastically reduce the power consumption of AI systems [29]. Additionally, hardware accelerators like tensor processing units (TPUs) have been developed specifically to handle AI workloads more efficiently, offering substantial improvements in energy efficiency compared to traditional GPUs and CPUs [30].

With this understanding, we can now proceed to outline the methodological framework used in the analysis of AI's role in global energy consumption.

While AI technologies present growing challenges related to energy demand, they also offer transformative potential for energy optimization. Emerging applications such as AI-driven climate modelling, smart grids, and intelligent energy management systems are powerful tools for reducing the environmental footprint of AI. These applications can enhance energy forecasting, improve demand-response strategies, and support the integration of renewable energy sources into power systems [2].

Smart grids, empowered by AI algorithms, can dynamically balance energy supply and demand, optimize power distribution, and reduce waste. AI-based predictive maintenance systems can also decrease unnecessary energy use and prolong the life cycle of infrastructure components [8]. Furthermore, climate modelling powered by AI can assist policymakers and scientists in better understanding and responding to environmental challenges, ultimately supporting climate resilience and sustainable development [9].

Despite these opportunities, the regulatory landscape for ensuring energy-efficient AI development remains underexplored. There is a pressing need for regulatory frameworks that promote energy transparency, enforce sustainability benchmarks, and incentivize the use of low-energy AI architectures [3]. These could include mandatory reporting standards for energy use, carbon footprint labelling for AI models, and green certification systems for data centers and AI developers.

In addition, the current metrics for assessing AI energy consumption lack standardization. There is minimal attention paid to how these metrics may reflect biases—such as differences in model size, data location, or training infrastructure—which can distort comparisons across applications [31]. Developing unbiased, standardized benchmarks for energy efficiency in AI will be essential to guiding responsible innovation.

Another crucial gap in current literature is the lack of detailed analysis of energy demand across different AI subfields. Large Language Models (LLMs) like GPT-3 and GPT-4 are extremely energy-intensive, requiring vast computational resources for both training and inference [30].

Computer Vision models, especially those used in real-time processing or edge devices, can also be demanding depending on resolution and processing frequency [21].

Reinforcement Learning, particularly in simulation-heavy environments like robotics or autonomous systems, often involves long training cycles with significant energy expenditure [22].

A granular breakdown of energy consumption by AI subdomain would enable more targeted strategies for energy efficiency and could help identify priority areas for optimization.

3 Methodology

The aim of this paper is to analyze the relationship between global energy consumption, the share of renewable energy, CO2 emissions, and AI revenues through regression analysis, providing insights into how AI's growth affects energy demand and environmental sustainability.

This study analysed the energy demand of Artificial Intelligence (AI) technologies using several key metrics, including global energy consumption, global carbon emissions (measured in MtCO2e), and the percentage of energy sourced from renewables. The approach involved a quantitative examination of statistical data to assess the environmental effects of AI technologies.

The research was driven by the following question: **How do AI technologies impact the environment in terms of energy usage and emissions?** Based on this, two hypotheses were developed:

- **H1:** There a statistically significant correlation between global energy consumption and AI revenues.
- **H2:** There a statistically significant correlation between AI revenues and the resulting greenhouse gas emissions.

The analysis was conducted using statistical tools such as DATAtab and jamovi, and the hypotheses were evaluated at a significance level of $\alpha = 0.05$. Data were obtained from the database of Precedence research, and Enerdata, providing a reliable basis for evaluating the energy consumption and emissions associated with AI technologies.

To assess whether the variables followed a normal distribution, the Shapiro-Wilk test was applied to the dataset. This test is particularly suitable for small sample sizes and evaluates the null hypothesis that the data is drawn from a normally distributed population. The variables tested included AI revenues, Share of renewables, Energy consumption, and CO_2 emissions. The results indicated no significant deviation from normality in any of the variables, with all p-values exceeding 0.05 (AI revenues: $p = 0.93$; Share of renewables: $p = 0.60$; Energy consumption: $p = 0.48$; CO_2 emissions: $p = 0.84$). These findings suggest that the assumption of normality holds, supporting the use of parametric statistical methods in subsequent analysis.

4 Results and Discussion

North America secured the largest market share in 2023, driven by the growing demand for automated and technologically advanced hardware and software across various industries, alongside favourable government policies encouraging the adoption of artificial intelligence (AI). A significant factor contributing to this growth was the 2019 launch of the American AI Initiative by the U.S. president, aimed at establishing the U.S. as a global leader in AI technology. This initiative provided guidelines for the practical application of AI in multiple industries and sectors. Additionally, North America is home to leading technology companies such as Facebook, Amazon, Google, IBM, Microsoft, and Apple, all of which have played crucial roles in advancing the AI market in the region [31].

Meanwhile, the Asia Pacific region is expected to experience the fastest growth in the AI market during the forecast period. Increased investments from various organizations in AI adoption are fuelling the demand for this technology. For instance, Baidu, a major tech company in China, has entered into agreements with investors to divest its financial services group, which offers consumer credit, wealth management, and other business-related services. Furthermore, the rising use of AI across industries such as automotive, healthcare, retail, and food and beverages are accelerating the expansion of the AI market in the Asia Pacific region (see Fig. 1).

Figure illustrates the distribution of AI subdomains in Europe as of 2023. It highlights the predominant position of robotics & automation. The chart emphasizes the significant role that these subdomain plays in shaping the AI landscape across Europe. However,

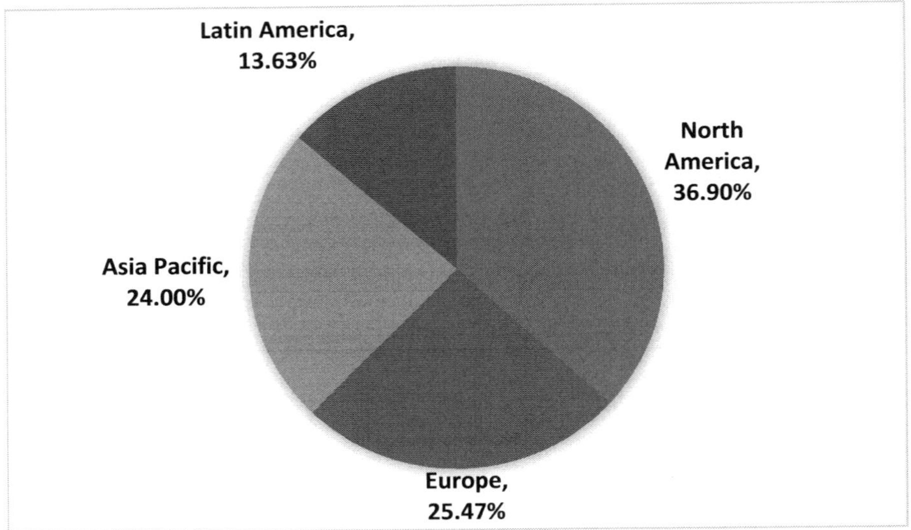

Fig. 1. AI market share in 2023.

Europe shows a more balanced focus across different subdomains, with robotics and automation (33%) and AI services (32%) being dominant. Machine learning (14%) plays a similar role to the USA, while NLP (7%) and computer vision (4%) have smaller shares in comparison (Fig. 2).

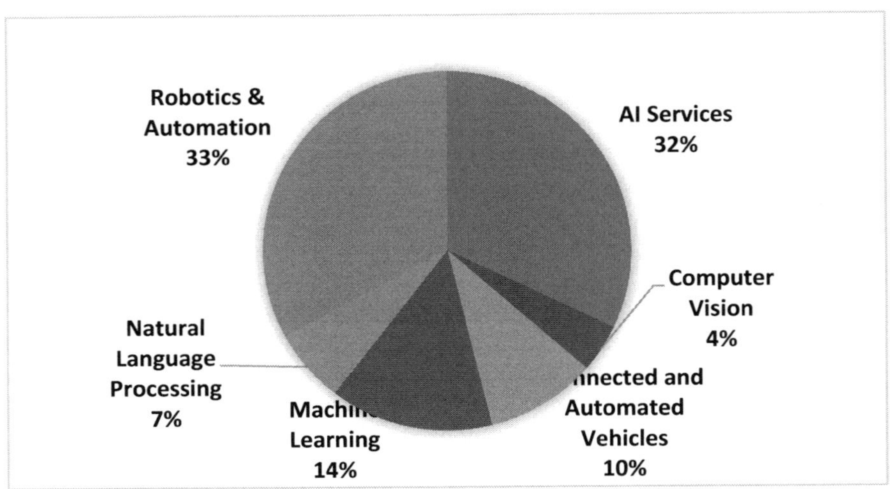

Fig. 2. AI subdomain structure in Europe.

Figure 3 shows the structure of AI subdomains in the United States in 2023, demonstrating the varying focus areas within the AI sector. In both regions, AI services represent a substantial portion of the AI landscape. Europe (32%) and the USA (28%) have similar emphasis on this subdomain, underscoring the widespread adoption of AI across various service sectors in both regions.

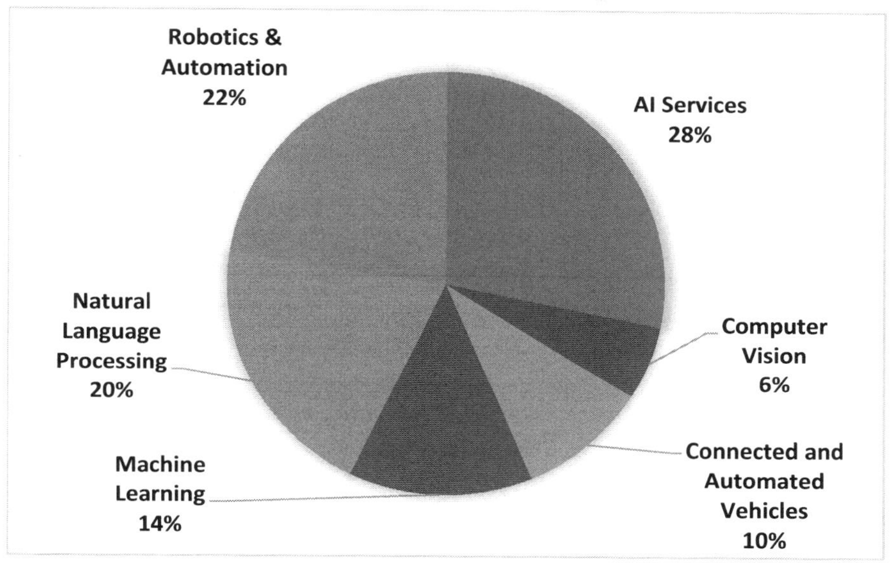

Fig. 3. AI subdomain structure in the USA.

The BFSI (Banking, Financial Services, and Insurance) segment accounted for the largest share of 17.1% in 2023 and is projected to experience substantial continuous growth (see Fig. 4). AI solutions are being increasingly adopted across the banking and finance sector for various purposes, including handling account inquiries, processing loan applications, detecting fraud, and monitoring credit scores. The BFSI sector is particularly well-suited for AI applications due to the vast amounts of data generated daily. Additionally, the growing demand for seamless, 24/7 service from the banking and finance industry is driving the segment's growth, as AI-powered tools can deliver efficient customer interactions and provide reliable outcomes for inquiries.

Table 1 represents the results of regression analysis. Both energy consumption and CO2 emissions increase with rising AI revenues. The slopes show a strong positive relationship, meaning as AI revenues grow, energy consumption and CO2 emissions grow significantly. The perfect R-squared suggests a very strong relationship, but this is likely due to the limited data points available for analysis. With a larger dataset, the R-squared might decrease, providing a more nuanced understanding.

According to the regression analysis, hypothesis H_1 and H_2 were confirmed.

In both research and practice, the implementation of ML applications often prioritizes a single evaluation criterion, such as accuracy, explainability, or cost-effectiveness. However, multi-objective optimization offers solutions that better align with a business's strategic goals, as highlighted by the experts interviewed. The Sustainable Machine

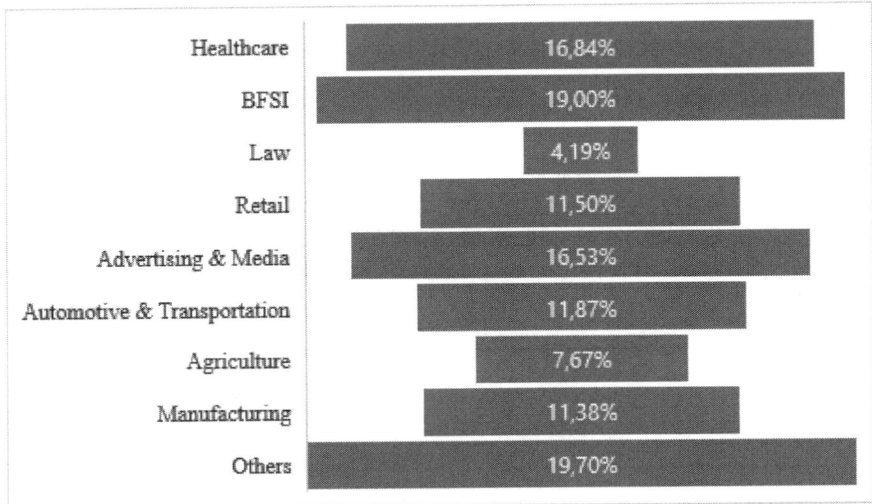

Fig. 4. AI market revenues structure (2023).

Learning Business Strategy (SMLBS) framework allows for the additional consideration of overall sustainability, which was previously only partially addressed. For example, SMLBS can be used to assess whether a transparent and inherently explainable ML algorithm (e.g., QLattice) provides advantages in terms of both accuracy and energy efficiency compared to post-hoc explanation techniques (e.g., SHAP values) commonly used in explainable AI (XAI) applications. Moreover, SMLBS can account for the higher energy consumption of resource-intensive applications (such as large server farms) and the associated costs due to carbon pricing, making energy consumption a quantifiable factor in economic assessments, as noted by several of the experts interviewed.

SMLBS also offers potential for expansion and integration due to its technology-agnostic and general approach. It can function as a meta-model that incorporates existing frameworks and tools. For instance, data-driven methodologies could be integrated by building on established frameworks like CRISP-DM.

Firstly, the study assumes that AI technologies will continue to grow and impact energy consumption in a linear fashion. However, future advancements in AI and energy-efficient technologies (such as neuromorphic computing or specialized hardware like TPUs) could drastically alter these trends, making the analysis less relevant over time.

Secondly, the study may not account for geographic differences in energy consumption patterns and AI development. For instance, energy consumption and emissions could vary significantly between regions depending on their energy mix, infrastructure, and regulatory environments. Finally, the analysis is based on recent data, which may not reflect long-term trends in AI and energy consumption. Rapid changes in AI development or energy policies could render the findings less applicable in future scenarios.

Table 1. The results of regression analysis

Regression Statistics	
Multiple R	0,992898
R Square	0,985846
Adjusted R Square	0,971691
Standard Error	17,92999
Observations	3

ANOVA

	df	SS	MS	F	Significance F
Regression	1	22391,18	22391,18	69,64935	0,07592
Residual	1	321,4844	321,4844		
Total	2	22712,67			

	Coefficients	Standard Error	t Stat	P-value	Lower 95%	Upper 95%	Lower 95,0%	Upper 95,0%
Intercept	-6659,54	861,9759	-7,7259	0,081945	-17612	4292,905	-17612	4292,905
CO2 emissions	0,20347	0,02438	8,345619	0,07592	-0,10631	0,513254	-0,10631	0,513254

5   Conclusion

This research explores the relationship between AI revenues, energy consumption, and CO_2 emissions, aiming to understand the environmental impact of AI growth. The findings demonstrate a strong positive correlation between AI revenues and both energy consumption and CO_2 emissions. As AI revenues increase, energy consumption and greenhouse gas emissions rise significantly, as indicated by the linear regression analysis, where the slopes for energy consumption and CO_2 emissions were 3.336 and 5.938, respectively. The R-squared values of 1.0 for both dependent variables suggest a perfect fit within the dataset, indicating that AI revenues explain the variability in energy consumption and emissions effectively.

However, several limitations must be acknowledged, including the small sample size, which limits the generalizability of the results. While the strong correlations suggest a direct relationship between AI growth and environmental impact, the study does not imply causation, and other factors such as technological advancements and regulatory frameworks may also influence the outcomes. Furthermore, the reliance on limited data points means that future research should expand the dataset and consider additional variables, such as energy efficiency measures and the role of renewable energy sources, to provide a more comprehensive view.

In conclusion, this study provides a foundational understanding of how AI growth may contribute to rising energy demand and emissions, highlighting the need for sustainable practices in AI development. As AI continues to expand across industries, addressing its environmental footprint through innovations in energy-efficient technologies and policies will be crucial to balancing technological advancement with sustainability goals.

Acknowledgements. The research paper belongs to the outputs of the currently implemented research grants VEGA no. 1/0662/23 and VEGA no. 1/0465/23.

References

1. Barrie, I., Adegbite, A., Osholake, S.F., Alesinloye, T., Bello, A.B.: Artificial intelligence in climate change mitigation: a review of predictive modeling and data-driven solutions for reducing greenhouse gas emissions. World J. Adv. Res. Rev. (2024). https://doi.org/10.30574/wjarr.2024.24.1.3043
2. Serban, A., Lytras, M.D.: Artificial intelligence for smart renewable energy sector in europe—smart energy infrastructures for next generation smart cities. IEEE Access **8**, 77364–77377 (2020)
3. Hacker, P.: Sustainable AI Regulation. ArXiv, abs/2306.00292 (2023)
4. Veerraju, M.S., et al.: AI-powered Smart Grids: Energy Optimization. Nanotechnology Perceptions (2024). https://doi.org/10.62441/nano-ntp.vi.3613
5. Adapa, V.R.K.: AI for climate action: leveraging artificial intelligence to address climate change challenges. Inter. J. Multidisciplinary Res. (2024). https://doi.org/10.36948/ijfmr.2024.v06i05.29015
6. Kwiliński, A., Lyulyov, O., Pimonenko, T.: The impact of digital business on energy efficiency in EU Countries. Information **14**(9), 480 (2023)
7. Liu, L., Yang, K., Fujii, H., Liu, J.: Artificial intelligence and energy intensity in China's industrial sector: effect and transmission channel. Econ. Analy. Policy (2021)
8. Moghaddam, S.S.H., Dashtdar, M., Jafari, H.: AI applications in smart cities' energy systems automation. Repa Proceeding Series (2022)
9. Necula, S.-C.: Assessing the potential of artificial intelligence in advancing clean energy technologies in Europe: a systematic review. Energies (2023)
10. Koengkan, M., Fuinhas, J., Belucio, M.: The impact of battery-electric vehicles on energy consumption: a macroeconomic evidence from 29 european countries. World Electr. Vehicle J. **13**(2), 36 (2022)
11. Noorman, M., Apráez, B.E., Lavrijssen, S.: AI and energy justice. Energies **16**(5), 2110 (2023)
12. Akhter, M.N., Mekhilef, S., Mokhlis, H., Shah, N.M.: Review on forecasting of photovoltaic power generation based on machine learning and metaheuristic techniques. IET Renew. Power Gener. **13**, 1009–1023 (2019)
13. Das, U.K., et al.: Forecasting of photovoltaic power generation and model optimization: a review. Renew. Sustain. Energy Rev. **81**, 912–928 (2018)
14. Vargas, S.A., Esteves, G.R.T., Maçaira, P.M., Bastos, B.Q., Oliveira, F.L.C., Souza, R.C.: Wind power generation: a review and a research agenda. J. Clean. Prod. **218**, 850–870 (2019)
15. Karady, G.G., Holbert, K.E.: Electrical energy conversion and transport: an interactive computer-based approach. John Wiley & Sons, Hoboken, NJ, USA (2013)

16. Kumari, A., Gupta, R., Tanwar, S., Kumar, N.: Blockchain and AI amalgamation for energy cloud management: challenges, solutions, and future directions. J. Parallel Distributed Comput. **143**, 148–166 (2020)
17. Weron, R.: Modeling and Forecasting Electricity Loads and Prices: A Statistical Approach. John Wiley & Sons, Hoboken, NJ, USA (2007)
18. Yildiz, B., Bilbao, J.I., Sproul, A.B.: A review and analysis of regression and machine learning models on commercial building electricity load forecasting. Renew. Sustain. Energy Rev. **73**, 1104–1122 (2017)
19. Ntakolia, C., Anagnostis, A., Moustakidis, S., Karcanias, N.: Machine learning applied on the district heating and cooling sector: a review. Energy Syst. **13**, 1–30 (2022)
20. Wang, H., Zhang, N., Du, E., Yan, J., Han, S., Liu, Y.: A comprehensive review for wind, solar, and electrical load forecasting methods. Global Energy Interconnection **5**, 9–30 (2022)
21. Aslam, S., Herodotou, H., Mohsin, S.M., Javaid, N., Ashraf, N., Aslam, S.: A survey on deep learning methods for power load and renewable energy forecasting in smart microgrids. Renew. Sustain. Energy Rev. **144**, 110992 (2021)
22. García-Martín, E., Rodrigues, C.F., Riley, G., Grahn, H.: Estimation of energy consumption in machine learning. J. Parallel Distribut. Comput. **134**, 75–88 (2019)
23. Henderson, P., Hu, J., Romoff, J.: Towards the Systematic Reporting of the Energy and Carbon Footprints of Machine Learning. MICROTOME PUBL, BROOKLINE (2020)
24. Chen, Y.-H., Krishna, T., Emer, J.S., Sze, V.: Eyeriss: an energy-efficient reconfigurable accelerator for deep convolutional neural networks. IEEE J. Solid-State Circuits **52**, 127–138 (2017)
25. IEA Electricity 2024—Analysis and Forecast to 2026. https://www.iea.org/reports/electricity-2024
26. MarketWatch, https://www.marketwatch.com/story/nvidia-is-dominating-and-could-unlock-300-billion-in-ai-revenue-by-2027-analyst-says-915935c0
27. Thunder Said Energy, https://thundersaidenergy.com/2024/04/04/energy-and-ai-the-power-and-the-glory/
28. Saha, S., Sarkar, J., Dwivedi, A., Dwivedi, N., Narasimhamurthy, A.M., Roy, R.: A novel revenue optimization model to address the operation and maintenance cost of a data center. J. Cloud Comput. **5**(1), 1–23 (2016)
29. Watson, R.T., Boudreau, M.-C., Chen, A.J.: Information systems and environmentally sustainable development: energy informatics and new directions for the IS community. MIS Q. **34**(1), 23–38 (2010)
30. Elliot, S.: Transdisciplinary perspectives on environmental sustainability: a resource base and framework for IT-enabled business transformation. MIS Q. **35**(1), 197–236 (2011)
31. Patterson, D.A., Hennessy, J.L., Arvind, et al.: Data centres and AI energy consumption: addressing the environmental impact. In: Energy and AI Systems, pp. 23–45. Springer, Berlin (2021)
32. Schwartz, R., Dodge, J., Smith, N., Etzioni, O.: Green AI: towards the systematic reporting of the energy and carbon footprints of machine learning. Commun. ACM **63**(12), 54–63 (2020)
33. Roy, K., Jaiswal, A., Panda, P.: Towards spike-based neuromorphic computing: models, learning algorithms, and hardware implementations. Nature **575**(7784), 607–617 (2019)
34. Dedrick, J.: Green IS: concepts and issues for information systems research. Commun. Assoc. Inf. Syst. **27**, 11–18 (2010)
35. Precedence Research homepage. https://www.precedenceresearch.com/artificial-intelligence-market

The Productivity Paradox: Job Crafting in the Context of Generative Artificial Intelligence

Akanksha Malik Jamwal[1(✉)] and Swati Garg[2]

[1] Guildhall School of Business and Law, London Metropolitan University, London, UK
a.jamwal@londonmet.ac.uk
[2] Keele Business School, Keele University, Staffordshire, UK

Abstract. Gen AI, due its unique capability has restructured traditional work and presented different approaches to make work better. This paper seeks to examine how job crafting with Gen AI influences performance. When GenAI is used by employees to craft their jobs, it enhances their trust and reliance on the technology. This increased dependency may impact both individual and team performance, however this would be contingent on organisation's support of AI adoption and their overall commitment to values of the organisation.

Keywords: Artificial intelligence · Gen AI · Performance · Teams · Trust

1 Introduction

Generative artificial intelligence (GenAI) is a transformative technology in the workplace, with applications extending across multiple domains, including, marketing, customer service, design, and software development [1, 2]. At its core, GenAI uses machine learning algorithms, particularly deep learning models like generative adversarial networks and transformer-based models, to create content such as text, images, audio, and even code [3]. GenAI models, like GPT and DALL-E, leverage large datasets to produce human-like outputs, enabling organizations to improve both efficiency and quality of their work [4, 5]. GenAI based tools have revolutionized workflows, allowing employees to automate time-consuming tasks, generate innovative ideas, and streamline complex processes [6, 7]. Use of these tools have led to a significant modification of the job design, demands, required skill sets and boundaries of traditional work [8]. This trend has led to emerging discussions around the benefits of GenAI in workplaces and implications on how to manage it in the work environment [9].

One of the key benefits of GenAI is its ability to augment human creativity [10]. For instance, employees in marketing can utilize GenAI to generate campaign ideas, write content, or even design visuals based on specific brand guidelines. Similarly, in software development, generative AI models like GitHub's Copilot provide developers with code suggestions, significantly reducing time spent on routine coding tasks. By

S. Goel et al. (Eds.): AICON 2025, LNICST 672, pp. 150–158, 2026.
https://doi.org/10.1007/978-3-032-14805-6_10

automating repetitive or foundational tasks, GenAI allows employees to focus on more strategic and creative work, thereby enhancing productivity and fostering innovation within organizations.

GenAI's integration into the workplace has demonstrated tangible benefits in employee engagement and skill development [11]. With AI handling routine tasks, employees can engage in higher-level decision-making and creative problem-solving, resulting in greater job satisfaction and personal growth. Additionally, as organizations increasingly adopt GenAI tools, employees are developing new technical skills to effectively collaborate with these tools, enhancing their digital literacy and adaptability in a tech-driven world. For instance, professionals in data-intensive fields like finance or logistics can use AI-generated insights to make informed decisions faster, ultimately contributing to organizational agility and competitive advantage [12].

In the context of human resource management (HRM), industry leaders and researchers have emphasized that Gen AI is helping with numerous HRM functions including recruitment, training and development, and performance management [13]. It is being used for responding to new hires' queries, automating paperwork related to pay and benefits, conducting training needs analysis and developing customised programs as per the identified needs [14, 15]. While the potential opportunities for Gen AI's applicability in HRM functions and the benefits of Gen AI integration for HRM leaders and organisations is receiving much attention [16], opportunities for employees' use of Gen AI and the its potential impact on them is still emerging.

Existing studies have focused on the impact of AI adoption by organisations on employees' attitudes and behaviours. As such, there is an increasing focus on how organisational AI adoption will impact employees' work engagement [17, 18], professional identity [19], and trust in AI [20]. However, the adoption of GenAI presents a challenging transformational space characterised with several challenges, including the risk of over-reliance on GenAI created content and potential job displacement. As more organizations integrate GenAI into their workflows, the focus on ethical AI, transparency, and continuous skill alignment for employees becomes crucial.

In our study, we focus on the adoption or use of Gen AI by employees for job crafting. We propose that employees use Gen AI to craft their jobs and this job crafting using Gen AI will develop an increased reliance on Gen AI which will eventually impact their as well as their team's performance levels. We will use social cognitive theory and self-determination theory to explain the proposed differential impact of job crafting using GenAI on individual and contextual performance. The study would contribute to professionals working in all fields, and particularly those working in the areas of generative artificial intelligence, human resource management, labour laws, and as it would provide them insights for design of policies around GenAI use.

In the next section, we outline the foundation of the conceptual model by exploring literature on job crafting and examining how crafting through generative can influence performance, grounded in established theoretical frameworks.

2 Theoretical Model

2.1 Job Crafting – Meaning and Existing Research

From the past few decades, considerable importance has been placed on employees' proactive behaviour [21]. Several constructs have emerged during this time, focusing on the same underlying features: employees' self- started initiatives aimed at making changes for improving the future. Taking charge, personal initiative, job crafting, and feedback seeking are examples of such constructs [21]. In this research, we focus on job crafting, which represents employees' efforts to modify their jobs on their own. In the foundational paper published in Academy of Management Review journal, Wrzesniewski and Dutton [22] introduced job crafting to the world of academic research as "actions [that] employees take to shape, mould, and redefine their jobs (p. 180)." The authors also suggested that individuals make efforts to change their jobs by modifying or redefining tasks and relationships on their jobs and their thoughts about their jobs. Using job demands and resources theory, Tims and colleagues [23] defined job crafting as "the changes that employees may make to balance their job demands and job resources with their personal abilities and needs (p. 174)." As per their conceptualisation, job crafting represents employees' proactive efforts at modifying the level of resources and the level of demands on their jobs. Accordingly, employees may increase structural and social resources (for instance, social support, job autonomy and feedback on work) and challenging demands (for instance, challenging clients and projects), and may decrease hindering demands (for instance, time pressures and work overload) at their jobs.

The conceptualisation by Tims and colleagues [24] garnered a lot of attention, with several researchers using their scale to understand the drivers and consequences of job crafting at workplaces. Various meta-analyses and literature review studies have conceptualized job crafting and presented an operational definition as individuals' actions aimed at re-designing their jobs in order to improve the meaningfulness and fulfillment from their jobs [25, 26]. Job crafting is a self-started, future-focused behaviour aimed at making changes to one's job. These changes may include an increase in resources and a decrease in hindrances, with the purpose of navigating one's work requirements and progressing in career development.

Job crafting has been described as an effective way to respond to the inadequacies and complexity of contemporary jobs [27]. Employees who craft their jobs find their work meaningful, have positive work experiences and high person-organisation fit [28, 29], which in turns improves their efficiency, performance and satisfaction levels [23, 26]. Studies have also been undertaken to understand the individual predictors of job crafting, such as researchers [30] reported that proactive employees are predisposed to pursuing job crafting at their workplace. The employee's regulatory focus, whether they are driven by growth and challenges (promotion focus) or by security and obligations (prevention focus) would also influence the degree to which they craft their jobs [31]. However, evidence suggests that it's the interplay of personal and situational factors that would explain job crafting such that when employees perceive there is a misfit between their motivation or style and the environmental cues, they would engage in job crafting [26].

2.2 Job Crafting in the AI Context

Research on job crafting has evidenced that individuals are no longer dependent upon just the top-down processes of job redesign. Instead, they indulge in a bottom-up process of job redesign by actively modifying what they do at their work and how they do their work [22, 23]. Job crafting serves as an effective strategy to enhance the fitment of individuals with their jobs, especially now that jobs are continuously being transformed [32] such as crafting tasks and relationships on the job to adjust to generative AI adoption and usage in the workplaces [33]. Recent research proposes AI crafting, which are volitional acts to shape and redefine one's job to better adapt to the AI in workplace and effectively integrate AI into the work routines [34].

The evidence on job crafting in the context of AI gives insights into how AI accentuates crafting by employees and the possible outcomes of the same. Advancements in Gen AI can shape the way employees redefine and modify their jobs as it gives them the required tools to tailor their jobs to their strengths and interestsb [35]. Use of Gen AI helps them to automate repetitive tasks and focus on more meaningful work [9]. For example, employees could utilize AI tools like Claude AI, ChatGPT, Gemini and others to conduct data analysis, which would free their capacity (in terms of time, energy and other resources) to focus on more strategic and critical tasks. Likewise, employees can use AI to develop an in-depth understanding of their job role at their workplace, which may help them in appreciating their role's contribution to the organisational goals (task significance and task identity) and eventually bring more mindfulness in their actions and their decisions at their work [34]. AI could also facilitate preparation of better-quality outputs (presentations, strategy documents, minutes of meetings, etc.) that can help with improved communication and brainstorming sessions [36]. Research shows some evidence on how AI awareness can lead to feelings of anxiety [37]. The good news is that these feelings of anxiety can motivate employees to proactively modify or redesign their jobs, and that can help enhance their productivity [37].

Another study by He and colleagues [38] demonstrates that when leaders exhibit a welcoming attitude towards AI and show a sense of approval towards AI adoption, their attitude positively cascades down to other employees, who then get motivated to indulge in job crafting behaviours. Cheng and colleagues [39] explicate that when individuals perceive AI adoption by their organisation as a developmental demand or a challenge stressor, they are motivated to craft their jobs with a focus on gains and accomplishments, and when they view the same as a hindrance demand or as a hindrance stressor, they are motivated to craft their jobs with a focus on loss prevention. Important recent research introduced a new construct called 'AI crafting', which is defined as those self-initiated job modifications that are done by individuals to catch up with the adoption of AI happening in their workplaces [34]. The same research also shows that leaders' AI crafting cascades down to subordinates and they also get encouraged to pursue the same for their job roles, which leads to enhanced engagement and citizenship behaviours at the workplace. Overall, there is sufficient evidence indicating advent and adoption of AI motivating employees to pursue job crafting as it gives them the autonomy and a sense of ownership with what they do at work and how they do their work. In our paper, we propose that employees will craft their jobs using Gen AI and their frequent pursuit of job crafting using GenAI will have an impact on their performance.

Prolonged utilisation of Gen AI tools can result in employees being completely dependent upon AI, and that may have different consequences. Such kind of dependence can result in reduction in engagement, because people can perceive that use of AI has reduced their role in their job [40]. Deskilling could also be an outcome, especially if employees keep on relying on AI to do their work and overlook their own need to upskill themselves [41]. While using AI for most of their job tasks, employees may indulge in excessive job modifications or doing more than required on their jobs, which can eventually result in exhaustion/burnout or role conflict/ambiguity [40, 41]. This could also negatively affect their performance and their team dynamics at their workplace. For instance, Bansal et al. [42] describe that AI enables timely discussions, better communication amongst team members, and therefore it actually improves team dynamics and outcomes. They also suggest that if team members are engrossed in engagement with AI more than they are in engagement with each other, then the same AI use can lead to deteriotiration of team cohesion. People can start working from their own corners under such circumstances [43].

In this research, we suggest that job crafting using Gen AI would positively impact our reliance on Gen AI, such that individuals will have better trust on the outputs produced by Gen AI and would therefore show increased use of Gen AI for daily tasks. This reliance could impact the individual and team performance depending on how Gen AI tools and technology are embedded in the organisation and the attitude of the individuals towards the organisation (affective commitment towards organisation, identification with the organisation, etc.). Individual performance can be captured by using constructs such as in-role performance or improved self-efficacy of the individual, and contextual performance can be captured by using constructs such as team commitment, team cohesiveness [44], and an empowered team environment [45].

2.3 Theories Used

We base our initial discussions of the study on social cognitive theory (SCT) and self-determination theory (SDT). Social cognitive theory gives considerable importance to self-efficacy, as a key driver of employee motivation and performance at workplace [46, 47]. Self-efficacy is explained as "people's judgements of their capabilities to organize and execute courses of action required to attain designated types of performances" (46: 391). Researchers further explained that self-efficacy represents people's beliefs in their ability to gather the necessary resources and take suitable actions to fulfil their jobs' demands [48]. It is associated with crucial individual variables of self- regulation [49] and goal setting [50]. Therefore, it holds considerable significance as a construct which determines individuals' behaviour at their jobs. In our paper, we propose that when individuals pursue job crafting using AI, their self-efficacy in use of AI increases. Higher self-efficacy encourages frequent use, reinforcing trust in AI's capabilities and leading to greater reliance. Further, according to SCT, personal factors (such as attitudes and skills), and environmental factors (such as organisational culture) interact to influence behaviour. In an AI driven environment, employees' positive experience with generative AI and organisation's encouragement of Gen AI use as a job crafting tool can alter their attitude towards AI and shape their reliance.

According to SDT [51], individuals are driven by three basic needs: need for competence (need to feel mastery in one's occupation), need for autonomy (need to have control and freedom over one's life) and need for relatedness (need to feel connected with others in the workplace). These three needs drive individuals' behaviour and motivation in the workplace. These needs form the basis for intrinsic motivation and facilitate psychological empowerment of individuals [52]. The theory suggests that these needs could be enhanced or undermined based on whether the social conditions thwarts or supports the psychological needs [53]. If a reward or other external event, feedback or competition posed a danger to these basic needs, the individual begins to perceive an external locus of causality and undermine intrinsic motivation, however if an event or situation tend to enhance or support these needs, it prompts the use of internal perceived locus of causality and thus enhances intrinsic motivation of the individual [53]. When it comes to job crafting using AI, AI may help employees in fulfilling these three needs for them: by giving them more control over their tasks (autonomy), allowing them to utilize their skills (competence), and fostering positive connections with colleagues (relatedness). But, the sense of fulfillment of these needs may be a function of how AI is embedded in employees' workplace, such that if there is too much reliance on these systems, it may diminish employee's autonomy and the employees may avoid learning new skills or developing new ones. It can also lead to decrease in feelings of connectedness/relatedness, especially when AI starts doing more work than what was previously being done by way of being in groups and having social relationships at work. Therefore, it is essential to explore how Gen AI integration in the organisations may affect the fulfillment of these needs for employees and how this fulfilment of needs can affect employees' performance individually and in teams.

3 Work

This study is a developmental work that explores how job crafting using Gen AI can impact individual and team performance. The study aims to develop a conceptual model, which will subsequently be tested using a quantitative research approach. We hope to share a consolidated review of existing research on this topic along with our proosed empirical model in the conference and look forward to constructive feedback on our work.

References

1. Dwivedi, Y.K., et al.: So what if ChatGPT wrote it? Multi-disciplinary perspectives on opportunities, challenges and implications of generative conversational AI for research, practice and policy. Int. J. Inf. Manage. **71**, 102642 (2023)
2. Ooi, K.B., et al.: The potential of generative artificial intelligence across disciplines: perspectives and future directions. J. Comput. Informa. Syst., 1–32 (2023)
3. Banh, L., Strobel, G.: Generative artificial intelligence. Electron. Mark. **33**(1), 63 (2023)
4. Gambacorta, L., Qiu, H., Shan, S., Rees, D.M.: Generative AI and labour productivity: a field experiment on coding (No. 1208). Bank for International Settlements (Working paper, 1208) (2024)

5. Noy, S., Zhang, W.: Experimental evidence on the productivity effects of generative artificial intelligence. Science **381**(6654), 187–192 (2023)

6. Dell'Acqua, F., et al.: Navigating the jagged technological frontier: field experimental evidence of the effects of AI on knowledge worker productivity and quality. Harvard Business School Technology Operations Mgt. Unit Working Paper (24–013) (2023)

7. Ross, S.I., Martinez, F., Houde, S., Muller, M., Weisz, J.D.: The programmer's assistant: Conversational interaction with a large language model for software development. In: Proceedings of the 28th International Conference on Intelligent User Interfaces (IUI 2023), pp. 491–514. Association for Computing Machinery, New York (2023)

8. Tong, S., Jia, N., Luo, X., Fang, Z.: The Janus face of artificial intelligence feedback: deployment versus disclosure effects on employee performance. Strateg. Manag. J. **42**(9), 1600–1631 (2021)

9. Parker, S.K., Grote, G.: Automation, algorithms, and beyond: Why work design matters more than ever in a digital world. Appl. Psychol. **71**(4), 1171–1204 (2022)

10. Eapen, T., Finkenstadt, D.J., Folk, J., Venkataswamy, L.: How generative AI can augment human creativity. Harv. Bus. Rev. **101**(4), 56–64 (2023)

11. Cazzaniga, M., et al.: Gen- AI: Artificial intelligence and the future of work. International Monetary Fund (2024)

12. Sharma, R., Shishodia, A., Gunasekaran, A., Min, H., Munim, Z.H.: The role of artificial intelligence in supply chain management: mapping the territory. Int. J. Prod. Res. **60**(24), 7527–7550 (2022)

13. Ardichvili, A., Dirani, K., Jabarkhail, S., El Mansour, W., Aboulhosn, S.: Using generative AI in human resource development: an applied research study. Hum. Resour. Dev. Int. **27**(3), 388–409 (2024)

14. Sooraksa, N.: A Survey of Using Computational Intelligence (CI) and Artificial Intelligence (AI) in Human Resource (HR) Analytics. In: 7th International Conference on Engineering, Applied Sciences and Technology (ICEAST) (April 2021)

15. Yorks, L., Abel, A.L., Rotatori, D. Digitization, Artificial Intelligence, and HRD. In: Strategic Human Resource Development in Practice: Leveraging Talent for Sustained Performance in the Digital Age of AI. Springer (2021)

16. Budhwar, P., et al.: Human resource management in the age of generative artificial intelligence: perspectives and research directions on ChatGPT. Hum. Resour. Manag. J. **33**(3), 606–659 (2023)

17. Braganza, A., Chen, W., Canhoto, A., Sap, S.: Productive employment and decent work: the impact of AI adoption on psychological contracts, job engagement and employee trust. J. Bus. Res. **131**, 485–494 (2021)

18. Dutta, D., Mishra, S.K., Tyagi, D.: Augmented employee voice and employee engagement using artificial intelligence-enabled chatbots: a field study. Inter. J. Human Resource Manag. **34**(12), 2451–2480 (2023)

19. Strich, F., Mayer, A.S., Fiedler, M.: What do I do in a world of artificial intelligence? Investigating the impact of substitutive decision-making AI systems on employees' professional role identity. J. Assoc. Inf. Syst. **22**(2), 9 (2021)

20. Glikson, E., Woolley, A.W.: Human trust in artificial intelligence: review of empirical research. Acad. Manag. Ann. **14**(2), 627–660 (2020)

21. Parker, S.K., Collins, C.G.: Taking stock: Integrating and differentiating multiple proactive behaviors. J. Manag. **36**(3), 633–662 (2010)

22. Wrzesniewski, A., Dutton, J.E.: Crafting a job: revisioning employees as active crafters of their work. Acad. Manag. Rev. **26**(2), 179–201 (2001)

23. Tims, M., Bakker, A.B., Derks, D.: The impact of job crafting on job demands, job resources, and wellbeing. J. Occup. Health Psychol. **18**, 234–245 (2013)

24. Tims, M., Bakker, A.B., Derks, D.: Development and validation of the job crafting scale. J. Vocat. Behav. **80**(1), 173–186 (2012)
25. Bruning, P.F., Campion, M.A.: A role–resource approach–avoidance model of job crafting: a multimethod integration and extension of job crafting theory. Acad. Manag. J. **61**(2), 499–522 (2018)
26. Zhang, F., Parker, S.K.: Reorienting job crafting research: a hierarchical structure of job crafting concepts and integrative review. J. Organ. Behav. **40**(2), 126–146 (2019)
27. Demerouti, E.: Design your own job through job crafting. Eur. Psychol. **19**(4), 237–247 (2014)
28. Chen, C.Y., Yen, C.H., Tsai, F.C.: Job crafting and job engagement: the mediating role of person-job fit. Int. J. Hosp. Manag. **37**, 21–28 (2014)
29. Lu, C.Q., Wang, H.J., Lu, J.J., Du, D.Y., Bakker, A.B.: Does work engagement increase person–job fit? the role of job crafting and job insecurity. J. Vocat. Behav. **84**(2), 142–152 (2014)
30. Viet, P.Q., Tuan, T.A.: The impact of proactive personality on job performance through job crafting: the case of Vietcombank in Ho Chi Minh City. Bus. Econ. Res. **8**(3), 149–163 (2018)
31. Brenninkmeijer, V., Hekkert-Koning, M.: To craft or not to craft: the relationships between regulatory focus, job crafting and work outcomes. Career Dev. Int. **20**(2), 147–162 (2015)
32. Bindl, U.K., Parker, S.K.: New perspectives and directions for understanding proactivity in organizations. Proactivity at work, pp. 577–602 (2016).
33. Parker, S.K., Grote, G.: More than 'more than ever': revisiting a work design and sociotechnical perspective on digital technologies. Appl. Psychol. **71**(4), 1215–1223 (2022)
34. Li, W., et al.: Embracing artificial intelligence (AI) with job crafting: Exploring trickle-down effect and employees' outcomes. Tour. Manage. **104**, 104935 (2024)
35. Ayinde, L., Kirkwood, H.: Rethinking the roles and skills of information professionals in the 4th Industrial Revolution. Bus. Inf. Rev. **37**(4), 142–153 (2020)
36. Dhoni, P.: Unleashing the potential: overcoming hurdles and embracing generative AI in IT workplaces: advantages, guidelines, and policies. Authorea Preprints (2023)
37. Tan, T.K. Artificial intelligence and basic human needs: the shadow aspects of emerging technology. In: Ethics in Online AI-based Systems, pp. 259–278. Academic Press (2024)
38. He, G., Liu, P., Zheng, X., Zheng, L., Hewlin, P.F., Yuan, L.: Being proactive in the age of AI: exploring the effectiveness of leaders' AI symbolization in stimulating employee job crafting. Manag. Decis. **61**(10), 2896–2919 (2023)
39. Cheng, B., Lin, H., Kong, Y.: Challenge or hindrance? How and when organizational artificial intelligence adoption influences employee job crafting. J. Bus. Res. **164**, 113987 (2023)
40. Garcia, R., Thompson, L., Smith, A.: Strategies for mitigating AI-induced skill atrophy in professional environments. Harv. Bus. Rev. **101**(4), 98–107 (2023)
41. Ganuthula, V.R.R.: The Paradox of Augmentation: A Theoretical Model of AI-Induced Skill Atrophy. Available at SSRN 4974044 (2024)
42. Bansal, G., et al.: Does the whole exceed its parts? the effect of ai explanations on complementary team performance. In Proceedings of the 2021 CHI Conference on Human Factors in Computing Systems, pp. 1–16 (May 2021)
43. Zercher, D., Jussupow, E., Heinzl, A.: When AI joins the team: a literature review on intragroup processes and their effect on team performance in team-AI collaboration. ECIS 2023 Research Papers, 307 (2023)
44. Morgan, B.B., Jr., Lassiter, D.L.: Team composition and staffing. In: Swezey, R.W., Salas, E. (eds.) Teams: Their training and performance, pp. 75–100. Ablex Publishing (1992)
45. Jehn, K.A., Chatman, J.A.: The influence of proportional and perceptual conflict composition on team performance. Int. J. Confl. Manag. **11**(1), 56–73 (2000)
46. Bandura, A.: Social foundations of thought and action, vol. 2, pp. 23–28. Englewood Cliffs, NJ (1986)

47. Saks, A.M.: Longitudinal field investigation of the moderating and mediating effects of self-efficacy on the relationship between training and newcomer adjustment. J. Appl. Psychol. **80**(2), 211–225 (1995)
48. Wood, R., Bandura, A.: Social cognitive theory of organizational management. Acad. Manag. Rev. **14**(3), 361–384 (1989)
49. Kanfer, R.: Motivation theory and industrial and organizational psychology. In: Dunnette, M.D., Hough, L.M. (eds.) Handbook of industrial and organizational psychology, pp. 75–170. Consulting Psychologists Press, Palo Alto, CA (1991)
50. Locke, E.A., Latham, G.P.: Work motivation and satisfaction: light at the end of the tunnel. Psychol. Sci. **1**(4), 240–246 (1990)
51. Deci, E.L., Ryan, R.M.: Self-determination theory. Handbook Theories Of Soc. Psychol. **1**(20), 416–436 (2012)
52. Gagné, M., Deci, E.L.: Self-determination theory and work motivation. J. Organ. Behav. **26**(4), 331–362 (2005)
53. Deci, E.L., Olafsen, A.H., Ryan, R.M.: Self-determination theory in work organizations: the state of a science. Annu. Rev. Organ. Psych. Organ. Behav. **4**(1), 19–43 (2017)

The Role of Generative AI in Supporting Neurodiverse Individuals: Literature Insights and Future Directions

Srishti Gupta[✉] and Sanjay Goel

Massry School of Business, University at Albany, SUNY, Albany, NY, USA
{sgupta4,goel}@albany.edu

Abstract. Neurodiversity emphasizes the natural variation in human cognition, celebrating the unique strengths and perspectives that neurodiverse individuals bring to society. This paper explores the role of artificial intelligence (AI) in supporting neurodiverse individuals, focusing on both traditional and generative AI systems. Current trends reveal two primary applications: (1) detecting, diagnosing, and treating neurodiverse conditions and (2) enhancing cognitive abilities and promoting wellbeing. The shift from a medical model to a social and ecological model underscores the need for inclusive and strengths-based AI systems that empower neurodiverse individuals across various domains, such as education, employment, and social interaction. By identifying design requirements—including customizability, ethical considerations, and responsible design practices—this paper highlights how generative AI can address current gaps and expand opportunities for neurodiverse populations. Future research should prioritize participatory design, inclusive datasets, and applications that holistically support neurodiverse individuals in achieving their potential.

Keywords: Neurodiversity · Generative AI · Inclusive Design

1 Introduction

There are over 13 million adults in the United States with an autism spectrum disorder (ASD) or attention-deficit/hyperactivity disorder (ADHD); this includes approximately 1-2 Neurodiversity refers to the natural variation in human cognition and behavior. Rather than viewing neurological differences as deficits, the concept of neurodiversity emphasizes the unique strengths and perspectives that individuals with different neurological wiring bring to society. Neurotypical, on the other hand, describes individuals whose neurological development and functioning fall within the dominant societal standards [6]. Some common neurodiverse conditions include attention-deficit/hyperactivity disorder (ADHD), autism spectrum disorder (ASD), dyslexia, down syndrome, and cerebral palsy. While neurodiverse individuals face certain challenges in conventional social and learning environments, they also possess unique strengths, such

S. Goel et al. (Eds.): AICON 2025, LNICST 672, pp. 159–170, 2026.
https://doi.org/10.1007/978-3-032-14805-6_11

as, hyperfocus, creativity, pattern recognition, visual-spatial skills, attention to detail, and innovative thinking [14]. There is a growing movement to recognize neurodiversity not as a series of disabilities, but as a spectrum of cognitive differences. By embracing neurodiversity and tapping into the resource pool of neurodivergent workforce, organizations can leverage the strengths and perspectives of these employees to improve creativity and performance of the organization. This shift necessitates understanding and accommodation rather than treatment and normalization. Recognizing and valuing neurodiversity is not just an ethical imperative, but a strategic advantage. By embracing the unique cognitive processes of neurodivergent individuals, society can benefit from their contributions in various fields, including education, technology, and the workplace [11].

Although the term neurodiversity encompasses a range of cognitive and intellectual disabilities, much of the research in information and computational sciences focuses heavily on Autism Spectrum Disorder (ASD) and, to a lesser extent, Attention-Deficit/Hyperactivity Disorder (ADHD). Autism Spectrum Disorder is the most frequently discussed neurodiverse condition. Many studies examine the characteristics of ASD, prevalence rates, and strategies for supporting individuals with ASD, including the application of AI [2,12,16,18,19,22]. ADHD is the second most frequently explored neurodiverse condition in this context [9,11,17]. Some studies address the challenges faced by individuals with ADHD, while others investigate AI-based interventions to support them. Dyslexia is also mentioned in several studies, which discuss it as a neuro- diverse condition with unique strengths and challenges. These studies explore potential AI applications designed to assist individuals with dyslexia.

Other neurodiverse conditions, such as Tourette's Syndrome, Down Syndrome, Cerebral Palsy, Epilepsy, Bipolar Disorder, Dyspraxia, Depression, and Alzheimer's Disease, are either briefly mentioned or absent in the recent literature reviewed. However, when specifically searching for these disabilities, some research does emerge, though much of it adopts a medical model perspective. This means the focus is often on detection, diagnosis, and treatment rather than broader applications, such as leveraging AI for support [4,13,20].

Advances in generative AI provide a tremendous opportunity to support learning of neurodiverse students who often struggle to keep up with other students in the class. The goal is not to separate these students but to equip them, so they are able to compensate for their shortcomings and are able to keep up with the class curriculum. Neurodiverse students can leverage AI tools such as text-to-speech for efficient notetaking, those with speech and communication difficulties can utilize AI tools to express themselves effectively and participate in classroom discussions when they wouldn't have been able to in the past. AI can also be used to create personalized curricular content catering to different learning needs for instance text-to-speech and speech recognition tools can break down barriers for students with dyslexia or auditory processing issues. Similarly, lesson plans can incorporate visual aids like charts, diagrams, icons, and color coding to present information in a clear, structured way, breaking down complex concepts into manageable chunks, and allowing for easy navigation and comprehension, for neurodiverse students who often struggle with traditional text-based learning methods.

There remains a significant gap in AI and technology research for these conditions. This disparity may stem from differences in the diagnostic processes and inherent nature of these disabilities compared to ASD and ADHD. Addressing this gap represents an important opportunity for future research. The current research on AI design for neurodiversity can be broadly categorized into two main areas: (1) the use of AI to detect, diagnose, and treat neurodiverse individuals, and (2) the use of AI to enhance cognitive abilities and promote the wellbeing of neurodiverse individuals in various social contexts.

Several studies focus on leveraging AI to identify and diagnose neurodiversity, particularly in conditions such as Autism Spectrum Disorder (ASD) and Attention Deficit Hyperactivity Disorder (ADHD). AI and deep learning techniques are advancing the detection and diagnosis of neurodiverse conditions, particularly Autism Spectrum Disorder (ASD) and Attention Deficit Hyperactivity Disorder (ADHD). For ASD, [16] demonstrated how AI can analyze behavioral features from video data to detect the condition, offering a faster diagnostic process without compromising accuracy. Researchers have also explored AI-powered tools like Robot Intelligent Modules (RIM) and Behavior Manager (BM) to assist in autism treatment. [1] highlight the use of federated learning, combined with classifiers such as logistic regression and support vector machines, to analyze data from children and adults for detecting autistic traits. Deep learning techniques, including facial image analysis, are being applied for ASD detection, with studies using computer vision to estimate engagement intensity in children with ASD. For ADHD, [9] explored the use of deep learning, particularly Convolutional Neural Networks (CNNs), to improve the accuracy and reliability of ADHD screening and diagnosis in children. Their work reviewed various deep learning models, such as those analyzing EEG data and employing computer vision tech- niques, showcasing the ability of these technologies to process large datasets and extract implicit patterns critical for diagnosis.

The second major area of research focuses on utilizing AI to support and enhance the cognitive abilities and wellbeing of neurodiverse individuals. Research has increasingly focused on leveraging AI and emerging technologies to enhance the cognitive abilities, communication skills, and social interactions of neurodiverse individuals. The Neurodiversity Reciprocating Wellbeing Artificial Intelligence (NRWAI) framework, proposed by [6], aims to enhance cognitive functioning and wellbeing through personalized AI-driven learning experiences and support systems tailored to the unique needs of neurodiverse individuals. Additionally, [22] highlight the potential of AI to reduce cognitive load during social interactions, addressing a key challenge for many neurodiverse individuals. AI is also being used to create virtual environments where neurodiverse individuals can practice essential social skills, such as communication and interaction, as discussed by [19]. An example is the "emotion translator" prototype described by [22], which helps users understand and express emotions during conversations. These advancements illustrate the broader applications of AI in enhancing communication skills and self-regulation for neurodiverse populations. Emerging technologies such as voice assistants, wearables, and virtual reality further contribute to supporting neurodiverse users in areas like executive functioning, communication, and interpersonal skills. [14] emphasize the importance of involving neurodiverse users in the design process to create inclusive and effective solutions.

Our focus in this research is on the second area of research i.e., support and enhance cognitive abilities and well-being of neurodiverse individuals especially towards the goal of integrating them in society seamlessly by compensating for any lack of abilities. The rest of the paper discusses the extant literature on the topic as well as future directions of research.

2   Shift from Medical Model to Social Wellbeing

The two topics—AI for Detecting, Treating, and Diagnosing Neurodiverse Individuals and AI for Enhancing Cognitive Abilities and Wellbeing—can be discussed in light of [8], which contrasts the traditional medical model of dis-ability with the social and ecological model. The medical model views disability as a pathology with the goal of curing or normalizing individuals to resemble typically developing peers. AI research aligned with this model often focuses on detecting autism through behavioral and biological markers tied to diagnostic criteria. These models emphasize identifying and categorizing atypical traits. However, the medical model perspective often fails to recognize the societal barriers that contribute to disability and can overlook the strengths and unique perspectives of neurodivergent individuals. This has led to a growing shift in re-search in recognizing that disability is a complex phenomenon arising from the interaction between an individual's characteristics and the environment in which they live. Hence, interventions should be tailored to individual needs and preferences, addressing both individual challenges and environmental barriers. This perspective promotes the development of AI-driven solutions that are inclusive, celebrate neurodiverse strengths, and create environments where individuals can thrive [10,11]. This shift in focus has led to innovations in AI design and development to support neurodiverse individuals in a variety of contexts such as education, interpersonal communication, and social wellbeing.

2.1   AI for Cognitive Enhancement and Wellbeing

AI-driven technologies have significantly improved cognitive accessibility for neurodiverse individuals, serving as gateways to new modes of interaction and understanding. These tools enhance cognitive abilities and promote well-being by providing personalized learning experiences tailored to individual needs and learning styles. AI-powered assistive technologies also play a crucial role in supporting various aspects of daily living, including sensory processing and emotional regulation. By offering individualized support, these tools enhance the quality of life and overall well-being of individuals with cognitive disabilities [7].

The adaptability of AI enables personalized learning, adaptive feedback, and context-aware interactions, which address the unique challenges faced by neurodiverse learners. Such capabilities can lead to improved learning outcomes and a deeper sense of well-being, helping individuals thrive in educational and everyday contexts [6]. Through its ability to tailor support to diverse needs, AI continues to transform opportunities for cognitive accessibility and empowerment among neurodiverse populations.

2.2 AI for Communication and Social Skills

AI has significant potential to create environments that foster communication and social interaction among neurodiverse individuals. For example, [15] highlights the effectiveness of the ECHOES project, which used AI-powered tools to motivate social interaction and communication in autistic children who might otherwise struggle with these skills. The project underscores the importance of blending AI and human support to create a comprehensive and adaptable learning environment. The presence of a human practitioner provided individualized support and intervention, addressing each child's specific needs and enhancing the overall effectiveness of the AI tools.

Similarly, conversational agents have been employed to help children with Autism Spectrum Disorder (ASD) develop emotional and social skills [18]. These agents act as personal assistants, narrate social stories, and facilitate communication. Generative AI, which leverages deep learning to create content, shows great promise in personalizing and adapting emotional learning experiences, particularly for children with high-functioning autism. Beyond serving as personal assistants, AI tools for communication and social support must move beyond mere detection and labeling of emotions. Instead, they should facilitate the co-construction of emotional understanding between autistic and neurotypical conversation partners.

For instance, [22] explored the use of AI-driven virtual environments where neurodiverse individuals could practice essential social skills like communication and interaction. One innovation was the development of an "emotion translator," designed to encourage active interpretation, negotiation, and shared meaning making regarding emotions. This approach fosters a more collaborative and dynamic communication process, emphasizing mutual understanding rather than one-sided adaptation. By integrating these tools into interactive environments, AI can play a transformative role in enhancing social and emotional learning for neurodiverse individuals.

2.3 AI for Education and Employment

AI has significant potential to advance education and employment opportunities for neurodiverse individuals by addressing their unique challenges and leveraging their strengths. In education, wearable technology, such as smartwatches, can monitor student activity and provide real-time interventions to support learning. These devices can collect sensor data to train activity recognition models capable of identifying and differentiating between activities like reading, writing, or being off-task. For example, if the smartwatch detects prolonged inactivity, it could issue a gentle reminder to reengage with the task, helping neurodiverse students maintain focus and improve their learning outcomes. The development of such tools requires inclusivity and careful consideration of diverse student populations, ensuring that AI systems are free from biases and designed to meet a wide range of needs [21].

In the realm of employment, AI-powered tools can address barriers faced by neurodiverse individuals in job searching and workplace integration. These tools can assist with tasks such as resume writing, interview preparation, and skill development, while also fostering more inclusive work environments. For instance, AI-driven job matching systems can pair neurodiverse job seekers with employers who value their specific skills and are prepared to offer necessary accommodations. Similarly, AI can analyze job descriptions to identify key skills and requirements, tailoring resumes and cover letters to better align with specific opportunities. Virtual interview coaches provide another avenue of support, offering feedback on communication style, eye contact, and body language to help neurodiverse individuals build confidence. AI can also support neurodiverse employees in managing their emotions and sensory sensitivities, which are often critical challenges in workplace settings. Tools designed to identify triggers and develop coping strategies can help individuals navigate sensory overload and social interactions effectively [2, 5].

3   Design Requirements for AI for Neurodiversity

The existing literature identifies several critical design requirements for AI systems aimed at supporting neurodiverse individuals. These requirements emphasize the need for personalization, inclusivity, and ethical considerations to ensure technology effectively meets the unique needs of this population. These design requirements have been summarized in Table 1.

3.1   Customizability: Tailoring AI Systems to Individual Needs

Customizability is a cornerstone of effective AI design for neurodiverse populations, recognizing that a one-size-fits-all approach is inherently inadequate. AI-powered tools for learning and communication can offer personalized experiences that adapt to individual cognitive patterns, sensory sensitivities, and learning styles. For example, AI applications designed for learners with ADHD can adjust the pace and delivery of educational content based on the learner's attention span and engagement level. These tools might provide multiple modalities, such as visual or auditory options, to align with individual preferences and enhance comprehension [7].

In social communication, AI-driven technologies have shown promise in creating tailored interventions. The ECHOES project, for instance, utilized an AI-powered virtual agent named Andy to support neurodiverse children in developing social and communication skills. By adapting to the child's actions and

Table 1. Design Requirements for AI in Neurodiversity

Category	Requirement
Customizability	Personalized tools that adapt to cognitive patterns, learning styles, and sensory preferences. Customizable interfaces for sensory needs, such as brightness and sound adjustments. Adaptive social tools, like emotion translators and tailored learning experiences.
Strengths-Based Approaches	Emphasize individual strengths in education and employment. Support job-seeking with collaborative tools and job simulations.
Ethical Considerations	Train AI on diverse datasets to mitigate biases. Ensure equitable access and culturally inclusive design. Maintain transparency in decision-making processes.

providing individualized support, Andy created a more engaging and effective learning environment. Similarly, EmoEden, an AI tool powered by large language models (LLMs), personalizes emotional learning for children with High Functioning Autism (HFA) by generating tailored visual and textual content. This individualized approach helps children better understand emotions in ways that resonate with their abilities and preferences [15, 18].

Customizability also extends to tools that bridge emotional understanding. For example, a prototype featuring a customizable matrix of emotion pictograms allowed autistic adults to create personalized emotion taxonomies. These tools help address challenges in interpreting and expressing emotions, fostering more meaningful social interactions [22].

3.2 Strengths-Based Approaches: Focusing on Abilities, Not Deficits

A strengths-based approach shifts the focus from compensating for perceived deficits to leveraging the unique abilities of neurodiverse individuals. In education, AI-powered tools can identify and highlight students' strengths, offering personalized learning plans that emphasize areas of excellence. For instance, if a learner exhibits exceptional problem-solving skills, the AI could design tasks that build on this ability, fostering confidence and motivation.

In employment, AI can similarly support strengths-based practices by helping employers identify and capitalize on neurodiverse candidates' unique talents. For example, AI systems can analyze resumes and work histories to detect patterns of success, helping match candidates with roles that suit their abilities. Job simulations powered by AI can allow candidates to demonstrate their skills in real-world contexts, offering both employers and candidates a clearer understanding of fit [11].

Collaborative job-seeking platforms present another opportunity for strength- based approaches. These systems can facilitate communication and preparation by enabling neurodiverse individuals to collaborate with family members, mentors, and experts. Features such as socially supported communication tools can help users refine emails to potential employers, ensuring appropriate tone and structure. Similarly, mock interview simulations with AI can provide constructive feedback, helping neurodiverse individuals develop their skills in a supportive environment [2].

3.3 Ethical Considerations: Ensuring Fairness, Inclusivity, and Transparency

Ethical considerations are paramount in designing AI systems for neurodiverse individuals, given the potential for algorithmic bias and unequal access to technology. AI algorithms often learn from datasets that may not fully represent the diverse range of cognitive abilities and experiences, risking the perpetuation of existing biases. For example, an AI tool developed to assist dyslexic students might be less effective if trained predominantly on data from neurotypical learners, potentially misinterpreting their needs or providing suboptimal support [7]. To mitigate such risks, diversity in training data is critical. Including inputs that reflect the lived experiences of neurodiverse individuals ensures that AI systems can address a broader spectrum of needs. Counterfactual data augmentation, which involves simulating alternative viewpoints and scenarios, can help AI systems develop a more nuanced understanding of neurodiverse conditions, reducing oversimplifications and biases [11].

Equitable access to AI-powered tools is another essential ethical consideration. Without targeted efforts, the digital divide could deepen, leaving socioeconomically disadvantaged neurodiverse learners behind. Addressing this requires not only the provision of technology but also robust training for educators and comprehensive support systems for learners. Designing culturally sensitive and inclusive tools is equally important to ensure that all students, regardless of background, can benefit from AI-enhanced learning.

Transparency is also crucial for building trust and fostering informed use of AI tools. Neurodiverse users, as well as educators and employers, should have a clear understanding of how AI systems operate, their limitations, and any potential biases. Educating users about AI interactions prepares them to navigate the digital world more effectively and empowers them as informed participants [7].

3.4 Responsible and Inclusive Design Practices

Responsible design and implementation are essential to ensuring that AI systems for neurodiversity truly meet the needs of their users. User-centered design (UCD) principles advocate for the active involvement of neurodiverse individuals throughout the design process, from conceptualization to evaluation. Frameworks like the Diversity for Design (D4D) approach encourage participatory methods that adapt to users' needs, leveraging strengths while minimizing potential difficulties [3].

Sensitivity to neurodiversity in design requires continuous learning and adaptation. Developers must prioritize creating interfaces that accommodate sensory sensitivities, such as reducing visual clutter or offering multiple interaction modes (e.g., text and voice). Additionally, AI tools should complement, rather than replace, human expertise, particularly in areas like diagnostics, where the nuanced judgment of a professional is indispensable [15].

4 Future Research Opportunities Identified for Generative AI in Neurodiversity

Generative AI presents unique opportunities to transform how technology supports neurodiverse individuals. Unlike traditional AI systems, generative AI can adapt dynamically to individual needs, addressing gaps in therapeutic, educational, and daily living support.

One promising area is **personalized learning**. Generative AI can create tailored educational tools that adapt to individual cognitive strengths and weaknesses. Frameworks like the Neurodiversity Reciprocating Wellbeing Artificial Intelligence (NRWAI) demonstrate how personalized feedback and rewards can enhance engagement and learning outcomes [6]. Similarly, **adaptive communication** tools, such as emotion translators can help neurodiverse individuals navigate social interactions by facilitating mutual understanding [22]. We need to be able to create customized learning plans for neurodiverse students that best match the cognitive abilities of neurodiverse individuals. Currently, the lesson plans for such individuals are done manually that can overwhelm caregivers and teachers. Generative AI can help create initial custom learning plans for individuals more efficiently, providing support to caregivers and educators.

Another area where AI technologies can enhance the quality of life on neurodiverse individuals is by providing them compensating technologies for their disability. For instance, providing real speech to text convertors for hearing impaired, visual to audio summarization for visually impaired, and text to speech conversion for speech impaired individuals. Using these tools in real-time can enable such individuals to normalize themselves in the society and become more self-reliant. This will reduce both the burden of caregivers as well as contributing to societal productivity through participation in jobs requiring higher levels of cognitive skills.

Generative AI also offers potential for **just-in-time therapeutic interventions**, addressing challenges that traditional therapies cannot. Smartwatches and other wear- able devices powered by AI can provide real-time emotional and behavioral support, helping individuals manage transitions and navigate complex tasks [18]. Additionally, AI-driven job-matching systems could revolutionize employment opportunities by aligning neurodiverse skills with workplace needs, promoting inclusivity and reducing barriers. Generative AI enables a shift from deficit-based models to **strengths-based paradigms**. By focusing on unique neurodiverse abilities, generative AI can challenge stereotypes, foster inclusivity, and empower individuals to thrive in diverse social contexts [11]. These opportunities highlight the transformative potential of generative AI to enhance neurodiverse lives.

Designing generative AI for neurodiverse individuals requires a holistic approach that embraces diversity and prioritizes inclusion. This entails moving beyond existing adaptations to create systems that recognize neurodiversity as a valuable form of human variation. A critical consideration is the **prioritization of participatory design**, where neurodivergent individuals are actively involved throughout the development process [2]. Shifting from "design for" to "design with" ensures that systems reflect lived experiences and diverse perspectives. Overcoming scalability challenges in participatory design requires innovative recruitment strategies, combining online and offline methods, and leveraging advanced tools like natural language processing to analyze large datasets. Equally important is the creation of inclusive datasets. These datasets should capture the full spectrum of neurodiverse experiences, ensuring representation across demographics, disabilities, and cultural contexts [22]. Open-sourcing anonymized data can accelerate collaboration and reduce biases in AI systems. Generative AI must also account for **intersectionality**, addressing the unique challenges faced by individuals with multiple marginalized identities. Finally, generative AI should expand into domains beyond education and employment, such as **mental health, financial management, and social activities**. By providing tools for emotional regulation, personalized budgeting, and accessible navigation, generative AI can holistically support neurodiverse individuals. These considerations will ensure that generative AI is not only assistive but also empowering, enabling individuals to lead fulfilling and independent lives.

5 Conclusion

Artificial intelligence has the potential to transform the lives of neurodiverse individuals by addressing their unique challenges and leveraging their strengths. From enhancing cognitive abilities and communication skills to supporting education and employment, AI-driven solutions are shifting from a medical model to a strengths based and socially inclusive paradigm. Generative AI, in particular, offers unprecedented opportunities for personalized, real-time support, enabling neurodiverse individuals to thrive in diverse contexts. To achieve this vision, the design and development of AI must prioritize customizability, inclusivity, and ethical considerations. Incorporating neurodiverse perspectives through participatory design, creating representative datasets, and addressing biases are essential to building systems that reflect the diversity of human experiences. Future research must continue exploring innovative applications of generative AI, expanding its reach into areas like mental health, financial management, and social activities. By fostering a collaborative and inclusive approach, AI can become not just a tool for assistance but a catalyst for empowerment, enabling neurodiverse individuals to contribute meaningfully and achieve independence in all facets of life. This holistic perspective positions AI as a transformative force in realizing the full potential of neurodiversity.

References

1. Anjum, J., Hia, N.A., Waziha, A., Kalpoma, K.A.: Deep learning-based feature extraction from children's facial images for autism spectrum disorder detection. In: Proceedings of the Cognitive Models and Artificial Intelligence Conference, pp. 155–159 (2024)
2. Ara, Z., et al.: Collaborative job seeking for people with autism: challenges and design opportunities. In: Proceedings of the CHI Conference on Human Factors in Computing Systems, pp. 1–17 (2024)
3. Benton, L., Vasalou, A., Khaled, R., Johnson, H., Gooch, D.: Diversity for design: a framework for involving neurodiverse children in the technology design process. In: Proceedings of the SIGCHI conference on Human Factors in Computing Systems, pp. 3747–3756 (2014)
4. Brügge, N.S., et al.: Towards privacy and utility in tourette TIC detection through pretraining based on publicly available video data of healthy subjects. In: 2023 IEEE International Conference on Acoustics, Speech and Signal Processing (ICASSP), ICASSP, pp. 1–5. IEEE (2023)
5. Burton, L., Carss, V., Twumasi, R.: Listening to neurodiverse voices in the workplace. Ought J. Autistic Cult. **3**(2), 11 (2022)
6. Chen, E., Meng, J., Dogan, S.: Towards a framework of AI-driven solution for neurodiverse learning: cognition, technologies and wellbeing. Technol. Wellbeing
7. Deetjen-Ruiz, R., Daniel, M.P., Telus, J., Deetjen, L.: Advancing cognitive accessibility: the role of artificial intelligence in enhancing inclusivity. PriMera Sci. Eng. **4**(2), 58 (2024)
8. Dwyer, P.: The neurodiversity approach: what are they and what do they mean for researchers? Hum. Dev. **66**(2), 73–92 (2022)
9. Gao, R., Deng, K., Xie, M.: Deep learning-assisted ADHD diagnosis. In: Proceedings of the 3rd International Symposium on Artificial Intelligence for Medicine Sciences, pp. 142–147 (2022)
10. Hall, K., Arora, P., Lowy, R., Kim, J.G.: Designing for strengths: opportunities to support neurodiversity in the workplace. In: Proceedings of the CHI Conference on Human Factors in Computing Systems, pp. 1–14 (2024)
11. Hutson, P.: Embracing the irreplaceable: the role of neurodiversity in cultivating human-AI symbiosis in education. Int. J. Emerg. Disruptive Innov. Educ. VISIONARIUM **2**(1), 5 (2024)
12. Li, J., et al.: MMASD: a multimodal dataset for autism intervention analysis. In: Proceedings of the 25th International Conference on Multimodal Interaction, pp. 397–405 (2023)
13. Malé, J., Fortea, J., Aranha, M.R., Heuzé, Y., Martínez-Abadías, N., Sevil- lano, X.: Towards the discovery of down syndrome brain biomarkers using generative models. arXiv preprint arXiv:2409.13437 (2024)
14. Motti, V.G.: Designing emerging technologies for and with neurodiverse users. In: Proceedings of the 37th ACM International Conference on the Design of Communication, pp. 1–10 (2019)
15. Porayska-Pomsta, K., et al.: Blending human and artificial intelligence to support autistic children's social communication skills. ACM Trans Comput. Hum. Interact. (TOCHI) **25**(6), 1–35 (2018)
16. Shelke, N.A., Rao, S., Verma, A.K., Kasana, S.S.: Autism spectrum disorder detection using AI and IoT. In: Proceedings of the 2022 Fourteenth International Conference on Contemporary Computing, pp. 213–219 (2022)

17. Tamdjidi, R., et al.: Chatgpt as an assistive technology to enhance reading comprehension for individuals with ADHD (2023)
18. Tang, Y., et al.: EmoEden: applying generative artificial intelligence to emotional learning for children with high-function autism. In: Proceedings of the CHI Conference on Human Factors in Computing Systems, pp. 1–20 (2024)
19. Wang, J., Hu, M.: The application of artificial intelligence in the recognition, diagnosis, and treatment of autism. In: Proceedings of the 2023 4th International Symposium on Artificial Intelligence for Medicine Science, pp. 882–886 (2023)
20. Yang, J., Por, L.Y., Leong, M.C., Ku, C.S.: The potential of chatgpt in assisting children with down syndrome. Ann. Biomed. Eng. **51**(12), 2638–2640 (2023)
21. Zheng, H., Mahapasuthanon, P., Chen, Y., Rangwala, H., Evmenova, A.S., Genaro Motti, V.: WLA4ND: a wearable dataset of learning activities for young adults with neurodiversity to provide support in education. In: Proceedings of the 23rd International ACM SIGACCESS Conference on Computers and Accessibility, pp. 1–15 (2021)
22. Zolyomi, A., Snyder, J.: An emotion translator: speculative design by neurodiverse dyads. In: Proceedings of the CHI Conference on Human Factors in Computing Systems, pp. 1–18 (2024)

AI Behavior and Society

Exploring the Potential of Voice Interaction for Gamified Education in Children with ADHD

Rithvik Hariprasad[1] , Aryamann Anand[2] , and T. M. Navamani[1]([✉])

[1] School of Computer Science and Engineering, Vellore Institute of Technology, Vellore, India
`navamani.tm@vit.ac.in`
[2] Department of Computer Science and Engineering, Amity University, Noida, India

Abstract. Human-Computer Interaction (HCI) presents opportunities for creating intuitive and user-focused learning tools, especially for children with Attention Deficit Hyperactivity Disorder (ADHD). Concentration and hyperactivity are the hallmarks of ADHD, which makes it challenging for the individual to complete basic tasks such as reading. A promising approach is a method of gamification for learning that utilizes speech-based voice inputs for control. This study provides a novel approach towards the harmonious use of HCI principles and Natural Language Processing (NLP) for integrating features such as user-speech inputs, audio cues, and speech-to-text conversion using Mel-Frequency Cepstral Coefficients along with keyboard-based input mechanisms and captivating visuals for retaining user attention. Implementing inputs through speech removes the need for equipment such as a mouse, keyboard, controller, etc. This eliminates the need for additional purchases of such devices, thereby reducing overall costs and making a learning platform free of cost. This study explores the potential of HCI and NLP for creating practical learning tools.

Keywords: Human-computer interaction · Signal processing · Natural language processing · education · speech-to-text conversion · attention deficit hyperactivity disorders

1 Introduction

Human-Computer Interaction (HCI) enhances user accessibility to different tools and platforms. HCI principles guide software developers on how to cater to the user's needs. It is required to improve the performance and usability of the interface, which can be accomplished through visualization methods and design principles [1]. Although gamification of learning is an excellent method for engaging users with learning disabilities, it is only effective when the cognitive load on the user is kept to a minimum [2]. The study by Shaban et al. [2] provides promising techniques to address these challenges. The authors suggest a practical design to decrease cognitive load while at the same time maintaining engagement throughout the activity. This can be done by enabling the users to learn at their own pace, using audio cues to signal that the answer is correct or incorrect, and maintaining minimalistic yet aesthetic design choices to avoid visual overload.

S. Goel et al. (Eds.): AICON 2025, LNICST 672, pp. 173–181, 2026.
https://doi.org/10.1007/978-3-032-14805-6_12

Attention Deficit-Hyperactivity Disorder (ADHD) causes excessive levels of inattention and hyperactivity [3]. The symptoms appear during early childhood and persist throughout the lifespan of the individuals. Learning in children with ADHD is heavily affected during the early years. A study by Fleming et al. [4] depicted that children with ADHD struggled in terms of education as well as health, even when receiving medication. Therefore, there is a need for gamification of the learning process for children with ADHD, which is more enjoyable and effective compared to traditional teaching methods [5]. As Putra et al. [5] discussed, design, player, and content must be considered when developing the learning platform.

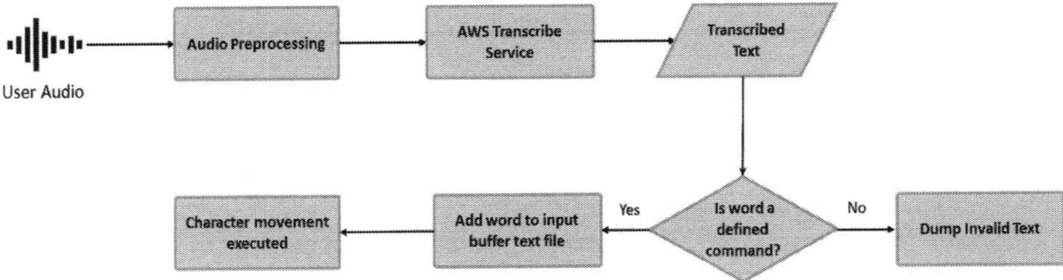

Fig. 1. Flowchart representing the speech to input validation process

Gamification is an effective method for various purposes beyond entertainment. The process of gamification is widely used in the field of rehabilitation [6]. In a study by Nath et al. [7], the authors devised virtual reality-based tasks for post-stroke-based rehabilitation. In another study [8], authors have developed a method of increasing users' inclusivity by implementing voice-based inputs. Numerous studies have also shown that games can be an efficient method for assessing and treating ADHD. A systematic review [9] investigated the effectiveness of gamified learning tools in diagnosing and treating ADHD in children under 18. The study observed that the tools that involved neurofeedback training had promising outcomes, and the researchers even observed that it was an effective method of targeting ADHD symptoms and improving cognitive capacity. In another study [10], the authors developed a game based on a supermarket simulation for assessing ADHD tendencies. This is predicted by using machine learning models using the player's data, points, and time. In a study [11], authors observed the effect of learning games on the concentration levels of children with ADHD. The learning activities were a constant stimulant for extended periods of concentrated learning. Therefore, the participants who had earlier displayed low levels of attention now showed enhanced focus and reduced hyperactivity. This highlights the need for continuous stimuli to maintain the children's focus. A study [12] showed that big lettering, clear topics, distinct colors, and shapes are important and effective design recommendations for capturing visual stimuli of children with ADHD. The authors also stated that people with ADHD require more assistance and for more extended periods. Park et al. have presented a study [13] depicting that games can improve reading ability and attention and decrease hyperactivity in children with ADHD.

This study aims to develop a gamified approach to increase learning among children with ADHD. This study discusses using HCI and NLP for a voice-input-based system to increase inclusivity and capture attention. NLP-based AWS speech-to-text transcribe API is used to detect the best input command. As presented in studies [12, 13], the HCI design principles are customized for better engaging children but also minimalistic and aesthetic [2]. Efforts have also been made to decrease the user's cognitive load by including options for setting the time between questions and summarization after a set of questions to encourage recollection.

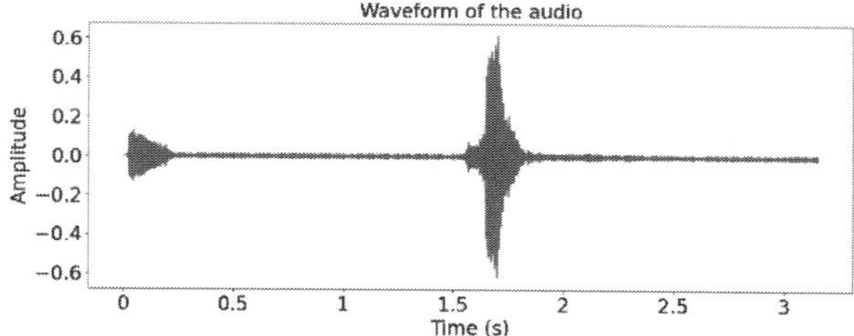

Fig. 2. Visualization of the waveform of test user 1 saying the command 'Jump'.

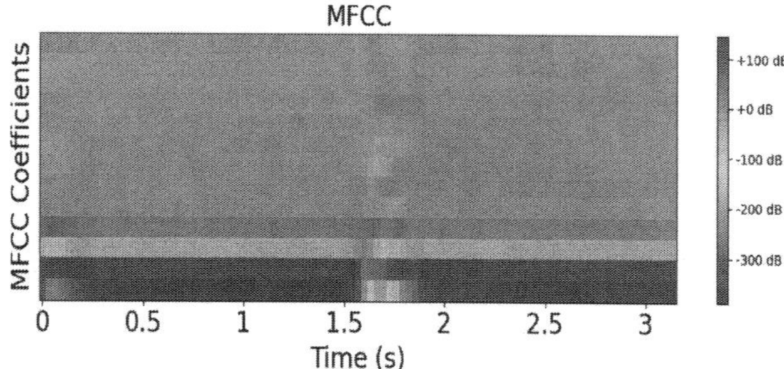

Fig. 3. The MFCC parameter visualized for test user 1 saying the command 'Jump'.

2   Materials and Methods

2.1   Platform Development

The learning platform in this study was developed using Unity, a popular cross-platform game development engine [14]. Unity is widely used by developers in the industry for its straightforward development interface. It was programmed in the programming language C#.

The game character's white color is in stark contrast to the game's background colors, where the distinct coloration helps highlight and draw attention to the character. This was proposed in an earlier study [12]. First, the repeating background was programmed, which, along with the player's running animation, gives the illusion of movement. Then, the 'QuestionManager.c' is programmed, which is responsible for changing the questions periodically, checking if the correct answer is chosen, increasing the score if the correct answer is picked, and spawning answer tiles corresponding to a given question. The

'AnswerTile.c' program controls the speed of the tile containing the answer, which, when chosen, removes both the answers from the screen and sends the answer that is selected to the Question Manager script to check and increase the score.

The game begins with the character walking while a question is displayed above. The question changes continuously as the game advances. For the current question, two tiles move toward the player, one with the correct answer and the other incorrect. The player must choose the correct answer for which the player must decide to jump to reach the tile if the correct answer tile is above and must decide not to jump if the correct answer is below. Each correct answer adds 1 point to the score, and after a regular interval of two questions, a summary is shown, which contains all the correct questions answered and their correct answer. This summary is used to increase memorization among the players. There is also a feature where the questions will be repeated until the correct answer is chosen to ensure learning. An additional system of audio cues is incorporated where if the correct answer is selected, the audio file says 'That's correct' followed by cheering. Still, if the incorrect answer is chosen, then the audio file that says 'Try again' is played, and the question repeats.

Fig. 4. The game interface when the game is first started.

2.2 Audio Preprocessing and Speech-to-Text Translation

The Amazon Web Services (AWS) Transcribe service [15] offered by AWS was used to translate speech to text. The Transcribe service is an automated speech recognition service that can take audio input from which it can produce transcripts. This feature is used via the API using Python.

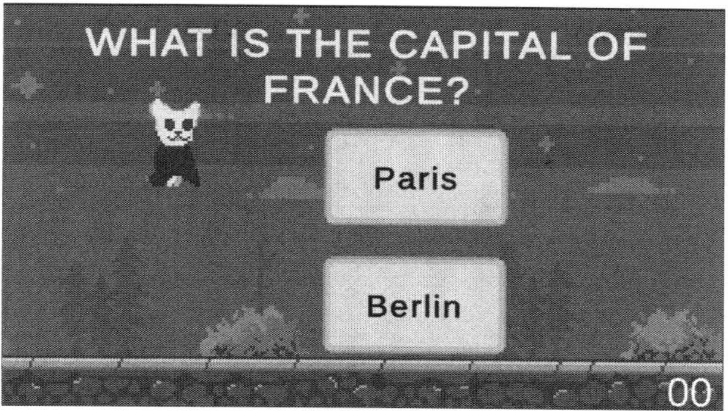

Fig. 5. The game interface when answer tiles appear.

2.3 Proposed Methodology

The overall process flow is visualized in Fig. 1. The audio taken via the microphone is first enhanced using audio preprocessing techniques, which consist of three primary methods: noise reduction, sound normalization, and filtering. For noise reduction, spectral subtraction minimizes background noise [16]. By subtracting the noise spectrum from the speech signal, this approach calculates the noise spectrum from quiet audio segments. Because of its computing efficiency, the technique may be used in real-time processing. Peak normalization is used to normalize the sound and to guarantee constant audio levels [17]. Therefore, the user's voice is steady and clear for the transcribe service. Bandpass filtering is applied to eliminate frequencies outside the specified range to remove noise and enhance the clarity of the voice inputs [18]. The preprocessed audio is converted to text using the AWS Transcribe service API. The process involves streaming audio through the microphone and relaying it to the AWS transcribe service. This study used the 'asyncio' library for asynchronous programming and the 'sounddevice' library to use real-time audio streaming. The rate of the AWS Transcribe API is set to 16,000 samples per second, and the audio is fed in short segments of 2048 audio samples. A queue is set up for the processing of each audio segment in the order of their occurrence. The language is set along with the location to store the transcribed text. It is recommended that the Waveform Audio File Format (WAV) be used with Pulse Code Modulation (PCM) encoding as it provides the best accuracy.

The API converts speech to text during transcription via Mel-Frequency Cepstral Coefficients (MFCC) [19, 20]. MFCC is a feature extraction technique for audio. MFCC presents the real cepstrum of a windowed signal derived using the Fast Fourier Transform and Discrete Cosine Transformation [21]. Compared to traditional spectral analysis methods, MFCC uses a nonlinear scale; it, therefore, filters out irrelevant sounds to focus more on speech patterns like the human auditory system. An acoustic vector can be acquired from a set of MFCC parameters that contains features such as phonetic information and sound attributes such as pitch and amplitude. For example, Fig. 2 visualizes the waveform of a test user saying the command 'Jump.' Fig. 3 then shows the MFCC parameters extracted from the same audio recording. As seen in Fig. 3, phonetic features can be extracted from the MFCC parameters as a transition between the different sounds in the word 'Jump,' which can be established by the changes in energy and frequency.

Fig. 6. The game interface when the correct answer is chosen.

The transcribed text is then checked for the presence of any defined commands. If the texts are commands, they are added to the instruction text file ('instruction.txt'). The instruction text file is a buffer, so only the necessary commands are fed into the player script. The character movement script ('PlayerScript.c') iterates through this instruction text to search for any presence of the input command 'Jump.' If found, the player movement script runs the required code to raise the character. After the command is performed, the text is removed from the instruction file to avoid repeated commands. After executing the command, the corresponding text is removed from the instruction file to avoid repeated commands. The user can also move the character using the keyboard input or the mouse left-click.

3   Results and Discussion

To conduct or study the construction of a learning platform for children with ADHD, the game's design was first developed, as depicted in Fig. 4. The designs were made considering the design principles of HCI and those discussed in previous works [12, 13] as discussed above. The design was made to be aesthetically pleasing yet minimalistic to avoid distractions. The high contrast of the player character to the background draws the user's attention to the character's movements and position. This thereby helps increase visibility and recognition. Considering the pacing, the answer tiles to be chosen are slowed to provide more time for the user to select; this can be later changed using the UI.

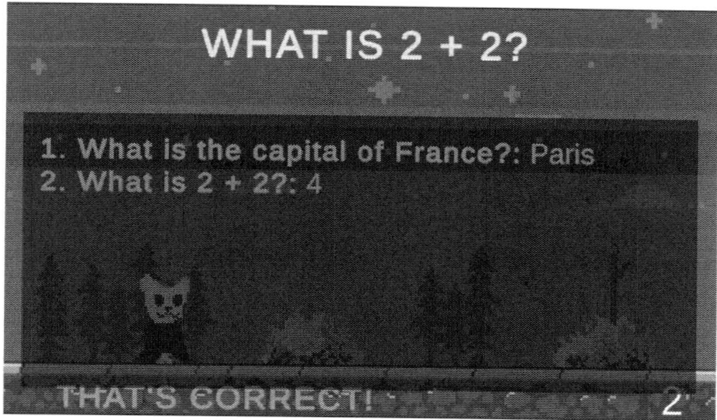

Fig. 7. The game interface with a summary of answers

The process begins with the display of a question at the top of the screen. After a brief delay to allow the player sufficient time to read and comprehend the question, answer tiles start moving toward the player, as depicted in Fig. 5. The delay before the answer tiles and the slow-paced answer tiles encourage the users to read the text quickly and facilitate timely responses. If the answer tile at the top contains the correct answer, the user must either say the words 'Jump' or 'Up,' or the additional option of using key binds as input; this will make the character jump upwards, selecting the answer at the top. Suppose the correct answer tile is chosen, as shown in Fig. 6. In that case, an animation of the character celebrating is played as well as the message 'That's Correct,' and an audio is played saying the same, followed by cheering celebrations. If the incorrect option tile is chosen, the message 'Try again' is displayed, and an audio message is played saying the same. The question is then repeated until corrected; this allows for learning by correction and repetition. After every two questions are answered, the performance summary is shown along with the correct answers so that the user can review their choices to improve learning via recollection. The summarization feature is depicted in Fig. 7.

This approach aims to encourage learning among children with ADHD by gamification of the learning process compared to the traditional book-based learning methods not aimed towards addressing issues such as easy distraction and hyperactivity. It further promotes education as well as enjoyment among the users. Furthermore, when the answers are selected, the system of audio cues offers a method of rewarding the user with cheers if correct. With HCI principles, the interface becomes more user-friendly and effortless. The concepts of NLP enhance user interaction using the user's speech, making the learning tool more accessible and engaging by incorporating voice-based inputs. The introduction of the system of voice inputs also removes any need for additional equipment such as a keyboard, mouse, or special controllers, thereby minimizing overhead expenses.

In this study, the observed limitation can be worked upon to increase its efficacy further. The voice input process carries some latency as the tool uses the AWS API. This is because continuous calls are made to the API along with the audio data, and therefore, the delay is primarily due to the heavy processing overload.

4 Conclusion

This study presents a unique approach to developing a learning tool for children with ADHD. The developed tool uses aesthetic yet minimalistic design principles and incorporates guidelines from other related works on the subject. The tool, thereby, is devised with the diverse needs of the ADHD community kept in mind. The learning tool offers a means to education via gamification technologies, and implementing voice-based inputs adds an immersive layer to the learning experience. The additional means of voice-based inputs to the regular key-binding gameplay make the tool more affordable and accessible, as it does not restrict people with motor disabilities. In the future, the aim is to integrate more advanced NLP networks for converting speech to text, eliminating the need for API-based service. This will reduce the overall latency and provide a better user-friendly experience.

References

1. Mannapperuma, C.: Human-computer interaction principles for developing web-based genomics resources. Umeå Universitet, Diss (2020)
2. Shaban, A., Pearson, E.: A learning design framework to support children with learning disabilities incorporating gamification techniques. In: Extended Abstracts of the 2019 CHI Conference on Human Factors in Computing Systems, pp. 1–6 (2019)
3. DuPaul, G.J., et al.: Parent and teacher ratings of attention-deficit/hyperactivity disorder symptoms: factor structure and normative data. Psychol. Assess. **28**(2), 214–223 (2016)
4. Fleming, M., et al.: Educational and health outcomes of children treated for attention-deficit/hyperactivity disorder. JAMA Pediatr. **171**(7), e170691–e170691 (2017)
5. Putra, A.S., et al.: Gamification in the e-learning process for children with attention deficit hyperactivity disorder (ADHD). In: 2018 Indonesian Association for Pattern Recognition International Conference (INAPR), Jakarta, pp. 1–6. IEEE (2018)
6. Bonnechère, B., et al.: The use of commercial video games in rehabilitation: a systematic review. Int. J. Rehabil. Res. **39**(4), 277–290 (2016)
7. Nath, D., et al.: Design and validation of virtual reality task for neuro-rehabilitation of distal upper extremities. Int. J. Environ. Res. Public Health **19**(3), 1442 (2022)
8. Hariprasad, R., Dhariwal, N., Swarnalata, P.: Voice stimulated inclusive multiplayer game development with speaker recognition. In: 2023 Third International Conference on Smart Technologies. Communication and Robotics (STCR), vol. 1, pp. 1–6. IEEE, Hyderabad (2023)
9. Penuelas-Calvo, I., et al.: Video games for the assessment and treatment of attention-deficit/hyperactivity disorder: a systematic review. Eur. Child Adolesc. Psychiatry, 1–16 (2020)
10. Santos, F.E., et al.: Assessment of ADHD through a computer game: an experiment with a sample of students. In: 2011 Third International Conference on Games and Virtual Worlds for Serious Applications, Athens, pp. 104–111. IEEE (2011)
11. Raniyah, Q., Syamsudin, A.: Centerred concentration for ADHD children via educational game. In: International Conference on Special and Inclusive Education (ICSIE 2018), Bandung, pp. 422–426. Atlantis Press (2019)
12. Galeos, C., Karpouzis, K., Tsatiris, G.: Developing an educational programming game for children with ADHD. In: 2020 15th International Workshop on Semantic and Social Media Adaptation and Personalization (SMAP), Zakynthos, pp. 1–6. IEEE (2020)

13. Park, K., et al.: Fairy tale directed game-based training system for children with ADHD using BCI and motion sensing technologies. Behav. Inf. Technol. **38**(6), 564–577 (2019)
14. Unity. https://unity.com/. Accessed 21 May 2024
15. AWS Transcribe Service. https://aws.amazon.com/transcribe/?nc=sn&loc=0. Accessed 24 May 2024
16. Karasözen, E., West, M.E.: An adaptive spectral subtraction algorithm to remove persistent cultural noise. Bull. Seismol. Soc. Am. **112**(5), 2297–2311 (2022)
17. Simaliak, M., et al.: Audio loudness normalization and measurement of broadcast programs. In: Proceedings of EIIC-The 2nd Electronic International Interdisciplinary Conference, Prague, pp. 1–6. IEEE (2013)
18. Jiang, J.: Audio processing with channel filtering using DSP techniques. In: 2018 IEEE 8th Annual Computing and Communication Workshop and Conference (CCWC), Las Vegas, pp. 545–550. IEEE (2018)
19. Biswas, M., et al.: Automatic spoken language identification using MFCC based time series features. Multimedia Tools Appl. **82**(7), 9565–9595 (2023)
20. Ezzat, S., El Gayar, N., Ghanem, M.M.: Sentiment analysis of call centre audio conversations using text classification. Int. J. Comput. Inf. Syst. Ind. Manag. Appl. **4**(1), 619–627 (2012)
21. Dave, N.: Feature extraction methods LPC, PLP and MFCC in speech recognition. Int. J. Adv. Res. Eng. Technol. **1**(6), 1–4 (2013)

Virtual Character-Based Study of the Combined Effect of Turn-Taking Behavior and Speech Speed on Conversational Atmosphere

Masahide Yuasa[✉]

Shonan Institute of Technology, Fujisawa, Kanagawa 251-8511, Japan
`yuasa@sc.shonan-it.ac.jp`

Abstract. In the field of human-computer interaction, researchers have explored methods to enhance the turn-taking abilities of conversational agents and robots in interactions with humans. Previous studies have shown that variations in turn-taking patterns (e.g., overlaps and gaps) can influence the perceived conversational atmosphere, and thus, their effect on human perceptions has been examined. However, the combination impact of turn-taking behavior and speech speed on conversational atmosphere remains underexplored. To address this, we developed a conversational simulator featuring virtual conversational characters with simple shapes and meaningless utterances to investigate how the combination of turn-taking and speech speed influences the identification of a conversational atmosphere. The characters followed basic turn-taking rules, and the simulator controlled their turn-taking behaviors. We conducted an experiment in which participants observed scenes generated by the simulator. A two-way repeated-measures ANOVA was performed, examining the effects of turn-taking behaviors (overlap, no-gap-no-overlap, gap) and speech speed (fast, medium, slow). Results indicated that fast speed was perceived as creating a competitive atmosphere, even when turn-taking adhered to no-gap-no-overlap patterns. This finding will contribute to developing conversational agents/robots that have the same capacity to judge conversational atmosphere as humans.

Keywords: Conversational Agent · Character · Turn-taking · Speech Speed · Overlap · Gap

1 Introduction

In the area of human-computer interaction, it is well established that turn-taking behaviors provide not only turn management but also influence the impressions formed during everyday conversations [1]. Consequently, how turn-taking patterns affect human senses has been studied [1, 2]. Reference [3] examined the relationship between conversational atmospheres and turn-taking patterns, suggesting that individuals might infer conversational atmospheres based on the degree of overlap or gaps during interactions.

However, the combined effect of speech speed and turn-taking patterns on the identification of conversational atmospheres has not been thoroughly investigated. Speech

S. Goel et al. (Eds.): AICON 2025, LNICST 672, pp. 182–191, 2026.
https://doi.org/10.1007/978-3-032-14805-6_13

speed is believed to also influence the perception of conversation, and the interaction between speech speed and turn-taking may significantly impact how individuals perceive conversations. Despite this, the specific effects of these variables remain largely unknown.

In this study, we developed a conversational simulator featuring virtual characters to examine how the combination of speech speed and turn-taking behavior influences the identification of conversational atmospheres. The findings from this study could contribute to the development of conversational agents and robots that can perceive conversational atmospheres, such as whether a conversation feels friendly or competitive, as illustrated in Fig. 1. Moreover, this research may aid in designing conversational agents that can evaluate whether the atmosphere of a human conversation is appropriate to participate in.

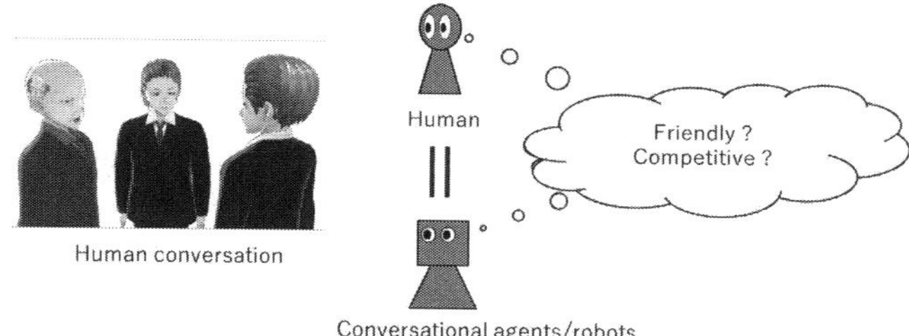

Fig. 1. Contributions of this study. Our investigation contributes to the development of conversational agents/robots that can identify conversational atmospheres like humans.

2   Previous Studies

Previous studies have reported that turn-taking behaviors, such as overlaps and gaps, not only manage the transition of speaking turns among participants [4–6] but also convey social meanings [7], influence the tension level of conversation [8], and reflect interpersonal attitudes [9].

Ter Maat et al. investigated the impressions created by different turn-taking behaviors. Their study examined the emotional responses and impressions associated with turn-taking patterns [1, 2], identifying factors such as agreeableness and assertiveness through variations in turn-taking behaviors. However, their research was limited to vocal expressions, as they did not incorporate the use of agents' body movements.Another study [3] proposed a classification of conversational types based on the degree of overlap or gap between speaking turns. The first type, referred to as a "competitive conversation, " was characterized by excessive overlaps [8, 10]. The second type, termed 'friendly conversation,' involved moderate overlap [10]. The third type, known as "formal/well-mannered conversation, " was distinguished by the presence of gaps between turns [11, 12]. Although these conversational types are categorized based on turn-taking behaviors, the relationship between turn-taking patterns and speech speed has not been thoroughly established.

It has also been reported that speech speed varies based on factors such as politeness, gender, and whether the speaker is a native or non-native speaker [13–16]. Yu et al. found that the speaking rate of a conversational agent affected the perception of the speaker's trustworthiness [17]. Dowding et al. investigated users' preferences for system speech rate, finding that fast speakers preferred faster system speech, while slower speakers preferred slower speech [18]. Xie et al. examined the influence of varying speech rates in conversational agents. They reported that users preferred the feedback speed to increase in response to their own faster speech rate [19].

While studies have explored the effects of changes in speech speed, the combined effect of speech speed and turn-taking behaviors on the overall conversational atmosphere remains largely unexplored. If conversational agents and robots have only knowledge about the effects of one element and lack knowledge regarding the effect of the combined effect of two factors, the difference between agents/robots and humans will occur. Thus, our study aimed to gain insights into the combined effect of these two factors, integrate our knowledge for conversational behaviors, and contribute to the development of conversational agents and robots that can perceive conversational atmospheres like humans do.

3   Conversational Simulator and Turn-Taking Rules

Building on previous studies [3, 8], we developed a conversational simulator featuring virtual characters. Figure 2 illustrates a conversation scene generated by the simulator. The simulator was built using WebGL, and the 3D characters were sourced from an external website [20]. To minimize biases related to character appearance, the virtual characters were designed as abstract, simple shapes with no facial expressions. Their heads and bodies could rotate, allowing them to look at the speaking character by aligning their head and body movements. The characters' mouth movements were synchronized with their vocal utterances.

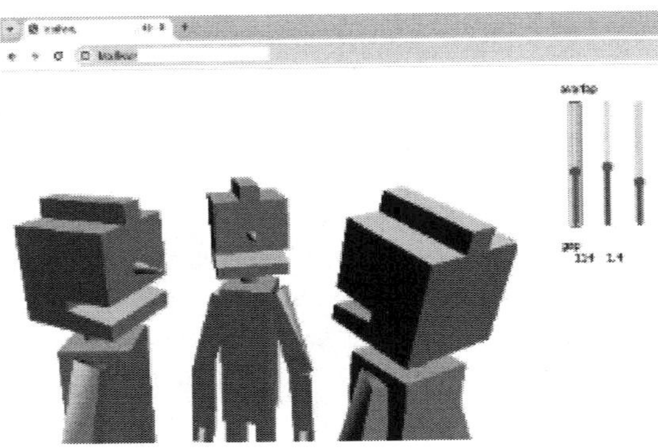

Fig. 2. A conversation scene in our simulator

To focus solely on conversational behavior, the virtual characters spoke in meaningless utterances such as "blah-blah-blah, yadda-yadda-yadda, or banana-banana-banana. " This approach, inspired by previous experiments that used non-human or filtered voices [1–3], helped isolate the effects of conversational behavior from verbal content.

Each utterance lasted for approximately 6.6 s, with consistent length across characters. Drawing on the findings of earlier research [3], we implemented typical conversational behaviors for the virtual characters (see Fig. 3):

1. When a character begins speaking, the other characters direct their gaze toward the speaker.
2. While speaking, the active character looks straight ahead.
3. Before finishing, the speaking character turns to look at the next designated speaker.
4. Once the speaker finishes, the next speaker starts; in cases of overlap, the new speaker does not wait for the previous one to complete their turn.

The simulated conversation then returns to the first behavior, with the next speaker selected automatically before the current speaker finishes, and this cycle continues.

Fig. 3. Character behaviors in our simulator

4 Experimental Design

4.1 Turn-Taking Patterns and Speeds of Speech

We prepared three types of turn-taking patterns: overlap, no-gap-no-overlap, and gap, based on the experimental results from a previous study [3] and our preliminary experiment. The duration of the overlap was set to approximately -1.9 s, which might be perceived as sufficient overlap. Similarly, the gap duration was set to approximately $+1.9$ s, which might be understood as a sufficient pause[1].

We utilized a voice synthesis tool (TTSMP3 [21]) to generate meaningless vocalizations (e.g., "blah-blah-blah"). The speech speed of these utterances was set to approximately 110 words per minute (wpm), which is generally perceived as a clear speaking rate [22]. This speed served as the baseline for our experiment. Using the audio processing library SoundTouchJS [23], we adjusted the speech speed of the utterances to

---

[1] These durations were based on formulated 'k-values' in the previous study [3]: k = 70 (-1.9 s), k = 100 (0 s), and k = 130 (+1.9 s).

create two additional conditions: approximately 150 wpm (1.4x faster than the baseline), representing fast speech, and approximately 90 wpm (0.8x slower than the baseline), representing slow speech [24].

The pitch of the utterance remained unchanged when the speech speed was adjusted. Although the length of the utterances was stretched or compressed based on the speech speed, the number of words remained consistent across all conditions.

4.2 Experimental Procedure and Participants

Using the three turn-taking patterns and three speech speeds, we produced nine unique scenes with the conversational simulator and recorded them as nine separate videos for participant evaluation. The resolution of each video was 450 x 275 pixels, which was sufficient for participants to answer the questions. Each video lasted approximately 30–40 s. Participants were not required to watch the videos to the end. The videos were presented to participants in random order.

While watching each video, participants were asked to rate it on a 7-point Likert scale. For example, they could rate the friendliness of the conversation as "not friendly". (−3)), "neither" (0) to "friendly" (+3). Based on previous studies [3] and our preliminary experiments, we selected three items, "competitive," "friendly," and "well-mannered" to evaluate each video.

Prior to viewing the videos, participants were informed that the study focused on modeling human conversations. They were also told that the behaviors of the virtual characters in the videos were modeled on human conversational behaviors and voices observed in real interactions. Participants were asked to infer how the three characters were communicating with each other based solely on their movements and vocalizations.

The participants were recruited for the experiment from Amazon Mechanical Turk (a crowdsourcing website). An informed consent procedure approved by our institution was used. Only those who consented participated in the experiment. Participants were paid points that could be redeemed on shopping sites.

4.3 Hypothesis

Based on previous findings, we hypothesized that speech speed would influence participants' comprehension of conversational atmospheres. The following hypothesis was formulated:

Hypothesis: Participants' ratings would be influenced not only by turn-taking patterns but also by speech speed, and an interaction effect between turn-taking and speech speed would be observed.

5   Results

The experiment included 56 participants after excluding inappropriate responses.[2] Figure 4 shows the average ratings for "competitive," "friendly," and "well-mannered." (The values were converted from "−3 to + 3" to "0 to 6.") A two-way repeated-measures analysis of variance (ANOVA) was conducted on the responses, Factor A being turn-taking patterns and Factor B being speech speed.

There was a significant interaction effect between turn-taking and speech speed for "competitive" ($F(4,220) = 2.509$, $p = 0.042 < .05$, $\eta_p^2 = 0.044$). Table 1 shows the results of the simple main effects of "competitive" in each condition. In the multiple comparisons using the Bonferroni method, there were significant differences. Table 2 shows the results of the comparisons. We can see that the B1(Fast) level differed from other levels and that the "No-gap-no-overlap" pattern had no difference from the "Overlap" pattern. Similarly, the A1(Overlap) level had no significant difference in speech speed.

Regarding "friendly," there were significant main effects for Factor A($F(2,110) = 46.876$, $p < .01$, $\eta_p^2 = 0.46$) and Factor B($F(2,110) = 7.141$, $p < .01$, $\eta_p^2 = 0.115$), and there was no interaction effect. In the multiple comparisons using the Bonferroni method, there were significant differences. For Factor A, "Overlap" < "No-gap-no-overlap" and "Overlap" < "Gap" ($p < .05$, mean square error (MSE) $= 3.447$, alpha' $= 0.0167$). Regarding Factor B, "Fast" < "Medium" and "Fast" < "Slow" ($p < .05$, MSE $= 2.861$, alpha' $= 0.0167$).

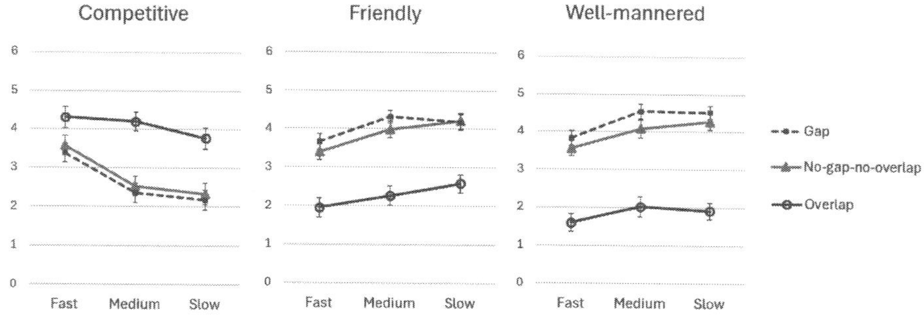

Fig. 4. Averages ± S.E. for "competitive," "friendly," and "well-mannered."

---

[2] We used participants with a specified qualification of 'HIT Approval Rate greater than 90%', which meant a high grade on the site. Participant-age groups were 21–30 (13%), 31–40 (41%), 41–50 (23%), 51–60 (14%), and 61 and above (9%).

Table 1. Results of simple main effects for "competitive." (+ $p < .10$, * $p < .05$, ** $p < .01$)

A: Turn-taking		B: Speech Speed	
A at B1(Fast)	$F(2,110) = 4.54$ *	B at A1(Overlap)	$F(2,110) = 2.79$ +
A at B2(Medium)	$F(2,110) = 14.60$ **	B at A2(No-gap-no-overlap)	$F(2,110) = 9.41$ **
A at B3(Slow)	$F(2,110) = 11.31$ **	B at A3(Gap)	$F(2,110) = 10.40$ **

Table 2. Multiple comparisons using the Bonferroni method for "competitive." (* $p < .05$, alpha' $= 0.0167$)

A at B1(Fast) Level	B at A1(Overlap) Level
(MSE = 2.9562)	(MSE = 1.6152)
Overlap = No-gap-no-overlap n.s	Fast = Medium n.s
Overlap > Gap *	Fast = Slow n.s
No-gap-no-overlap = Gap n.s	Medium = Slow n.s
A at B2(Medium) Level	B at A2(No-gap-no-overlap) Level
(MSE = 3.9464)	(MSE = 2.6083)
Overlap > No-gap-no-overlap *	Fast > Medium *
Overlap > Gap *	Fast > Slow *
No-gap-no-overlap = Gap n.s	Medium = Slow n.s
A at B3(Slow) Level	B at A3(Gap) Level
(MSE = 3.7904)	(MSE = 2.2425)
Overlap > No-gap-no-overlap *	Fast > Medium *
Overlap > Gap *	Fast > Slow *
No-gap-no-overlap = Gap n.s	Medium = Slow n.s

In the case of "well-mannered," there were significant main effects for Factor A($F(2,110) = 67.613$, $p < .01$, $\eta_p^2 = 0.551$) and Factor B($F(2,110) = 9.317$, $p < .01$, $\eta_p^2 = 0.145$), and there was no interaction effect. In the multiple comparisons using the Bonferroni method, there were significant differences. Regarding Factor A, "Overlap" < "No-gap-no-overlap" and "Overlap" < "Gap" ($p < .05$, MSE $= 4.405$, alpha' $= 0.0167$). Regarding Factor B, "Fast" < "Medium" and "Fast" < "Slow" ($p < .05$, MSE $= 1.925$, alpha' $= 0.0167$).

6   Discussion

6.1   Verification of Hypothesis and Considerations from Experimental Results

The experimental results showed a significant interaction effect between turn-taking patterns and speech speed for the "competitive" rating. At the fast speech level (B1), the "no-gap-no-overlap" pattern did not differ significantly from the "overlap" pattern, even though the "overlap" pattern was perceived as more "competitive" than the "no-gap-no-overlap" pattern at other speech speeds. This result indicates that participants' responses were influenced not only by turn-taking patterns but also by speech speed. It suggests that speech speed plays a significant role in the perception of conversational atmospheres, partially supporting our hypothesis.

However, for the "friendly" and "well-mannered" ratings, there was no interaction effect between turn-taking and speech speed. This suggests that the turn-taking pattern operated independently of speech speed, with both factors affecting the ratings of "friendly" and "well-mannered" separately. Moreover, in the case of the "no-gap-no-overlap" pattern, fast speech did not reduce the ratings of "friendly" and "well-mannered, " even though fast speech significantly increased the ratings of "competitive. "

It is possible that the reason fast speech influenced the perception of "competitive" turn-taking is related to the role of turn-taking in managing the control of speaking turns at the end of utterance. Reference [25] examined the behavior of speakers toward the end of their utterances and found that certain behaviors express a strong desire to take control of the conversation. Fast speech may create the impression of a strong desire to take the floor, which could explain the increase in "competitive" ratings. Further experiments focusing on competitive turn-taking are needed to explore these relationships in greater detail.

6.2 Limitations

To isolate the effects of turn-taking and speech speed, and to avoid content-related biases, we used meaningless words in the experiment. However, future studies should employ more practical utterances to better reflect real-world conversations. Additionally, while we used simplified characters to eliminate bias related to appearance, future experiments with more realistic characters are needed to obtain deeper insights into how the conversational atmosphere is perceived.

Furthermore, cultural differences in conversational norms must be considered. In our experiment, 55% of participants were from the U.S., 43% from India, and 2% from other countries. Although this study is the first to explore the combined effects of turn-taking and speech speed, further experiments with a more diverse range of participants are required to gain more comprehensive insights.

7 Conclusions

In this study, we conducted an experiment to investigate the relationship between turn-taking behaviors and speech speed. The results confirmed an interaction effect, showing that fast speech speed significantly influences the perception of competitive conversations. This finding can contribute to the development of conversational agents and robots capable of making judgments about the conversational atmosphere (e.g., determining whether a conversation is competitive) and joining human conversations. Additionally, our use of abstract characters and meaningless words in a bottom-up approach provides insights into cognitive psychology, which aims to the understanding of the internal models.

Further experiments addressing generational gaps, cultural differences, and other factors are necessary to deepen these findings.

8 Conflicts of Interest

The author declares no potential conflicts of interest with respect to the research, authorship, and/or publication of this article.

Acknowledgment. We are grateful to the persons who participated in our experiments.

References

1. Ter Maat, M., Heylen, D.: Turn management or impression management? In: Proceedings of IVA2009, vol. 5773. Springer, Heidelberg (2009). https://doi.org/10.1007/978-3-642-04380-2_51
2. Ter Maat, M., Truong, K.P., Heylen, D.: How turn-taking strategies influence users' impressions of an agent. In: Proceedings of IVA2010, vol. 13, pp. 441–453 (2010). https://doi.org/10.1007/978-3-642-15892-6_48
3. Yuasa, M.: Investigation of the relationship between turn-taking behaviors and conversational atmospheres using virtual characters. Trans. Hum. Interface Soc. **26**(2), 259–262 (2024). https://doi.org/10.11184/his.26.2_259
4. Sacks, H., Schegloff, E.A., Jefferson, G.: A simplest systematics for the organisation of turn-taking for conversation. Language **50**(4), 696–735 (1974). https://doi.org/10.2307/412243
5. Goffman, E.: Interaction Ritual: Essays on Face-to-Face Behavior. Doubleday Anchor New York (1967)
6. Schegloff, E.A.: Overlapping talk and the organization of turn-taking for conversation. Lang. Soc. **29**, 1–63 (2000). https://doi.org/10.1017/S0047404500001019
7. Coates, J.: No gap, lots of overlap: turn-taking patterns in the talk of women friends. In: Graddol, D., Maybin, J., Stierer, B. (eds.) Researching Language and Literacy in Social Context, pp. 177–192. Multilingual Matters, Clevedon (1994)
8. Yuasa, M.: Can animated agents help us create better conversational moods? In: Proceedings of HCII2014 (2014)
9. Ravenet, B., Cafaro, A., Biancardi, B., Ochs, M., Pelachaud, C.: Conversational behavior reflecting interpersonal attitudes in small group interactions. In: Proceedings of IVA2015, pp. 375–388 (2015). https://doi.org/10.1007/978-3-319-21996-7_41
10. Dunne, M., Ng, S.H.: Simultaneous speech in small group conversation: all-together-now and one-at-a-time? J. Lang. Soc. Psychol. **13**, 45–71 (1994). https://doi.org/10.1177/0261927X94131004
11. Fairclough, N.: Discourse and Social Change. Polity Press (1992)
12. Hakulinen, A.: Conversation types. In: Verschueren, J., Östman, J.O., Blommaert, J., Bulcaen, C. (eds.) Handbook of Pragmatics, pp. 101–120. John Benjamins (1999)
13. Quené, H.: Multilevel modeling of between-speaker and within-speaker variation in spontaneous speech tempo. J. Acoust. Soc. Am. **123**(2), 1104–1113 (2008). https://doi.org/10.1121/1.2821762
14. Jacewicz, E., Fox, R.A., Wei, L.: Between-speaker and within-speaker variation in speech tempo of American English. J. Acoust. Soc. Am. **128**(2), 839–850 (2010). https://doi.org/10.1121/1.3459842

15. Munro, M.J., Derwing, T.M.: Modeling perceptions of the accentedness and comprehensibility of L2 speech: the role of speaking Rate. Stud. Second Lang. Acquisit. **23**(4), 451–468 (2001). http://www.jstor.org/stable/44486957
16. Ofuka, E., McKeown, J., Waterman, M., Roach, P.: Prosodic cues for rated politeness in Japanese speech. Speech Commun. **32**, 199–217 (2000). https://api.semanticscholar.org/CorpusID:10838259
17. Yu, Y., and Levitan, S.I.: What makes a conversational agent sound trustworthy? Exploring the role of acoustic-prosodic factors. In: Proceedings of Speech Prosody 2024, pp. 1240–1244 (2024). https://doi.org/10.21437/SpeechProsody.2024-250
18. Dowding, S., Gutwin, C., Cockburn, A.: User speech rates and preferences for system speech rates. Int. J. Hum.-Comput. Stud. **184** (2024). https://doi.org/10.1016/j.ijhcs.2024.103222
19. Xie, Y., Qu, J., Zhang, Y. et al.: Speaking, fast or slow: how conversational agents' rate of speech influences user experience. Univ. Access Inf. Soc. **2023** (2023). https://doi.org/10.1007/s10209-023-01000-2
20. Social-exp.site. https://social-exp.site/. Accessed 17 Sept 2024
21. TTSMP3. https://ttsmp3.com/. Accessed 17 Sept 2024
22. What's your speech rate?. https://www.write-out-loud.com/speech-rate.html. Accessed 17 Sept 2024
23. SoundTouchJS. https://github.com/cutterbl/SoundTouchJS/. Accessed 17 Sept 2024
24. How fast do you speak and type?. https://www.typingmaster.com/speech-speed-test/. Accessed 17 Sept 2024
25. Yuasa, M., Mukawa, N., Kimura, K., Tokunaga, H., Terai, H.: An utterance attitude model in human-agent communication: from good turn-taking to better human-agent understanding. In: CHI Extended Abstracts 2010, pp. 3919–3924 (2010)

Author Index

A
Abinaya, M.   119
Anand, Aryamann   173
Anbazhagan, E.   51
Annamalai, R.   3, 51
Arafat, N. H. M.   85

B
Bartekova, Maria   138

C
Chaitanya, Tekumudi Vivek Sai Surya   3
Chaurasia, Brijesh Kumar   22
Chiran, B. K.   40
Chow, Kam-Pui   70

D
Divakara, B. C.   108

G
Ganesh, Bachu   3
Garg, Swati   150
Goel, Sanjay   159
Gupta, Srishti   159

H
Hariprasad, Rithvik   173
Hazela, Bramah   22
Hemadarshini, M. P.   40

J
Jamwal, Akanksha Malik   150

K
Khare, Ankit   22

L
Lam, Yi Anson   70

M
Majduchova, Helena   138
Mishra, Awanish   22

N
Nagarathna, C. R.   40, 108
Nandini, G.   40, 108
Navamani, T. M.   173

R
Ramya, M.   108
Romanova, Anita   138

S
Srinivas, Seema   108
Suchithra, R. B.   108
Suchithra, T.   108
Sudharson, S.   3, 51
Sun, Weiqing   85
Swetha, K. R.   40

V
Vadivu, G.   119
Vamsi Krishna, V.   51
Verma, Aman Kumar   40
Vernekar, Karthik Dinesh   40

Y
Yiu, Siu-Ming   70
Yuasa, Masahide   182

Made in the USA
Monee, IL
07 July 2026

56547422R00114